The Sentimental Revolution

FRENCH WRITERS OF 1690–1740

OTHER BOOKS BY GEOFFROY ATKINSON

The Extraordinary Voyage in French Literature before 1700 (1920).

The Extraordinary Voyage in French Literature from 1700 to 1720
(1922).

Les Relations de voyage du 17ᵉ siècle et l'évolution des idées (1924).

La Littérature géographique française de la Renaissance (1927); *Supplément* (1936).

The Works of François Villon with text, translation, and introduction
(1930).

Les Nouveaux horizons de la Renaissance française (1935).

Les Idées de Balzac (5 vols., 1949, 1950).

Afternoon (poetry), (1950).

Le Sentiment de la Nature et le retour à la vie simple (1690–1740),
(1960).

Students and External Readers	Staff & Research Students
DATE DUE FOR RETURN	**DATE OF ISSUE**
~~15 MAR 1968~~ ~~13. MAR 1974~~	~~JUL 1971~~
~~8 DEC 1969~~ ~~14.MAR 79~~ 0 0 1 9	
~~12 MAR 1970~~ ~~27.JUN79~~ 0 0 2 0	
~~11 2 MAR 1970~~	25. 06. 86.
~~2 2 JUN 1970~~ ~~0 0 2 3~~	
~~16. MAR 1973~~	
~~13 MAR 1974~~ ~~7 851~~	

**Any book which you borrow remains your responsibility
until the loan slip is cancelled**

THE
Sentimental Revolution

FRENCH WRITERS OF 1690–1740

By Geoffroy Atkinson

EDITED BY ABRAHAM C. KELLER

University of Washington Press / Seattle and London

Copyright © 1965 by the University of Washington Press
Library of Congress Catalog Card Number 64–18424
Manufactured by American Book–Stratford Press, Inc., New York
Printed in the United States of America

Author's Preface

THE CHIEF PURPOSE of this study is to bring to the knowledge of those interested in the half-century from 1690 to 1740 a number of emotional statements from authors who are no longer read. This purpose would be largely achieved if readers were only to go carefully through the passages quoted and omit reading the commentary. Whether or not anyone reading in that manner agrees with the conclusion, which presents, in general terms, the historical implications of the passages reproduced, he may nevertheless be better informed about some of the social and emotional facts of French history during the admittedly complicated period of transition from the heyday of absolutism under Louis XIV to another very different epoch.

Almost forty years ago, when preparing to write *Les Relations de Voyages du XVIIe siècle et l'évolution des ideas,*[1] I had already come to believe that "what is important in the history of ideas is always their expression and frequency of expression by different authors, for the date of onset of ideas is impossible to find." Since then, in studying sixteenth-century authors and finding that a number of them had already expressed what are ordinarily labeled as "eighteenth-century ideas," I became even surer that neither ideas nor human emotions have dates of onset, although the form and the expression of both obviously vary from one period to the next, in accordance with changes in the public, with contemporary taste, and perhaps even more with religious, political, and economic facts.

If one believes this to be true, it is difficult to set definite limits in time to "The Enlightenment," about which much has been written as if it were possible to place it here and not there. On the contrary, an enlightenment certainly began to appear in France at least as early as the time of Amyot, Jean Bodin, and Montaigne in the 1500's. It went into a marked eclipse among the best authors for fifty or sixty years in

[1] (Paris: E. Champion, 1924), p. 22.

v

the century following, but rose rapidly again in more open questioning of traditional institutions and beliefs between the late seventeenth century and the publication of the *Encyclopedia* in 1750.

The rationalistic protest against tradition in France from 1600 until the mid-eighteenth century has been studied and presented in the works of French critics of the first magnitude. Since Gustave Lanson began that study in 1907, Paul Hazard, Daniel Mornet, and lately Professor René Pintard have shown, in brilliant fashion and from quite divergent points of view, this part of intellectual history. In doing so, they have greatly helped to destroy the time-honored but quite false "literary history," limited to great authors, neatly arranged in "centuries with conflicting characteristics." That sort of cataloguing is as misleading as political history limited to the actions by and for the prominent people of each age. Such highly selective interpretations omit the broader fact that the majority of men in any period rejoiced or grieved over personal experiences and over political events. Furthermore, it is often the mediocre writers, who are eventually forgotten, who foreshadow the great statements to be made later by authors of genius, as it is sometimes the sentiment of a large number of unimportant people which eventually influences political events.

Those familiar with French literature have long understood that the expression of personal emotions was frowned upon by the dictators of literary taste in the time of Louis XIV, whereas numerous sentimental novels and plays appeared in the period immediately following. Yet there has been no general examination of the growth of sentimental writing—on subjects other than love—or any attempt to trace this fundamental change in the literate public within so short a space of time.

A useful contribution might be made, therefore, by one who had read the many volumes of periodicals, the large number of second-rate novels, plays, poems, uninspiring accounts of travel in Europe and elsewhere, letters, diaries, memoirs, and sermons, even the few books on natural science, all of which were published during a transitional period of fifty years.

The first result of that reading, which had taken a number of years, appeared in a small volume published in February, 1960, on *The Sentimental Appreciation of Nature and the Return to the Simple Life*.[2] The

---

[2] G. Atkinson, *Le Sentiment de la nature et le retour à la vie simple* (1690–1740), (Société de Publications romanes et françaises, Vol. LXVI [Geneva: E. Droz; Paris: Librairie Minard, 1960]).

present volume on the growth of expressions of compassion and of some other feelings within the same period is consequently the second in a series of studies. Here again, I am attempting to find some of the truth about changes in French society, not exclusively in "high society," whose members did not do most of the writing. It was not "good form" among nobles, or among logical rationalist *philosophes* for that matter, to indulge in personal confession. But the rapidly growing number of literate commoners constituted an increasing reading public which absorbed the outpourings of authors or fictional characters who were able to confess their own feelings without the reservations instilled by an earlier literary tradition.

The few scores of quotations given in the first volume of these studies, devoted to nature and the out-of-doors, may have helped to demonstrate what thoughtful people had already suspected: that Rousseau did not invent the emotional appreciation of natural beauty in French. For the fact is that Jean-Jacques Rousseau was born and lived to be more than thirty years of age during a period when minor French authors were already writing with emotion on these subjects, as well as on the urge to leave the cities and take up the simple and virtuous ways of country people. Of course, those less gifted writers did not possess the intellectual grasp or stylistic cogency which were to make Rousseau a world figure in literature.

In dealing with such an aesthetic matter, it seemed appropriate to quote passages in the original. And, to avoid the back-and-forth awkwardness of two languages, one for the quotations and another for the commentary, that study was written in French. But in the present volume, where the form of the emotional expressions deploring cruelty or oppression and praising compassion or altruism is of far less importance, I have used English throughout. The truly significant fact is that French writers between 1690 and 1740 were sympathetic toward the unfortunate and outspoken in their condemnation of the cruel no matter what the rank, and that is of importance to human rather than to purely literary history.

G.A.

Amherst, Mass.
September, 1960

Editor's Preface

THE LATE Professor Geoffroy Atkinson virtually finished this volume before his death, and in preparing the manuscript for publication I have tried to avoid violence to his style or intent. The changes of detail that accuracy and clarity in a final version would demand, or the occasional shifting of a quotation from one place to another—alterations often suggested by trusted colleagues in the same field of study—would, I feel sure, have been made by Professor Atkinson himself had he lived to see his book through the press. I have contributed an index, found and arranged the originals of the author's translation (except for several instances indicated in the notes, where the original was unavailable to me), arranged the bibliography, and compiled a list of Professor Atkinson's writings.

Notes for a final volume on the period 1690–1740, which Professor Atkinson planned and to which he refers in one place, were given to me by Mrs. Atkinson after his death, in accordance with his wish, and such a volume is in preparation.

A.C.K.

Seattle, Washington
December, 1965

Contents

The Sentimental Revolution

FRENCH WRITERS OF 1690–1740

CHAPTER I

Famine, Plague, and Bankruptcy

I

IT IS much easier to study the growth of pity and humanitarian doctrine, which is what concerns us here, than to trace the opposite factors contributing to a marked lack of charity for one's fellow beings which one finds in Paris during the Regency of 1715–23. Moral condemnation of public conduct during that period has long been a commonplace feature in the writing of French history. It may suffice to mention the duels between little *abbés* over mistresses, the general gambling and speculation, and the promotion of Guillaume Dubois, a man of notoriously bad character, to Cardinal and Prime Minister.

It is not likely that those who misbehaved with such gusto had suddenly, upon the death of Louis XIV, thrown all restraint to the wind. It would be oversimplification to imagine any one cause of so complicated a change. If we turn back from the small respect for Christian morality in 1715–23 to another cause which can be identified in the preceding epoch, we may find a more fundamental root.

3

Two examples of religious fervor in the seventeenth century in France are well known. Pascal and Racine, two of the great literary figures of that period, gave up their manner of life after becoming persuaded of Jansenism and devoted their energies to it. Of all bleak doctrines in Catholic history, predicting damnation for all but a few elect, that vagary of Christianity most clearly resembled the preaching of Jonathan Edwards at Northampton, Massachusetts, in the 1730's. Jansenism was impotent, if not dead, by 1730 in France, but it did not die without a long struggle.

Pascal took time from prayer and meditation in 1656 and 1657 to write his *Lettres Provinciales* with the intention of destroying Jesuitism in France. But the struggle for power between Jansenists and Jesuits went on for fifty years, in part perhaps because of the Jansenist leanings of Madame de Maintenon and her influence upon Louis XIV.

The Jesuits suffered a temporary defeat in the "Chinese affair" at the end of the century. In 1698, Father Charles le Gobien published an account of the Chinese belief in a "Sovereign Ruler of Earth and Heaven." He explained furthermore that Jesuit missionaries had found this belief helpful in persuading people there about the Christian God, who was similarly believed to be the "Ruler of the Universe." The Faculty of Theology at Paris condemned the book as "false, brazen, scandalous, erroneous and insulting to the Holy Christian Faith." The condemnation was published in 1701 and the Jesuit book was publicly burned, but a few copies of Le Gobien's book escaped the flames.[1]

Jansenism did not profit long from this scandalous affair, however. It received a deathblow only a few years later, when its headquarters at Port Royal des Champs were ordered to be razed to the ground (1710) and its membership there to be dispersed among other Catholic institutions. Only five years later, the leading exponents of the Jesuits in Paris were exiled to the small town of Trévoux, many miles to the southeast.

Overlapping the years of this struggle between factions within the Church, there occurred what was probably the best known of Church quarrels during the reign of Louis XIV. In this instance, two very highly placed churchmen and a number of important nobles, both men and women, were involved. Madame Guyon (Jeanne-Marie Bouvier de la Motte), the instigator of the "Quietist" movement who would not re-

---

[1] G. Atkinson, *Les Relations de voyages du XVIIe siècle et l'évolution des idées* (Paris: Champion, 1924), pp. 89–98.

nounce her printed works or her beliefs after these had been condemned at Rome, was forced to spend seven years in prison, most of them in the Bastille. Archbishop Fénelon, a nobleman by birth, an outstanding author and a member of the French Academy of "immortals," was exiled by the King to spend the rest of life near his cathedral at Cambrai. Nor did Madame de Maintenon dare to support Fénelon or his noble friends who had espoused "Quietism" in Paris against the vehemence of Bossuet, the outstanding orator and churchman of his time.

Such persisting quarrels over doctrines were public affairs throughout Louis XIV's reign and the fortunes of victors and vanquished were dependent upon royal action. This fact may be considered as one reason why high-ranking officials in government came to look upon religion as primarily a matter of politics, and why many less important people had come, even before 1715, to look upon matters of doctrine as more important than questions of morality.

The common people obviously did not share in such changing attitudes. They looked upon their little parish priests as guides and counselors. But those in authority in France showed their attitude toward religious questions very clearly in the years of persecution of Protestants preceding the Revocation of the Edict of Nantes—which legally protected them.

The royal policy was a matter of public knowledge: Louis wished all loyal Frenchmen to be of the Catholic faith. Letters and sermons of 1685 show clearly that important people in Paris believed that most of the Protestants had already obeyed the King's request by that date and that only a few recalcitrant and untrustworthy subjects still clung to the "heresy."

It seems curious today, perhaps, that Protestants were first offered monetary rewards. But the fact is that the men in charge of such disbursements from the King's purse were astonished when those sums were refused by so many "stuburn people." A little persecution was, however, thought of as an efficient remedy. Nevertheless, "a little persecution" hardened the Protestant resistance, even before the official revocation of their rights as citizens, and religious, political, and military leaders expressed astonishment at the continued will to resist on the part of lower-class and middle-class Protestants, in Normandy, in the South of France, and especially in the Cévennes in the center of the country, where resistance flared up and continued for years.

Since religion had become primarily a political matter, it is not surprising that, after the death of Louis XIV, the example of the scandalous life of the Regent, the Duke of Orleans, served as a pattern for other people in Paris. The lives, schemes, and actions of the Regent, of the Scotsman John Law, and of the disreputable Cardinal Dubois were obvious signs of the change of emphasis that had taken place in religious fervor (at least in Paris) since the time of the pious Pascal and Racine. It seems likely that the antireligious efforts of French unbelievers, called the *philosophes,* would have had less influence later on, if it had not been for the scandalous examples set by certain nobility and churchmen during the years from 1715 to 1723. Indeed, from the time of Gassendi, La Mothe le Vayer, and other iconoclasts until the years of Pierre Bayle at the end of the seventeenth century, it was not socially in good taste to favor subversive doctrines.

II

Quite aside from the woes of the Protestants, whose exodus caused a reduction in manufacturing and foreign trade, the half century following 1690 was in many ways an unhappy period. Even before 1690, the constant drain upon the economy of the nation, for which the warlike ambition of Louis XIV was directly to blame, had been greater than even a prime minister like Colbert could conjure away. The Treaty of Nijmegen in 1678 had probably marked the end of good fortune in foreign adventures. Although the defeat of the French navy off Beachy head in 1690, off La Hogue in 1692, and the Treaty of Ryswick in 1697 pointed to dwindling respect for France in Europe, Louis XIV continued his campaigns in North America, on the Danube, in Spain, in Italy, and in Ireland.

From a political standpoint, sufficient reasons perhaps existed to justify the coercion of French Protestants into the Catholic fold. Protestant neighbors in England, Holland, and Germany, as well as the probably disloyal Protestants at home, were dangerous, according to the views of those who put religion into the category of politics and were intent only on national glory. But continuation of the wars proved inadequate, after 1678, to increase French power in Europe.

In addition to military reverses, other serious events disrupted the monarchy. Disastrous famine occurred in the 1690's, in 1709–10, and again in 1725. The popular notion of a unified and well-governed France is emphatically denied by the fact that, as early as 1709, a hungry horde had rattled the grill and shaken the gates at Versailles, shouting for bread. And, ten years after Louis XIV's death, in the city of Paris, a mob estimated at eighteen hundred openly pillaged food shops.

Then, in 1720, the Mississippi Bubble finally burst with a resounding explosion, following a heavy gambling spree involving many in the various classes, as well as many foreigners who had come to Paris hoping to make a fortune. The schemes of John Law fell apart; shares and bank-notes dropped to the point where many hundreds were beggared. During that same year, a plague afflicted Marseille at the other end of the country, a disaster of such proportions that a whole region in the South of France was sealed off by soldiers to preserve the rest of the kingdom.

The series of catastrophes must have impressed peasant, shopkeeper, police officer, and judge far more than the struggles for precedence among dukes at Court, so painstakingly related in the *Memoirs* of Saint-Simon. Even kindhearted men, it seems, could remain indifferent to the misfortune of the nation, or to the cruelty of customs which they had known from childhood. An examination of the reactions of two groups who lived through those years points to what were, in fact, fairly wide-spread feelings in France.

Because most writing by Protestant Frenchmen, at home and abroad, is so far from typical of that of the great majority of their compatriots, their work will be reported only very sparingly in this chapter. Their political animosity sometimes made their statements about misery and hunger less than charitable with regard to their fellow Frenchmen. The influence of Protestant authors becomes evident more and more, after 1730, upon rationalist *philosophes,* intent on criticizing the monarchical-Christian tradition.

Shortly before the Revocation of the Edict of Nantes, on September 28, 1685, a lady wrote to Count de Bussy Rabutin, Lieutenant General of the Armies of the King, as follows:

The King has done marvels against the Huguenots. This is a Christian and Royal enterprise and the authority he is using to bring them back to the Church will in the long run be the salvation of their people, or, at the very least, of their children, who will be brought up in the true Faith. The King will have blessings from Heaven for this. He lives in a most Christian manner. . . .[2]

On November 18, 1685, the general wrote to the lady:

In the past twenty years the King has almost uprooted this heresy in his Kingdom, by cutting off royal favor, by excluding Protestants from public office, in a word by removing opportunities for livelihood, without violence. If he continues to be fortunate in this project, he will have gained more profit and honor by the ruin of that religion than by winning battles and conquering Provinces.[3]

Clearly, Bussy Rabutin, like many of his contemporaries and their king, had believed during the years preceding the Revocation that Protestantism was almost extinct in France. Surely, those who were still convinced of "this heresy" could easily be brought to abjure it, if it were formally banned by the monarch and some violent pressure were applied here and there in recalcitrant cases. The failure of this policy soon caused more painful pressure than had been contemplated. Increased violence quite naturally caused a greater hardening of Protestant convictions, and violence on their part met violence on the part of the government in mountainous Central France.

In 1685 and 1686, Bishop Gilbert Burnet of England, a prolific writer and often a keen observer, passed through France. His testimony regarding the poverty and wretchedness of regions he traversed is striking. In his *Travels through France, Italy, Germany, and Switzerland,* which was translated into French and appeared at Rotterdam in 1688, we read on the second page:

As I came all the way from Paris to Lyons, I was amazed to see so much Misery as appeared, not only in Villages, but even in big Towns, where all the Marks of an extreme Poverty shew'd themselves both in the Buildings, the Cloaths, and almost in the Looks of the Inhabitants: And a general

2 "Le Roi fait des merveilles contre les Huguenots; c'est une œuvre Chrétienne et Royale, et l'autorité dont il se sert pour les ramener à l'union de l'Eglise, leur sera salutaire à la fin, et au pis aller à leurs enfans qui seront élevez dans la pureté de la foi. Cela lui attirera des bénedictions du Ciel. Il vit fort Chrétiennement. . . ." Lettre de Mme de Sc—, Paris, 28 septembre 1685, in Bussy Rabutin, *Lettres* (Paris: F. et P. Delaulne, 1697).

3 "En vingt ans de retranchement de grâces, d'exclusions de Charges publiques, en un mot de soustractions d'alimens sans violence, le Roi a presque déraciné cette hérésie de son Etat. S'il continue à être heureux dans ce projet, il aura gagné bien des Batailles et des Provinces, qui ne lui ont fait ni tant d'honneur ni tant de profit que la ruine de cette Religion." (18 novembre 1685), in *ibid.*

dispeopling in all the Towns, was a very visible Effect of the Hardships under which they lay.[4]

And again:

> Switzerland lies between France and Italy, that are both of them Countries incomparably more rich and better furnished with all the Pleasures and Conveniences of Life than it is; and yet Italy is almost quite dispeopled. . . . And France is in a great Measure dispeopled, and the Inhabitants are reduced to a Poverty that appears in all the Marks in which it can shew itself, both in their Houses, Furniture, Clothes, and Looks. On the contrary Switzerland is extreme full of People, and in several Places, in the Villages as well as in their Towns, one sees all the Marks he can look for of Plenty and Wealth; Their Houses and Windows are in good Case, the Highways are well maintained, all People are well clothed, and every one lives at his Ease . . . those Vallies are well peopled, and every one lives happy and at ease under a gentle Government: whilst other rich and plentiful Countries are reduced to such Misery, that as many of the Inhabitants are forced to change their Seats, so those who [*sic*] stay behind can scarce live, and pay those grievous Impositions that are laid upon them.[5]

We may, if we wish, allow somewhat for this Anglican author's observations and theories, and yet Burnet was a man known to be truthful and not likely to exaggerate. In short, he was reputed to be of judicious mind. La Bruyère had observed the stark poverty of French peasants in the 1680's and Jean-Jacques Rousseau remembered, many years afterwards, the peasant of 1731 in France who had food and wished to be hospitable, but who dared not give the traveling foreigner even a crust, until he became convinced that he was not a tax collector's spy.

Many others remained horrified by what they had seen. *A Continuation of the Treatise on the Enforcement of Regulations* by Le Clerc du Brillet appeared in Paris in 1738. The editor of the *Journal des Sçavans*, in March, 1739, commented that this author had written the first volume of his *Treatise* "after having observed the frightful dearth of everything in 1693."

Sébastien le Prestre de Vauban, the great authority on military fortifications, was of all men perhaps the most credible witness regarding the wretched state of France at the end of the seventeenth century and the

---

[4] Bishop Gilbert Burnet, *Travels through France, Italy, Germany, and Switzerland* (London: T. Payne, 1750), p. 2.

[5] *Ibid.*, pp. 42–43.

beginning of the eighteenth century. Authors as diverse as Voltaire, Fontenelle, Saint-Simon, and the Dominican, Father Labat, all admired and respected him, for Vauban was of outstanding honesty and sincerity, patriotic to the extent of opposing Louis XIV in the interest of France and at cost to himself.

In a letter to his friend, Roger Brulait Puyzieulx, Marquis de Sillery, written in June, 1699, Vauban wrote: "The unfortunate Peace of Ryswick has greatly lowered our standing among our neighbors and everywhere else."[6]

A month later, writing from Dunkirk, Vauban repeated the same opinion, but his patriotism won over his despondent thoughts, as it frequently did throughout his last years: "Not that the state of affairs and our recent conduct do not inspire many scornful thoughts among our neighbors; but they had better not be too sure, for one misstep does not necessarily lead to a fall."[7]

Pessimism was stronger in this upright patriot two months later, however. In his letter to Puyzieulx from Dieppe on September 16, 1699, a reaction of disgust appears in his reference to France ceding half the Island of Saint Christopher in the Antilles: "It seems that Frenchmen now have only the capacity to bring dishonor upon themselves."[8]

Continuing his inspection of fortifications along the coast, Vauban wrote the same friend from Saint-Malo: "In this region, people complain bitterly of the fact that commerce has ceased. This complaint is general in all the regions which I have passed through, to a degree which you cannot imagine."[9]

Over a year later, Vauban was still at work building or rebuilding coastal fortifications. From Toulon on the Mediterranean, in a region

6 "La malheureuse paix de Ryswick nous avoit extrêmement fait tomber de considération chez nos voisins et partout ailleur." Marquis de Vauban, *Lettres intimes addressées au marquis de Puyzieulx* (Paris: Ed. Bossard, 1924), Lettre de juin 1699; hereafter cited as Vauban, *Lettres*.

7 "Ce n'est pas que la situation de nos affaires et la conduite que nous tenons depuis quelque temps n'inspirent bien des pensées méprisantes à nos voisins; mais fol qui s'y fie, on ne tombe pas pour faire un faux pas." *Ibid.*, 12 juillet 1699.

8 "Il semble que les François ne soyent plus faits que pour se déshonorer." *Ibid.*, 16 septembre 1699.

9 "On se plaint fort, en ce pays-ci, de la cessation du commerce: la plainte est générale par tous les pays d'où je viens, à un point que cela ne se conçoit pas." *Ibid.*, 2 novembre 1699.

where famine in the 1690's and still other causes had reduced the population, he wrote:

France has certainly lost a good third of its subjects. And the two thirds who remain are not worth as much as the third lost . . . one part of the population, which is the greater part, tills the soil and does not profit by it, the other part appropriates its fruits . . . one possesses all the goods and property, uses them and dissipates them in superfluities, while the other is perishing of hunger and poverty. What is the remedy to this? I see none, for far from making life easier for the common people, the others find something new every day by which to oppress them.[10]

By August, 1704, this devoted soldier was in despair:

. . . in the interior of the Kingdom, everything is ruined; several Provinces even are leaning toward revolt: Auvergne and the Dauphiné are filled with malcontents; the Protestant inhabitants of the Cévennes keep a large body of our troops busy to no purpose. I am as good a Catholic as the next man, but I admit that, under such circumstances, I should not hesitate to grant those wretched people in the Cévennes free exercise of their religion. But, as the high capacity of His Majesty has judged the matter differently, he must be thinking more correctly than I.[11]

With the exception of his love of country, Vauban was anything but a man of tender feelings. He had been born, as he said, "the poorest gentleman in all France," orphaned and brought up in a rough profession. But his contemporary, Archbishop Fénelon, expressed much the same sense of ruin in the year of famine (1709) and in the spring which followed.

In a letter of December, 1709, Fénelon said:

The troops on this frontier are without money, and people are down to their last piece of bread each day. . . . The soldiers keep languishing and dying,

[10] "Il est certain que la France a perdu un grand tiers des siens et que les deux tiers qui restent ne valent pas le tiers perdu . . . l'une, qui est la grande, cultive la terre et n'en profite pas, et l'autre s'en approprie les fruits . . . l'une possède tous les biens, les mange et dissipe en superfluités et l'autre meurt de faim et de misère. Quel moyen de remédier à cela? Je n'en sais aucun; car loin de soulager les peuples, on invente tous les jours quelque chose de nouveau à leur préjudice." *Ibid.,* 4 décembre 1700.

[11] ". . . au dedans du Royaume. Tout y est ruiné; plusieurs provinces mêmes ont du penchant à la révolte: l'Auvergne et le Dauphiné sont remplis de mécontents; ceux des Cévennes nous occupent inutilement un bon corps de troupes. Je suis un aussi bon catholique qu'un autre; mais je vous avoue que, dans une conjoncture comme celle-ci, je n'hésiterais pas à laisser aux malheureux des Cévennes le libre exercice de leur religion. Mais comme la haute capacité de S.M. l'a jugé autrement, il faut bien qu'elle pense plus juste que moi." *Ibid.,* 19 août 1704.

whole units are wasting away and do not even have hope of improvement.
. . . It seems to me there is reason to fear an enemy invasion next year.
. . . I have no fear for myself, or for my personal fortune; but I love
France and am devoted, as I should be, to the King and to the Royal
Family.[12]

The following April he wrote as follows about his fears:

Everything I hear our principal officers and officials say makes me fear
great misfortunes. We are short of everything; the soldiers are so starved
and listless that nothing vigorous can be expected of them. By all appearances, the campaign will begin soon.[13]

If two serious famines and diverse military reverses, as well as de-
creased manufacturing and exports had reduced some of the certainties
of belief of only a few years earlier, some signs of such a change in the
officials' attitude should become apparent. One should expect to find
that even in high places the fever of persecution of Protestants might
have cooled somewhat before 1720. This supposition is perhaps ade-
quately supported by the fact that Monsieur d'Arnadin, Doctor of the
Sorbonne and Royal Censor of Books, allowed the first part of the
following sentence to appear in a book by Guillot de Marcilly, printed
in Paris in 1719:

Although there are a number of decent people who left France, believing
it their duty to do so because of their religion, it is equally certain that a
large number of ignorant scum-of-the-earth, while making France a better
place by their departure, have spread about in this Republic [Holland] and
elsewhere.[14]

12 "Les troupes y manquent d'argent, et on est chaque jour au dernier morceau de
pain. . . . Les soldats languissent et meurent, les corps entiers dépérissent, et ils n'ont
pas même l'espérance de se remettre. . . . Il nous est permis, ce me semble, de craindre
que les ennemis ne nous envahissent la campagne prochaine . . . je n'ai aucune peur
pour ma personne ni pour mon intérêt particulier: mais j'aime la France, et je suis attaché,
comme je le dois être, au roi et à la maison royale." Lettre XVIII, au duc de Chevreuse,
Cambrai, 5 décembre 1709, in *Œuvres complètes de M. François de Salignac de La
Mothe Fénelon*, Vol. VIII. Edition unobtainable (ed.).

13 "Tout ce que j'entends dire à nos principaux officiers et aux intendants, fait
craindre de grands malheurs. On manque de tout; les soldats sont affamés et si languis-
sants, qu'on n'en peut rien espérer de vigoureux. Selon toutes les apparences, la campagne s'ouvrira bientôt." Lettre XXII, au duc de Chevreuse, Cambrai, 7 avril 1710, in
ibid.

14 "Quoiqu'il y ait un nombre d'honnêtes gens qui soient sortis du royaume croyant
le devoir faire par motif de religion, il est constant aussi qu'il y a une infinité de
canailles ignorantes qui, purgeant la France par leur sortie, se sont répandues dans cette
République et ailleurs." Guillot de Marcilly, *Relation historique et théologique d'un
voyage en Hollande* (Paris: Jacques Estienne, 1719), p. 8.

That the author of this sentence was a gentleman boastful of having shaken the Protestant belief of the Marquis de Longallerie, who had escaped to Holland, is significant. Perhaps, by 1719, gentlemen were gentlemen, even if Protestant refugees!

Although official torture of prisoners to extract confessions continued in France for many years after 1720, the torture of anyone, even slaves, by private individuals was forbidden in the *Edicts of the King for the Administration of Justice in Louisiana*, published at Versailles in March, 1724. This document, which will be referred to again later, contains one very illuminating article: "Article XXXVIII. We forbid the torture of slaves by authority of private persons. These may only chain them and beat them with rods or with ropes."[15]

In 1726, Mademoiselle Charlotte-Elisabeth Aïssé, the respected friend of a number of noblemen, wrote in a letter: ". . . everything which happens in this kingdom clearly foretells its destruction. How wise you are to maintain the laws and to do so severely, for innocence is preserved in that way."[16]

Jesuit missionaries in Louisiana were moved by the ill-treatment of Frenchwomen taken prisoners by the Natchez Indians at the time of the revolt. Father Mathurin Le Petit testified as follows, about the year 1730: "We could not forbear being affected, when we saw arrive in this city [New Orleans] the Frenchwomen whom the Natchez had made slaves."[17] But in the same passage, this good Jesuit, who believed in law and order, also said:

Three of the most refractory Negroes, who had taken sides most clearly with the *Natchez*, were abandoned to the mercies of the Indians. They were burned alive with a cruelty which inspired all other Negroes with a new

[15] "Deffendons de faire donner de leur authorité privée la question ou torture à leurs esclaves . . . leur permettons seulement, de les faire enchaisner et battre de verges ou de cordes." *Le Code noir, ou Edit du Roy servant de Réglement pour le gouvernement et l'Administration de la Justice . . . le commerce des Esclaves Nègres dans la Louisiane* (Versailles, mars 1724), Art. XXXVIII.

[16] ". . . tout ce qui arrive dans cette monarchie, annonce bien sa destruction. Que vous êtes sages vous autres de maintenir les loix, et d'être sévères! Il s'ensuit de là l'innocence." Mlle de Aïssé, *Lettres à Mme C . . . , depuis l'année 1726 jusqu'en 1733* (Paris: Lagrange, 1787), Lettre IV, p. 44.

[17] "On ne put s'empêcher d'être attendri, lorsqu'on vit arriver en cette Ville les femmes Françaises, que les Natchez avaient fait leurs esclaves." Le Petit, "Lettre au Procureur des Missions de l'Amérique septentrionale," datée à la Nouvelle Orléans, 12 juillet 1730, *Jesuit Relations and Allied Documents. Travels and Explorations of the Jesuit Missionaries in New France, 1610–1791* (76 vols.; Cleveland, Ohio: The Burroughs Bros. Co., 1900), LXVIII, 198–99.

horror of the Savages: a blessing may result for the safety of this Colony. . . .[18]

Nearly four hundred women and children of these savages were captured when French troops were sent to conquer the rebelling Natchez tribe. These captives were sold in the West Indies as slaves, for the benefit of the Mississippi "Company" through which, since the time of Law, Frenchmen had been exploiting Louisiana.

None of the Jesuit Missionaries seems to have protested against these official actions to instill fear in Negroes or Indians in the Louisiana colony—which would tend to indicate little change toward compassion in the New World since the time of Pizarro and Cortez farther south.

A similar lack of imagination and absence of tenderness toward those who were not French is evident in the account of events in Montreal which was sent by a Jesuit to France in 1735:

> An Algonquin, in a drinking-bout, with three stabs of a knife killed a poor soldier who was quietly working in a house at Montreal. The Algonquin thought he would escape punishment because he was drunk and did not know what he was doing. He was condemned notwithstanding to be hanged; but as the executioner was away, they smashed his head instead.[19]

The unemotional and matter-of-fact manner in which Father Nau told of these events in his letter "from near Quebec" in October, 1735, betrays no criticism of the manner of execution of the Algonquin. The method used was just as expeditious as that of the regular executioner in killing the offender as an example to others. Possibly the brutal and unusual execution convinced other savages of the seriousness of the crime, and the men in charge of affairs in France and in her colonies were apparently unconscious of the ferocity of their ways, perhaps because they were matters of day-to-day experience.

III

Letters and memoirs of this period have an abundance of general laments about crookedness and injustice, like Montesquieu's: "In Paris,

---

18 "On a abandonné aux Tchactas trois Nègres des plus mutins, et qui s'étaient déclarés le plus pour les Natchez; ils les ont brûlés vifs avec une cruauté qui a inspiré à tous les Nègres une nouvelle horreur des Sauvages: il en peut résulter un bien pour la sûreté de la Colonie. . . ." *Ibid.*

19 "Un Algonquin dans l'Ivresse tua de trois coups de couteau un pauvre soldat qui travaillait tranquillement dans une maison de Monréal. L'Algonquin . . . crut en être quitte pour dire qu'il étoit yure [ivre] et qu'il ne sçavoit pas ce qu'il faisoit, mais on ne laissa pas de le condamner à être pendu, et parce que le bourreau étoit absent on luy cassa la tête." *Ibid.*, pp. 266–67.

you will find a very large number of worthy people on foot, and the majority of coaches filled with scoundrels,"[20] and minutiae like the Marquis de Dangeau's: "On Tuesday, April 1st, 1718, the Duchess de Berri went to Saint-Cloud to bathe early in the morning."[21] But there was also an important attempt to see, and to show others, how contemporary events looked to men of no standing in society.

Thus, in *Les Bourgeoises à la mode*, a comedy by Dancourt produced in 1692, the serving-woman Lisette says: "The good times are over, Madame Amilin; people of quality have no extra money today."[22] In the same author's comedy, *Le Moulin de Javelle*, first played in 1696, that meeting-place of amorous and adulterous couples near Paris constitutes the scene of a play. Its whole tone, except for the language used, lacks the seemly and decorous air often associated with the reign of Louis XIV, at least until the year 1700. In the fourth scene, Madame Bertrand, the proprietress of the establishment, says: "I don't know how many ladies who spend the winter here with Dukes and Marquises almost never come in summer with any but legal officials and young dandies from the Saint-Honoré district."[23] The countess to whom this speech is addressed says that everybody who is anybody is off with the Army. And the serving-girl, Finette, agrees, "Yes. The way things are now, you have to take what you can find. Summer is the dead season."[24]

In 1695 a book, supposedly written by Pierre le Pesant de Boisguilbert, appeared without authorization, perhaps at Rouen, entitled, *Detailed Account of France: The Cause of the Diminution of its Wealth, and the Ease of Remedying the Situation, by Furnishing in One Month All the Money the King Needs, and Making Everyone Richer.* The

---

[20] "A Paris, vous trouverez à pied une infinité de gens de mérite et la plupart des carrosses pleins de faquins." Montesquieu à Msgr. Cérati; 1740, *Lettres*.

[21] "Madame la duchesse de Berry alla dès le matin à Saint-Cloud se baigner." Marquis de Dangeau, *Journal* (Paris: Firmin Didot, 1859), Vol. XVII, mardi, 1er avril.

[22] "Le bon tems est passé, Madame Amelin; les gens de qualité n'ont point aujourd'hui d'argent de reste." Dancourt, *Les Bourgeoises à la Mode* (Comédie. Représentée pour la première fois le 15 novembre 1692), Acte I, scène 12, in *Choix de Pièces du Théâtre françois, Chef-d'œuvres de Dancourt* (4 vols.; Paris: Les Libraires associés), Vol. II.

[23] "Je ne sais combien de Dames qui sont ici tout l'hiver avec des Ducs et des Marquis, n'y viennent presque, l'été, qu'avec des Procureurs et des petits-Maîtres du quartier S. Honoré." Dancourt, *Le Moulin de Javelle* (1696), scène 4, in *ibid.*

[24] "A l'heure qu'il est, on se prend où l'on peut; en été c'est la saison morte." *Ibid.*

commercial theory of this book is of less importance here than its remarks on the sad state of finance and commerce in 1695, a year of famine:

> In fact, arbitrary taxation forces the Merchant to conceal his money and a Farmer to let his land lie fallow, for if the first did business and if the second ploughed his land, they would both be overwhelmed with taxes by those powerful people who themselves can decide to pay nothing, or very little.[25]

In the following year, a notorious scamp, François Gacon, published his *Satirical Discourse in Verse,* in which the advantages to be gained by going into bankruptcy are explained to a client by a lawyer.

> Go into bankruptcy, he said,
> There is no other way for you,
> An Easy step, and in one week
> I'll show you how to gain the sum
> Of a hundred thousand crowns.[26]

Another indication of protest against high taxation appeared in 1701, supposedly by a former judge, also without indication of printer or place and, of course, without royal privilege, entitled *Memoirs for the Restoration of Commerce in France.* "Jean Le Pelletier," or whoever actually wrote this book, proposed a government by businessmen as a solution to many difficulties that sprang from the practice of rent-farmers.

With frequent mention of "the sufferings of the common people," the author advanced the following: "Nothing is more opposed to the interests of a hereditary Monarchy than groups or Companies with extraordinary privileges, for they destroy commerce and reduce the number of men in business."[27]

---

25 "En effet, la Taille arbitraire contraint un Marchand de cacher son argent, et un Laboureur de laisser sa Terre en friche; parce que si l'un vouloit faire Commerce, et l'autre labourer, ils seroient tous deux accablez de Taille par les personnes puissantes, qui sont en possession de ne rien payer, ou peu de chose." Pierre le Pesant de Bois-guilbert, *Le Détail de la France: La Cause de la Diminution de ses Biens, et de la facilité du Remède, en fournissant en un mois, tout l'argent dont le Roy a besoin, et en enrichissant tout le monde* (n.p., 1695), p. 214.

26 "Faites, lui disoit-il, au plûtôt Banqueroute,/ Pour sortir d'embarras il n'est point d'autre route,/ La chose est fort aisée, et dans huit jours au plus,/ Je vous fais d'un seul coup gagner cent mille écus." [François Gacon], *Discours satiriques en vers* (Cologne: n.p., 1696), pp. 66–67.

27 "Rien n'est donc plus opposé à l'intérêt d'une Monarchie héréditaire, que les Partis ou les compagnies privilégiées, car ils détruisent les Négoces et diminuent le nombre des Négociants." Jean Le Pelletier, *Mémoires pour le rétablissement du commerce en France* ([Rouen?]: n.p., 1701), p. 71.

The diatribes of refugee Protestants which appeared in the monthly magazine, *Mercure historique et politique,* published in Holland for many years, often indulged in wishful thinking. In France itself, the following prediction, for example, was surely much less credited than in Holland: "With the exception of a very few, all Christian Nations, Catholic as well as Protestant will join in breaking this union [of the Spanish Monarchy and the French Dauphin]."[28] Yet the magazine's correspondents in France fed the editors accurate, and frequently prophetic commentaries. Remarks like the following, dated February, 1702, must have alarmed partisans of the "Sun King" Louis XIV as much as they pleased the Protestant refugees:

> But what is astonishing is that there should exist bold enough people in France and in the capital of the Realm, not only to condemn what is done at Court, but also to compose and circulate satires aimed at such a Sovereign Prince and such an absolute Ruler as Louis XIV. This causes one to speculate and to draw conclusions, if one is given to reflection. People are already speaking of the "Setting Sun" and of the "Rising Sun." . . . Frenchmen, both great and small, are so discontented over being heavily burdened with taxes and being reduced to abject poverty, in order to preserve for Philip V a Kingdom which can only end by being dismembered, that hatred and despair blind them and do not permit them to reflect (as subjects have been urged to do for so long) that one must never write anything against powers which can punish.[29]

The "setting of the sun of Louis XIV" can perhaps be partially explained by another statement in the section of this periodical entitled "News From France" in May of the same year: "Money is becoming

---

[28] "Tout ce qu'il y a des Puissances Chrétiennes, tant Catholiques que Protestants, si l'on en excepte un très petit nombre, se ligueront avec l'Empereur pour tâcher de rompre cette union. . . ." *Mercure historique et politique* (The Hague: 1692–1720), XXXII (1702), Avant-propos.

[29] "Mais ce qu'il y a de surprenant, c'est qu'il y ait des gens assez hardis en France et dans la Capitale du Royaume, non seulement pour fronder ce qui se fait à la Cour, mais pour composer et débiter des Satires contre un Prince aussi Souverain et aussi absolu que l'est Louis XIV. Cela fait faire bien des réflexions aux spéculatifs et tirer bien des conséquences. On parle déjà de Soleil couchant et de Soleil levant, . . . les François tant grands que petits sont si mécontens qu'on les accable d'impositions, et qu'on les réduise à la dernière misère pour conserver en son entier à Philippe V une Monarchie qui ne peut être à la fin que démembrée, que le dépit et le désespoir les aveuglent, et ne leur permet pas de faire cette réflexion recommandée aux Sujets depuis si long-temps; qu'il ne faut jamais écrire contre ceux qui peuvent proscrire." *Ibid.,* février 1702.

scarcer every day. New ways of getting money, or of extracting it from the purses of private individuals, are being worked at continually."[30]

In July, 1703, in the editors' "Comment on the News from France," we read:

> The more one considers the population of France, the more one is surprised that they do not rise up everywhere, after the example of the dissatisfied folk of the Cévennes; for after all, it is hard to imagine anything more wretched than their condition, or more frightful than their destiny.[31]

Once the violent persecution of the Protestants had been launched, the spirit of revolt against the power of the throne was constantly in evidence among Protestant authors, almost a century before the 1789 Revolution. Opinions such as the following, which appeared in the *Mercure historique et politique,* were typical among the subjects of Louis XIV at the time of the famine of 1709:

> [January, 1709] Money has become so rare and costs so much to borrow that it is difficult to find any at six per cent per month.[32]
>
> [April, 1709] Letters which we receive from the Provinces in France are all filled with the wretched poverty suffered there because of the shortage of food and the great damage caused by this long and harsh winter. Money is still very scarce.[33]
>
> [June, 1709] Troops are used to make the roads safe, for they are no longer safe [otherwise], because of the great number of people driven to despair, who rob passers-by.[34]

IV

Commentaries written by those of no particular social standing in the days immediately following the death of Louis XIV were sometimes bitter. One nearly forgotten author of the period who deserves better

---

30 "L'argent devient plus rare de jour en jour en France, et l'on travaille continuellement à de nouvelles affaires pour en trouver et pour le faire sortir des bourses des particuliers." *Ibid.,* mai 1702.

31 "Plus on considère les peuples de France et plus on est surpris qu'ils ne se soulèvent partout à l'exemple des Mécontens des Sévennes [*sic*]; car enfin on ne peut rien concevoir de plus triste que leur condition, ni de plus affreux que leur destinée." *Ibid.,* juillet 1703, p. 67.

32 "L'argent est d'une rareté et cherté, qu'on a peine à en trouver à six pour cent par mois." *Ibid.,* janvier 1709, p. 702.

33 "Les lettres qu'on reçoit des Provinces de France, ne sont remplies que de la misère qu'on y souffre, par la disette des vivres, et par les grands dommages que ce long et rude hiver y a causez. L'argent y est toujours rare." *Ibid.,* avril 1709, p. 409.

34 Original unavailable (ed.).

recognition today was Robert Chasles. His *Memoirs* do not go beyond the year 1716. They were still in manuscript in the collection of Gabriel Hanotaux until published in Paris in 1931, although Chasles' novel and his annals of a trip to the East Indies were known and the novel reprinted before 1735. His realism of description and effective expression of dislikes merits much quotation here.

In the first and second chapters of his *Memoirs*, he pronounces a terrible judgment of the King who had just died:

> Louis XIV has died with few regrets on the part of his subjects, although he had been the object of their adoration. This prince lost the love of his subjects by the ridiculously devout life in which he was plunged during his last thirty years. The suppression of the Edict of Nantes began the downfall of France, by the money which those who chose banishment took with them, and by the manufacturing . . . which those voluntary exiles took to neighboring countries.[35]

Evidence abounds in his writings that Chasles was both business-minded and anticlerical in ways which were certainly not unusual among "Catholics." His hatred and distrust of the Protestant English is mitigated only by his favorable opinion of their religious toleration:

> They love their King, as long as he does not attack their religion or their privileges. But as soon as he violates his oath and attacks these, they consider themselves free of their oath to him. It is perfectly certain that King James would have died still a reigning King, if he had not undertaken to make his religion dominant and if he had had Father Peters hanged on London Bridge.[36]

In the following passage Chasles expresses some of the feeling which undoubtedly gave rise to his political and economic opinions. The explosive and personal resentment against the wretched condition of the poor and against the brutality of public officials is noteworthy.

[35] "Louis XIV est mort avec peu de regrets de ses sujets, quoiqu'il en eût été l'adoration. Ce prince a encore perdu l'amour de ses sujets par la dévotion ridicule où il a été plongé les trente dernières années de sa vie. La suppression de l'édit de Nantes a commencé la perte de la France, par l'argent que ceux qui s'en sont bannis ont emporté avec eux, et par les manufactures . . . que ces bannis volontaires ont portées chez nos voisins." Robert Chasles, *Un Colonial au temps de Colbert: Mémoires de Robert Challes, Ecrivain du Roi* (written before 1717), edited by A. Augustin-Thierry (Paris: Plon, 1931), p. 4; hereafter cited as Chasles, *Mémoires*.

[36] "Ils aiment leur Roi, tant qu'il n'attaque pas leur religion ni leurs privilèges. Mais, sitôt qu'il viole l'un ou l'autre, ils se tiennent quittes du leur. Il est très certain que le roi Jacques serait mort sur le trône, s'il n'avait pas entrepris de rendre sa religion dominante et s'il eût fait pendre le P. Peters sur le pont de Londres." *Ibid.*, p. 23.

This wretchedness has been carried to such a point that I have myself seen two things which posterity will find it hard to believe. One took place at Saint-Maixent in Poitou. A woman whose husband had died about two weeks earlier was eight months pregnant. Furthermore, she had four living children. This woman had just been ordered dispossessed for unpaid taxes. The scoundrelly bailiffs assigned to collect taxes were taking from this poor woman's home everything they could carry away. The unfortunate creature ran after them. Her complaints, cries, and lamentations drew a great number of spectators. . . . In spite of the poor woman's being very close to childbirth, a constable, or a bailiff, was brutal enough to strike her. She gave birth at that moment . . . and died a quarter-hour later, screaming imprecations by the hundred against those who had caused her death and asking God's vengeance upon them.[37]

Over fifty pages farther on, Chasles is still cursing officials, tax-farmers, and moneylenders who oppress the people:

Wretches and scoundrels, who do not see, or who refuse to see, that by reducing their contemporaries to abject poverty they are likewise condemning future generations, and themselves are inviting curses to be heaped upon them! The wealth of such men, gained by evil means, will not pass to the third generation![38]

Many confessors complain that unmarried women who confess to them admit sins of the flesh, and some confess having had abortions, because they did not have money to pay the fee for publishing marriage-bans in church.[39]

The death of Louis XIV was, of course, a feature of all diaries and

---

37 "Cette misère a été portée à un tel point, que j'ai vu par moi-même deux choses, que certainement la postérité aura peine à croire. L'une est arrivée à Saint-Maixent, en Poitou.
Une femme, dont le mari était mort, il n'y avait que quinze jours ou environ, qui était grosse de plus de huit mois, ayant en outre quatre enfants vivants, venait d'être exécutée pour la taille. Les coquins d'huissiers des tailles emportaient de chez cette pauvre femme tout ce qu'il pouvaient emporter. Cette malheureuse courait après eux. Ses plaintes, ses cris et ses lamentations attirèrent un grand nombre de spectateurs. . . . Tout près d'accoucher qu'était cette malheureuse, un archer ou un huissier fut assez brutal pour la frapper. Elle accoucha dans le moment . . . et mourut elle-même, un quart d'heure après, vomissant mille imprécations contre les auteurs de sa mort, dont elle demandait à Dieu la vengeance." *Ibid.,* p. 43.

38 "Malheureux et misérables, ceux qui ne voient pas, ou ne veulent pas voir, qu'en réduisant leurs contemporains à la misère ils y condamnent également les générations à venir et s'exposent à être maudits dans la suite! Leur bien, mal acquis, ne passera point à la troisième génération." *Ibid.,* p. 101.

39 "Beaucoup de confesseurs se plaignaient de ce que leurs pénitentes s'accusassent de pécher contre la chair et plusieurs de s'être fait avorter, parce qu'elles n'avaient pas le moyen de payer le contrôle des bans de mariage." *Ibid.,* p. 102.

memoirs relating to the year 1715, for no king had died in France within the memory of virtually any but centenarians. The telling of Louis XIV's death naturally varied in the writing of different men.

One suspects, in the *Journal du Marquis de Dangeau* for that momentous day, that the author might have liked to say more than:

> The King died this morning [September 1, 1715], at eight twenty-two, and gave up the ghost without difficulty, as a candle goes out. He had been unconscious all night. Immediately after his death, the duke of Orleans and all princes of the blood went to bow to the young king.[40]

Jean Buvat, probably the most typical lower bourgeois whose own record we have, remembered the event as many others did, observed from the streets, or from the court of the palace:

> An officer appearing at a palace window, came out on the balcony with a black plume on his hat to announce in a loud voice, "The King is dead!" Having withdrawn, this same officer reappeared, having taken off the black plume and replaced it with a white one. He cried three times in loud tones, "Long live the King, Louis XV!"[41]

On the fourth of December in that year, the funeral of the Marchioness de Louvois took place. Those who are familiar with Saint-Simon's manner of relating the history of his time may compare the wealth of detail in the descriptions by Jean Buvat in reporting events in the Paris streets:

> Such a heavy rain fell toward evening that the funeral procession was greatly incommoded. It left [the Marchioness's] residence in the rue de Richelieu to proceed to the Church of Saint-Roch, which was her parish, and thence to the church of the Capucins, where she was buried in the magnificent tomb of the Marquis de Louvois, Minister and Secretary of State. . . . The body was carried by eight priests, who were greatly fatigued because of the weight, for it was placed in a lead casket, enclosed

---

[40] "Le roi est mort ce matin, à huit heures un quart et demi, et il a rendu l'âme sans aucun effort, comme une chandelle qui s'éteint. La nuit s'étoit passée sans aucune connoissance. Aussitôt qu'il a expiré, le duc d'Orléans est allé avec tous les princes du sang saluer le jeune roi. . . ." Dangeau, *Journal*, 1er septembre 1715.

[41] "Après la mort du Roi, un officier dans le moment, ayant un plumet noir sur son chapeau, parut à la fenêtre, et étant sur le balcon dit à haute voix: 'Le Roi est mort!' Le même officier s'étant retiré, et ayant quitté le plumet noir pour en prendre un blanc, parut une seconde fois le même balcon, et cria à haute voix par trois fois: '*Vive le roi Louis XV!*'" Jean Buvat, Ecrivain de la Bibliothèque du Roi, *Journal de la Régence* (*1715–1723*). Publié pour la première fois . . . par Emile Camparadon, Archiviste aux Archives de l'Empire (2 vols.; Paris: H. Plon, 1865), I, 47.

in another of oak, not to speak of the rain which kept falling in abundance.[42]

The visit of the Persian Ambassadors to Paris in 1715 was described at some length by Saint-Simon and served as a point of departure for the *Lettres Persanes* of Montesquieu in 1721. But Buvat, with characteristically lower middle-class Parisian prejudice, was not greatly impressed by the expensively dressed "foreigners." On the contrary, he detailed one feature of their visit which neither of his distinguished contemporaries would have considered proper to recount when writing of ambassadors.

According to Buvat, the ambassador of Portugal who arrived shortly after the departure of the Persians created some difficulty about staying in the house assigned to important visitors in the rue de Tournon near the Luxembourg Gardens.

> Those Infidels, because of their superstitions, had scruples about exposing themselves in the toilet arrangements of that residence, although these were very clean. Instead, they put all their nastiness into a barrel, which was found in one corner of the house, after their departure.[43]

Another indication of the attitude of many thousands of Parisians in Buvat's time may be noted in his unsympathetic references to those men and women who were being shipped off to Louisiana and other colonies in the New World. Buvat, observing the events in the streets of Paris, describes their departure without any sentimental pity whatsoever.[44] To him, and apparently to many other law-abiding Parisians, the exile of those offenders was a cleansing operation beneficial to the country. Yet this petty employee of the Royal Library makes us share his terror by his description of a lightning bolt striking the Church of Saint-Sulpice. We can imagine the parishioners of that celebrated church on Sunday, June

---

[42] "Le 4 de décembre, il tomba sur le soir une si grosse pluie que le convoi funèbre de madame la marquise de Louvois en fut très-incommode . . . Ce convoi, qui partit de son hôtel, rue de Richelieu, pour aller à Saint-Roch, sa paroisse, et ensuite à l'église des Capucines, où elle fut inhumée dans le superbe mausolée du marquis de Louvois, ministre secrétaire d'Etat. . . . Le corps était porté par huit prêtres, qui en furent fort fatigués pour la pesanteur, étant mis dans un cercueil de plomb revêtu d'un autre cercueil de bois de chêne, outre la pluie qui tombait en abondance." *Ibid.*, p. 112.

[43] "Comme ces infidèles avaient scrupule de s'exposer dans les lieux communs de cet hôtel, quoique très-propres et très-commodes pour cet usage, ils jetaient leurs ordures dans un tonneau, qui s'en était trouvé rempli dans un coin de la maison." *Ibid.*, I, 38.

[44] *Ibid.*, I, 118, 386, 422, 426; II, 22, 40, 63, 93, 96–97.

29, 1719, "lying flat on the floor, overcome with fear and with the smell of sulphur."[45]

This humble and unpretentious writer had what was then a rare ability —or perhaps what was then "the bad taste"—to tell of events with striking, realistic details. Buvat was a writer of "human interest stories" before there were newspapers for the mass of people who might have enjoyed them. His manner of telling a story is made remarkably clear through the use of details, in contrast to the vague descriptions of upper-class characters in many fashionable novels which were then being writ-ten. These last are today almost impossible to read, whereas unpreten-tious Buvat's pages are so alive that one is tempted to quote a great many of them.

For instance, on the same stormy Sunday that lightning struck Saint-Sulpice, he tells us that the vanes of a windmill near the suburb of Vincennes were torn off; and a horse being led past the mill by a peasant was killed by a singeing bolt of lightning. "Half the halter remained in the man's hand, the other half being consumed by fire, which also burned the horse."[46]

Two of Buvat's fuller accounts are reproduced here because of their unconscious revelation of the lawless times in which he lived and, further, because they illustrate the realistic ability of this gifted reporter.

An individual who said he had been an officer, dressed in scarlet, crippled in both legs and riding a small horse, was begging in that condition near Paris when, two leagues from Versailles, he asked alms of a carter who was passing with his dray. This man presented the beggar with a penny, saying, "Give me back three farthings."

"Not at all," said the cripple. "Give me money."

The carter replied, "I am a poor man, I can only give you what I offered."

The cripple pointed a pistol at him to kill him, but it failed to go off, as did his other pistol; this frightened the carter, who began to run away. But the cripple followed him, armed with a dagger. Seeing him without fire-arms, the carter took courage and slashed at him with his whip, winding the lash around his neck and dragging the cripple from his horse. The carter then seized the dagger and killed the man. After this, when returning to his cart, he met a group of police patrolling the road.

The chief of them, seeing that the carter was still frightened, asked him

---

[45] "[Le tonnerre répandit une puanteur de soufre si grande, que] en furent malades aussi bien que de frayeur, dont la plupart s'étaient couchées par terre." *Ibid.*, p. 404.

[46] ". . . la moitié du licol lui resta dans la main, l'autre moitié étant en poussière avec le cheval." *Ibid.*, p. 405.

the reason. He gave the carter time to recover his wits, then listened to his story.

"If this is true," the officer said, "nothing will be done to you. But take us where you left the body."

When they all got there, they searched it and found thirty gold *louis* in the pockets of the corpse, plus as many more gold pieces in his saddle-bags, together with a whistle. Whereupon the officer said, showing the carter the whistle, "Don't worry, my lad, this is your absolution."

Then, having advanced toward a small wood, he blew the whistle.

Four robbers appeared at once and were greatly surprised to be attacked by the police.[47]

The smallpox epidemic which broke out in Paris in August and September, 1719, wrought wide havoc in the capital, and before its effects had died down, the financial panic of May, 1720, aggravated the hardships of the population, especially of the "little people" like Jean Buvat, the library worker. John Law had, several years earlier, been allowed to institute a system of banknotes which could be redeemed in coin and which were accepted in payment of taxes. After a spectacular initial success, the system collapsed when the public, alarmed at an announced gradual reduction in the value of the notes, began a run on the treasury which led to a cessation of payments. It is against this back-drop of utter financial chaos that the following excerpts must be read.

Buvat seldom wrote of amusing incidents, like the dancing and drink-ing of the fishwives from the central market in the Garden of the

---

47 "Un particulier qui disait avoir été officier, vêtu d'écarlate, estropié des deux jambes, monté sur un petit cheval, demandant l'aumône en cet état à Paris, et étant à deux lieues de Versailles, la demanda à un charretier qui passait avec sa voiture, lequel lui présenta un sol en lui disant:—'Rendez-moi trois liards!' Ce n'est point cela, dit l'estropié, donnez-moi de l'argent. Le charretier répliqua:—Je suis un pauvre homme, je ne peux vous donner que ce que je vous offre. L'estropié lui présenta un pistolet pour le tuer, qui ne prit pas feu, non plus que son autre pistolet; ce qui effraya le charretier, de telle sorte qu'il se mit à courir pour s'échapper. L'estropié le poursuivit, un poignard à la main. Mais le charretier ne lui voyant plus d'armes à feu, reprit courage et lui fit un collier de son fouet, dont il le tira en bas de son cheval, se jeta sur lui, se saisit du poignard et l'en tua; après laquelle expédition, allant rejoindre sa charrette, il fut ren-contré par une brigade d'archers de la maréchaussée, dont le commandant, ayant vu le charretier tout effrayé, lui en demanda le sujet, et après lui avoir donné le temps de se remettre les sens, le charretier lui conta son aventure. —Si cela est comme tu le dis, reprit l'officier, il ne te sera rien fait; mène-nous seulement où tu as laissé le corps. Où étant, on le fouilla, on trouva dans les poches du mort trente louis d'or, et autant dans un bourson de la selle de son cheval, avec un sifflet, sur quoi l'officier dit au charretier:—Rassure-toi, mon ami, voilà ton absolution, en lui montrant le sifflet. Suis-nous seule-ment et ne crains rien; voilà deux archers qui garderont ta charrette jusqu'à ce que nous soyons revenus. Puis s'étant avancé vers un petit bois, l'officier se servit du sifflet: aussitôt il parut quatre voleurs qui furent bien étonnés de se voir attaqués et environnés de la maréchaussée. . . ." *Ibid.*, I, 254–55.

Tuileries on the occasion of the young king's recovery from illness. The wild behavior of those women, when supplied with plenty of the royal Burgundy, "from time to time pausing to drink the king's health again and shouting 'Long live the King, and the devil with the Regency!' " is amusing.[48] But most incidents in Buvat's diary are serious and give the impression of a period when calamities must have come to be expected.

In 1721, he wrote down what had been told him by a wheelwright of his acquaintance about an escape from the quarantined south of France by a Parisian woman whose husband had died there:

> . . . To return [to Paris] she had to cross the regions of Auvergne, Gévaudan, and Limoges. She said she had gone through more than twenty villages whose inhabitants had died of the plague. Then, being in great need, she entered the house of a priest in one of those villages, near the church, whose doors were open. She went up to a bedchamber and saw the priest dead in bed, gnawed by worms. Next, she went into another room, where the Father's servant-woman was in a similar state. Having opened a chest, this woman found the sum of five hundred *livres* in gold and silver coin, which she took for her needs. She continued her journey with great difficulty and in a starving condition, without finding anyone who could give her anything to eat. She found bread in some houses standing open, whose tenants had died and rotted in their homes or on the streets. And she gave money to soldiers who were on guard, to let her pass [the quarantine line], as she also did to come back into Paris.[49]

It seems doubtful that either the woman herself or the wheelwright to whom she gave these details of horror, could have told the tale with such brevity and effect. It is even hard to see how any of his distinguished contemporaries could have much improved upon Buvat's cogent and simple prose.

[48] ". . . de temps en temps se mettaient à boire à la santé du Roi et à crier: *Vive le Roi, malgré la Régence au diable!" Ibid.*, II, 281.

[49] ". . . pour s'en revenir, elle avait traversé l'Auvergne, le Gévaudan et le Limousin, qu'elle avait passé par plus de vingt villages dont les habitants étaient tous morts de la peste; que se voyant dans un grand besoin, elle était entrée proche de l'église dans la maison du curé d'un de ces villages, dont ayant trouvé la porte ouverte elle était montée dans une chambre où elle avait vu le curé mort dans son lit, rongé de vers; qu'ensuite elle était entrée dans une autre chambre où la servante du curé était en pareil état; qu'ayant ouvert un coffre, elle y avait trouvé une somme de cinq cents livres en or et en argent monnayé dont elle s'était saisie pour ses besoins; qu'elle avait poursuivi son chemin avec beaucoup de peine et dans un grand besoin, sans trouver personne qui pût lui donner à manger; qu'elle avait trouvé du pain dans quelques maisons ouvertes dont les particuliers étaient morts et pourris chez eux et dans les rues, et qu'elle avait donné quelque argent à des soldats de garde pour la laisser passer, comme elle avait fait pour s'en revenir à Paris." *Ibid.*, pp. 299–300.

A writer whose middle-class status was considerably higher and whose life was much more comfortable than that of the scrivener Jean Buvat, was Edmond-Jean-François Barbier. His diary from July to October, 1720, presents a testimonial from a different viewpoint. On the seventeenth of July in that catastrophic year men found the bank closed. It did not reopen again for a period longer than Parisians could face with any assurance. Barbier tells of those days of suspense as follows:

> Ever since Wednesday, July 17, the Bank has not been open and nobody is paying anywhere in the city. That is what has happened to the Bank which was so flourishing at the end of last year, when they would have asked a man who wanted to cash two million *livres* in notes whether he wanted gold or silver! . . . People have great difficulty getting along without money, and it continues to be sold openly in public: bills have gone down as much as fifty per cent, which is outrageous. No one wants them anywhere, so one is obliged to buy on credit.[50]

Like other writers of memoirs, diaries, plays, and novels, Barbier excoriates the tax farmers, many of whom had sprung from the working class but by devious means had risen to the point of being bankers and even marrying girls of good family and old names. Such a man was Crozat, first a servant, then a clerk, who became a millionaire through overseas trade even before the death of Louis XIV. Barbier recounts that this scoundrelly character met his match when Law cheated him of two million *livres*, "from which it is plain that this wretched Law is a proud, insolent cheat."[51]

A proof of the general detestation of Law is the following anecdote which Barbier relates with evident gusto in his entry for October 12, 1720:

> A thing happened that will teach Law the opinion people have of him. M. de Crochetel, an officer decorated with the Cross of Saint-Louis, unfortunately has servants in livery which has some resemblance to Law's livery. His private carriage was assailed by the common people with stones,

---

[50] "Depuis le mercredi 17 juillet, la banque n'a point été ouverte et l'on ne paye nulle part. Voilà où en est cette banque si florissante à la fin de l'autre année, où l'on aurait demandé à un homme qui serait venu changer deux millions de livres s'il voulait de l'or ou de l'argent! . . . En sorte qu'on se passe d'argent avec grande peine, et on le vend toujours à la place ouvertement: le billet a été jusqu'à cinquante pour cent de perte, ce qui est indigne, car on ne veut de billets nulle part, et on est obligé de prendre à crédit." E.-J.-F. Barbier, *Journal historique et anecdotique du règne de Louis XV* (Paris: Jules Renard, 1847), juillet 1720.

[51] "On voit par là que ce malheureux Law est fripon, fier et insolent." *Ibid.,* août 1720.

as he was passing through the rue Saint-Antoine. He showed them his Cross to no purpose. Then he had the presence of mind to hurry into the Church of the Great-Jesuits. He was pursued right up to the main altar and, as he jumped over the balustrade, got a great whack with a stick on the shoulder.[52]

After reading Barbier's account of those troubled times, one will certainly have greater patience with adventure novels of the period! What seem at first, in such novels, to be melodramatic incidents outrageously contrived are related briefly by Barbier as actual events. That someone's bastard was made an archbishop (p. 190), that a man who spoke no known language spent thirty-five years in the Bastille (p. 174), that girls were kidnapped from nunneries by young gentlemen (p. 197), that criminals escaped from the Chatelet prison (p. 203), that bakers' shops were looted (p. 224), all appear in his diary during times of violence in the capital.

The sins of the great are also recorded, and what may perhaps have been rumors are recounted as facts:

> The Regent made a great row, when he returned from Chantilly; but he was appeased in a short time, that is with money. They say four millions.[53]

> M. L'abbé Dubois [Foreign Minister at the time], a man of violent nature, always has a policy of going forward by violence.[54]

> L'abbé Dubois has been anointed Archbishop of Cambrai. . . . As he is generally considered a scoundrel, idle gossips keep saying that giving him this post is a secret means the Regent has invented to make Dubois take his first communion, because as Archbishop he will be forced to say mass.[55]

Between 1734 and 1736, an outstanding novel by Marivaux was published in five parts (Paris). Jacob, the hero of *Le Paysan parvenu*, is a peasant who has succeeded in rising to middle-class status in Paris. While recounting his rapid rise, Jacob also comments on the social revolution fermenting in French society, a phenomenon observed by many others besides Marivaux. The moral diatribes of this peasant hero would obviously have been impossible in the work of a talented author in the preceding century, when the distinction between classes was clearly defined and peasants were most often considered amusing clowns.

[52] Original unavailable (ed.).

[53] "M. le Duc a fait grand bruit à son retour de Chantilly; mais il fut apaisé en peu de temps, c'est-à-dire avec de l'argent. On dit quatre millions." *Ibid.*, mai 1720.

[54] Original unavailable (ed.).

[55] Original unavailable (ed.).

Jacob, retired with a comfortable fortune, begins his life story with the following reflections:

> I have seen a number of stupid chumps, who had no other merit in society and who recognized no merit in other people but the distinction of having been born in noble families, or in those holding high positions. I used to hear those chumps speak scornfully of many who were better men than they, simply because those men were not gentlemen. And some of those commoners who were scorned, although they were worthy of respect because of many good qualities, were weak enough to blush about their birth, to conceal it, and to try to assume an origin which hid their true descent, in order to protect themselves from the disdain of society.[56]

Many other writers as well as Marivaux expressed their outraged sense of moral decency during this period. Some of them, like Marivaux, were born in families of petty nobility. Many more were commoners. The volume of such moral preaching by laymen in the publications of this fifty-year period is great enough to warrant separate consideration in a later chapter. This important development in society—the separation of moral judgment from the religious tradition—is a feature of eighteenth-century history which the minor writers quoted in this volume undoubtedly helped to create.

[56] "J'ai pourtant vu nombre de sots qui n'avaient et ne connaissaient point d'autre mérite dans le monde que celui d'être nés nobles, ou dans un rang distingué. Je les entendais mépriser beaucoup de gens qui valaient mieux qu'eux et cela seulement parce qu'ils n'étaient pas gentilshommes; mais c'est que des gens qu'il méprisaient, respectables d'ailleurs par mille bonnes qualités, avaient la faiblesse de rougir eux-mêmes de leur naissance, de la cacher, et de tâcher de s'en donner une qui embrouillait la véritable, et qui les mît à couvert du dédain du monde." Pierre de Chamblain de Marivaux, *Le Paysan parvenu* (1735–40), 1ère Partie, p. 1; hereafter cited as Marivaux, *Le Paysan parvenu.*

CHAPTER II

Witnesses of War and Wretchedness

CRITICISM OF WAR did not, of course, originate in France in the eighteenth century, nor did praise of the "noble enterprise" come to an end in that century either. Yet the number of those who did not accept war as a necessary or proper occupation for civilized men appears to have increased in Europe, in proportion as men gained greater freedom to express their feelings against a long and noble tradition.

Without going back to the antiwar statements of the Greeks and Romans, known and admired by Frenchmen of the Renaissance, we might appropriately glance at such expressions in seventeenth-century France.

I

Marc Lescarbot, in his *La Conversion des Sauvages* (1610, p. 10), the Jesuit missionary Pierre Moreau in his *Relation du Brésil* (1651, p. 30), and Paul Boyer in his *Véritable Relation de l'Amérique Occidentale* (1654, p. 350), lamented the existence of war with conviction. It is amusing that the Protestant Lescarbot should have dedicated his book about North American savages, in which he deplored warfare, to Queen Marie de Médicis, who was not the most peaceful of queens. But there was greater freedom for French authors to express opinions early in the century than after 1660.

A scathing denunciation of wars between Christian rulers, published by the Jesuit Jean-Erard Foullon in 1648, was printed at Liège, far from Paris. Its title is *Les Causes des Guerres et de toutes les afflictions publiques,* and the text is not only sympathetic toward those who suffer, but sometimes ironical about the rulers who cause the suffering:

> All Infidel Rulers are now at peace, but among the Faithful those "High Priests and Sacrificers of Peace," as Tertullian calls our Rulers, are killing each other and thereby giving opportunity to Heresies and to Mohammedanism to extend their frontiers.[1]

Since many gentlemen were seeking and finding glory during the first forty or fifty years of Louis XIV's reign, and since the policy of their king was then definitely warlike, a statement like the one just quoted could not have been made "according to law and order." In fact, to an unprejudiced observer, the battles fought between Jesuits and Jansenists without gunfire and more particularly the armed battles against Protestants in the mountains of the Cevennes after 1685, might well have appeared to indicate anything but Christian charity and humility.

Although utopian novels of travel stressed the evils of war in the 1670's and thereafter, works like Foullon's often had to be printed and distributed surreptitiously. The first French novel still known and read today that condemned cruelty and warfare was Fénelon's *Adventures of Telemachus* (1699). Significantly, many readers of that extremely popular novel thought it to be a veiled criticism of the ambitious policies of Louis XIV, rather than the purported poetic and idealized story of wise rulers in ancient Greece ostensibly written for the instruction of the heir apparent to the throne.

By the year 1699, the glorious successes of the king, having reached their military zenith in the late 1670's, had diminished. Wars, diplomatic defeats, and famine had shaken earlier confidence in the efficacy and justice of the regime, at least in the minds of some of the French. Many nobles, of course, who remained politically and militarily busy, in gen-

---

1 Jean-Erard Foullon, S.J., *Les Causes des guerres et de toutes les afflictions publiques* (Liège: B. Bronckart, 1648), pp. 5–6.

eral were not to change their beliefs for a long time. Peasants, as one would expect, remained the most traditional group. In contrast to the nobility, no outstanding exceptions appeared among them to suggest changes in administration and policy that might benefit the kingdom.

It is to be expected that the middle-class writers of the half century studied here were most frequently to condemn warfare. Business—the backbone of the middle class—was endangered by the continuous wars entailing enormous taxation; the fortunes of those families who did not own land nor possess large benefices in the church were based upon trade and commerce.

A notable exception among nobles and great churchmen alike during the reign of Louis XIV was Archbishop Fénelon. His kindly doctrines were perhaps more frequently preached by little parish priests than by notables of the Church, who found it a proper part of their duty to remain strictly within the political framework of an absolute and a war-like monarchy.

It would be absurd to assume that Fénelon's writing was the "cause" of the condemnation of war in the first half of the eighteenth century, although his *Telemaque* went through at least fifty printings in the year 1699 and was read by a whole generation of Frenchmen. The popularity of his novel, beyond any other of its time, may reasonably be ascribed to the many readers, after 1699, who were sensitive to its musical prose, gentle homilies, and possible allusions to contemporary politics.

The condemnation of war was only one of a number of phases of the sentimental resurgence in French writing between 1690 and 1740. The best known of these phases is, of course, that of the *sensibilité,* or self-conscious understanding of love among young people. Another was the slowly growing sentimental appreciation of the beauty of nature, which has been traced in the preceding study on the emotions of this period.* A third and very striking sign of social change, if not of literary style, is the increased frequency with which pity was expressed for all sorts of unfortunate contemporaries—a subject to be presented in a later chapter.

As to disapproval of war, it may seem strange to a modern reader that otherwise sensitive men so rarely perceived or mentioned the obvious incompatibility between Christian charity and forbearance on the one hand and warlike urges on the other. Surely, if men were logical instead of primarily emotional, that dichotomy would have been remarked by

---

* Atkinson, *Le Sentiment de la Nature et le Retour à la Vie Simple* (1690–1740).

many. But neither had it been a consideration in the days when Christians were battling Saracens, conquering the New World, or engaging in civil wars on behalf of "religion" in the sixteenth century. It may be said in passing that George Fox and his followers in the Society of Friends, derisively called "Quakers," had been extremely unpopular in seventeenth-century England, at a time when two other religious groups had been shedding each other's blood. Another ingredient than logic must have been responsible for the growing expressions of pity and kindliness that began to appear in the work of many French writers between 1690 and 1740. The public, in accepting such printed expressions, was undeniably different from the public in France of 1660–80.

The fundamental Christian belief in kindness was inculcated during childhood in French families. It is not difficult to imagine, therefore, that adults were so outraged by hardness of heart among those with rank and power that "believers" and "unbelievers" both worked toward the disintegration of absolutism—which must always be cruel to survive. One is even led to consider whether all the intellectual and rational writings of eighteenth-century *philosophes* in France were as important in preparing for the political explosion of 1789 as the emotional outpourings of idealistic authors.

II

The *Mercure de France, Mercure Galant, Mercure,* and *Nouveau Mercure,* magazines published under various titles for "the best people" to read, contained the following articles on contemporary wars:

1688–89	Documents of the capture of Philipsburg
1690	Battle of Fleurus
1692	Siege of Namur *and* Battle of Steinkerke
1693	Campaign in Piedmont
1698	Journal of the Camp at Coudon
1702	Siege of Brisac
1707	Siege of Toulon
1715	Illness and Death of Louis XIV

At least for the noble and fashionable people in Paris and at the Court who dominated French society, military events must have been of great interest and personal concern. For all subjects of the king, the fact of wars and the sight of armed forces at close range must have constituted a part of daily observation during the last quarter century of

Louis' reign. Protestants who had left France, as well as those who fought in Protestant armies in Ireland and later in Spain, took keen interest in the enterprises of Louis XIV. Thus Jacques Basnage, a Protestant author and editor of high ability, at the end of a long and detailed account to J.-A. Turrettini, another Protestant pastor in Geneva, concerning the fighting on the Meuse River in the summer of 1702, wrote as follows:

> This is all I shall write to you today. We shall speak of books at some other time, but I thought it would please you to have a very accurate account of events which everyone is relating in his own way. You know that my information comes from a trustworthy source; that is why I have not wanted to write to you until I had a firsthand account. . . .
>
> I am, my dear Sir,
Yours to command
Basnage.[2]

In the north of France, as well as in the valley of the Meuse, the facts of warfare necessarily occupied the thoughts of all classes of men. Although there was no fighting in the immediate vicinity of his cathedral, Archbishop Fénelon was deeply disturbed by the depredations of French troops near Cambrai and by the general misery in France between 1709 and 1711.

> This whole region is ruined beyond repair by the troops, no matter what order our generals try to maintain among them.[3]
>
> If what many people say is true and the Spanish matter is now peaceably settled, it would be a good thing if we hastened to settle other matters too. We are in a bad way and, if we do not change greatly, war will continue. The interior of the realm is being exhausted. People have very little money and the population is wasting away with extreme suffering. This must be stopped.[4]

[2] "Vous n'aurez aujourd'hui de moi que cette relation, une autre fois nous parlerons de livres. Mais j'ay cru vous faire plaisir de vous faire un détail un peu exact d'une chose que tout le monde rapporte d'une manière très différente. Vous sçavez que mes nouvelles viennent d'une main assez sincère; c'est pourquoi je n'ay point voulu vous escrire que je n'en eusse reçu directement." Lettre de Jacques Basnage, 6 aoust 1702, in *Lettres inédites adressées de 1686 à 1737 à J.-A. Turrettini* (3 vols.; Paris and Geneva, 1887), I, 137.

[3] "Tout ce pays est ruiné sans ressource par les troupes, quelque bon ordre que nos généraux tâchent de faire garder." Lettre vi, Cambrai, à M. le Marquis de Fénelon, 26 septembre 1709.

[4] "S'il est vrai, comme beaucoup de gens l'assurent, que l'article d'Espagne est réglé pour la paix, il serait bien à désirer que l'on se hâtât de finir les autres articles. Nous sommes dans un mauvais train; et si nous ne changeons pas beaucoup, la guerre ne se redressera point. Le dedans du royaume s'use; on a peu d'argent, et cependant les peuples dépérissent par une extrême souffrance. Il faut finir." Lettre xxvii (sans adresse), 14 septembre 1711.

It is striking that François de Salignac de Fénelon, a nobleman and a distinguished cleric and above all a good Christian, should have written of the woes of France in 1711 in the same exasperated manner as that used, so many years later, by the Revolutionists who took the Bastille with the conviction that all this must be stopped.

The denunciation of war by the Quaker, William Penn, probably had been as little heeded by bellicose English noblemen as the words of the French Archbishop Fénelon were heeded in his country governed by an absolute monarchy. But William Penn had published in London (1695) *An Essay towards the . . . Future Peace of Europe . . .*, proposing a sort of League of Nations, or United Nations, to prevent war on a continent which was being, and which continued to be, bedevilled by it.

> . . . aggressors seldom getting what they seek . . . and the Blood and Poverty that usually attend the enterprise [of war] weigh more on Earth as well as in Heaven than what the Aggressors lost or suffered, or what they get by endeavouring to mend their condition . . . this seems the Voice of Heaven, and Judgment of God against those violent attempts. . . . Thus peace is maintained by Justice, which is a fruit of Government, as Government of Laws [springs] from Society and Society from Consent.[5]

These sentences have a familiar ring to those who remember the spirit of the "rights of man," of a "government of laws," and of "government based on the consent of the governed." The time was not ripe at that date for many in England or for more than a very few in France to respond to such statements. It is even doubtful if theories promulgated in either country by a Quaker could have been welcomed by many of his contemporaries. From the point of view of practical politics and conformity, Quakers were a peculiar group and Penn's essay cannot have greatly influenced even those rare Frenchmen who read English.

Both in England and in France, however, written indications expressed the weariness over a long war. The sight of disabled soldiers begging for alms must have been familiar in Paris as well as in London in the year 1698, although it is possible to read a great many books and periodicals of the time without finding reference to a single case. After the Napoleonic wars, French romantic authors pictured the "old soldier" in compassionate, even in lachrymose tones, but in 1698 Vigny, Hugo,

---

[5] William Penn, *An Essay towards the Present and Future Peace of Europe, by the Establishment of an European Dyet, Parliament, or Estates* (London, 1695), pp. 9–10.

Théophile Gautier, and Balzac were still a century and more away in the future.

The reason for the absence of such a sympathetic figure at the end of the 1600's in French, and in English writings as well, apparently lies in the low esteem of the public for the common soldier. An example is to be found in the play *Love and a Bottle* by George Farquhar, which appeared with success at Drury Lane in 1698. A crippled veteran could serve to amuse some of the London public at that time but seemed not to have stirred any emotion of pity. In the first act, Roebuck, a jolly chap with only one penny in his pocket, exclaims: "But hold—can't I rob honorably, by turning soldier?" He is then beseeched for alms by a one-legged man, who tells the sad tale of spending five years in the army, being crippled, and then forced to use a crutch for fifteen years. Roebuck asks the veteran, "Why wouldst thou beg of me? Dost think I am rich?" The beggar replies, "No, sir, and therefore I believe you charitable. Your warm fellows are so far above the sense of our misery, that they can't pity us."[6]

The current of literary influence was, of course, still running from France to England in 1698. Like Wycherley, Congreve, and Van Brugh, Farquhar was not above ransacking French comedies for characters and situations. But even if that current had been reversed and if this play by Farquhar had been translated into French, which it was not, it is hard to imagine a French author toward 1700 employing a one-legged veteran to stir the pity of his audience. In both countries the soldier in the ranks was thought of as a rascally man, ready to steal if still active and ready to whine and beg when disabled. Nor was this an illusion. In the absence of universal service, soldiers often were, in fact, rascals or criminals, impressed into military service.

The French authorities would certainly not have admitted the right of a French author to publish a denunciation of the continuing war in Europe such as Daniel Defoe's *Reasons Why This Nation Ought to Put a Speedy End to This Expensive War*, which appeared in 1711 and was doubtless addressed to English shopkeepers and merchants.

Defoe's text begins:

A mind possest with any Tenderness for the Miseries, Sufferings and Distresses of its Native Land, that has the Happiness of any Generous Principles . . . cannot look upon the present Condition of this Nation

[6] George Farquhar, *Love and a Bottle* (1698).

without being in the highest Degree affected. . . . How have we above Twenty Years groan'd under a Long and Bloody War?[7]

How many battles, as that near *Mons,* could we bear? There we conquered the *Mareschal de Villiers* and gain'd the Honor of the Field of Battle. But how lie the Bones of 22,000 of the best and bravest Soldiers in Christendom, sacrificed meerly [*sic*] to the Pique [*sic*] of Glory between Haughty Generals.[8]

This theme, the sacrifice of soldiers for the personal glory of their generals, had occurred in French writing before 1711 in the work of Vauban. But in the view of that high-minded French officer, as in that of Defoe, generals who sacrificed soldiers uselessly were depriving their nation of its strength and deserved to be punished severely. Unlike Defoe, Vauban, as we shall see later, expressed no heartfelt sympathy for the soldiers who were so killed.

III

In Switzerland, a nation renowned for its bravery and the fidelity of its soldiery, at least one sensitive citizen expressed a condemnation of war in much the same way as did men in England, France, and Holland by the time of Louis XIV's death. J. P. de Crousaz of the University of Lausanne[9] wrote as follows in the dedication of his *Traité du beau* (1715):

> The madness of war, spreading like a disease from one nation to the next, had finally embroiled all Europe; but your wisdom, Noble Sir, constantly attentive to our interests, took pains to keep this contagion away from us and managed to teach our people, who are thought to be born soldiers, to love peace.[10]

In this same year, the *Journal Littéraire* at The Hague began the preface of its second edition with the words:

> The peace which has just followed a long and bloody war, by which all of Europe was for so long afflicted, seems to promise a new life for the Arts

[7] [Daniel Defoe], *Reasons Why this Nation Ought to Put a Speedy End to This Expensive War* ([London]: J. Baker, 1711).

[8] *Ibid.,* p. 6.

[9] Crousaz was also one of the first of his time to extol the beauty of vast landscapes. See: G. Atkinson, *Le Sentiment de la Nature et le retour à la vie simple* (Geneva: Droz, 1960), p. 51.

[10] "La fureur de la Guerre se répandant, comme une maladie, de Nation en Nation, avoit enfin gagné toute l'Europe; mais Votre Sagesse, Monseigneur, continuellement attentive à nos intérêts, s'est appliquée à éloigner de nous cette contagion, et a sû faire aimer la Paix à des Peuples qu'on croit nez uniquement pour la Guerre." J.-P. de Crousaz, *Traité du beau* (Amsterdam: François l'Honoré, 1715), Epitre au Comte du Luc, p. 4.

and sciences, which but languish in the tumult of Arms. The interest of the Public, so long directed toward Sieges and Battles, will henceforth be directed toward events in the Republic of Letters.[11]

In this period, other periodicals continued to voice opinions in favor of peace. The *Journal des Sçavans* contains, for example, a review of *The Concept of a Perfect King*, a book now very rare, supposed to have been written by one Chansierges. Part of the review reads: "Kindliness, which this author makes the first mark of a perfect King, is according to him an inclination of the heart which urges us to be useful to mankind."[12]

The notion that warriors are essentially destroyers seems to have been rather freely expressed, even in moralizing novels intended for what must have been a far more sentimental and humanitarian public than we can easily imagine. In the early pages of *The Adventures of Aristée and Telasie* (1731), which Auvigny wrote for the sentimental public then reading the story of *Manon Lescaut,* a young nobleman who has gone hunting stops to reflect:

> Would my reputation be enhanced, even if I were to destroy all the deer in this forest? Wild boars are ravaging our countryside, destroying the hopes of the ploughman and of the vineyard-worker. It is on these ferocious animals that we must wage war.[13]

Two volumes of this novel, published in Paris in 1731, were termed "interesting" in a review appearing in the Holland edition of the *Journal des Sçavans* (May, 1731), an indication of the acceptance of this point of view.

In the following year, there appeared the first edition of the Abbé Prévost's novel, *Cleveland, or the English Philosopher.* Its hero suffers calamity after calamity through hundreds of pages, pausing, when each comes upon him, to reflect and to inflict his reflections and opinions upon the persistent reader. It is impossible for a modern reader to wade

[11] "La Paix qui vient de succéder à une longue et sanglante Guerre dont toute l'Europe a été si long-tems désolée, semble promettre une nouvelle vie aux Arts et aux Sciences, qui ne font que languir parmi le tumulte des Armes. La curiosité du Public attachée depuis si long-tems à des Sièges et à des Batailles, va désormais s'occuper des événemens de la République des Lettres." *Journal littéraire* (The Hague: T. Johnson, 1715), Vol. I, Preface.

[12] "La bonté, dont notre Auteur fait le premier caractère d'un Roi parfait, est selon lui, une inclination de notre cœur, laquelle nous porte à nous rendre utiles aux hommes." *Journal des Sçavans* (Amsterdam, juin 1724), review of M. Chansierges, *L'Idée d'un Roi parfaict* (Paris: G. Saugrain, 1723).

[13] Original unavailable (ed.).

through this once-popular novel without thinking of Voltaire's *Candide,* which appeared a quarter century later and lampooned romances of this type.

Cleveland, the bastard son of Cromwell, reared in a cave until almost full grown, does an admirable job of wandering in England, France, Virginia, Saint Helena, and the West Indies, pursued by fate and bemoaning his lot. He is quite specific on the subject of war:

> War has always horrified me. It is the shame of reason and humanity. Except for cases of righteous defense—which should cause us to moan, even after a victory—a battle is the greatest crime of madness and violence, and in my code of ethics a military hero is but a ferocious monster.[14]

IV

In spite of the foregoing evidence of a horror of war among upright and sentimental people, particularly after 1710, it would be an error to believe that such a strong force as the "noble tradition of arms" ceased suddenly.

The pessimism inherent in Christian metaphysics, as the ground for justifying war, is visible in the following statement:

> War has always existed: it is a misfortune of our human estate but must not be accounted a crime, unless we wish to blame the eternal decree of Providence, which has subjected all men to war. It is the means employed which are blameworthy . . . and the pretexts. Cain slew Abel. The human race is descended from them and shows the influence of its origin.[15]

A great many Frenchmen still adhered to this ancient, mystical belief that "trial by combat" indicated the favor or the disfavor of deity. A typical example would be the reaction, in 1711, of a humble and deeply

14 "La guerre m'a toujours fait horreur. C'est la honte de la raison et de l'humanité. Excepté le cas d'une juste défense, qui doit faire gémir, même après la victoire, une bataille est le dernier attentat où l'extravagance et la fureur puissent se porter; et dans les principes de ma morale, un héros guerrier n'est qu'un monstre féroce." Abbé Prévost, *Le Philosophe anglois, ou Histoire de Monsieur Cleveland, fils naturel de Cromwell,* écrite par lui-mesme, et traduite de l'anglois (8 vols.; Paris, 1731–39), here quoted from *Œuvres choisies* (Paris, 1823), Livre IV, II, p. 175; hereafter cited as Prévost, *Cleveland.*

15 "La guerre a été de tout temps: c'est un malheur attaché à la nature humaine, mais dont on ne doit pas lui faire un crime, à moins que de vouloir blâmer les décrets éternels de la Providence, qui y a soumis tous les hommes, ce sont les moïens dont on se sert, qui sont blâmables . . . et les prétextes. Caïn assoma Abel. Le genre humain descend d'eux, et se ressent de son origine." Robert Chasles, *Journal d'un voyage fait aux Indes orientales par une escadre.* . . . *commandée par Mr. Du Quesne* (Rouen: J.-B. Machuel le Jeune, 1721), I, 385–86; hereafter cited as Chasles, *Journal d'un voyage.*

religious Jesuit, Father Joseph Germain, after a storm in the Gulf of Saint Lawrence had destroyed an English expedition against Quebec. Father Germain was troubled and distressed by the drowning of many Protestants on those vessels and therefore "damned for all eternity." His contemporaries at Quebec, however, judged the event in more traditional terms:

> The inhabitants of that region, French and Savages, drew near to witness all the havoc. They saw a great number of dead bodies on the shore . . . the beach was covered with dead bodies at various places. Those who have seen them state that there are over three thousand dead. But the most lamentable thing in this shipwreck is that, inasmuch as they all have died in heresy, these were so many souls that were damned. . . . All are so thoroughly convinced that it is an effect of Heaven's intervention and that this defeat of our enemies is an extraordinary and miraculous manifestation of Divine Providence in our behalf, that, as an act of thanksgiving, on the Sunday following the receipt of the news, the *Te Deum* was solemnly chanted in the Cathedral. In the evening, a large bonfire was lighted, and while it burned the soldiers fired several salvos . . . in the presence of 50 English prisoners who had been captured, on various expeditions by our Savages.[16]

It is to the honor of Father Germain not to have shared these feelings of triumph, as it is to the credit of humane authors like William Penn, Daniel Defoe, and the indefatigable reformer, the Abbé de Saint-Pierre, to have hoped for something better than warfare on earth.

[16] "Les habitans de ces terres François et sauvages s'étant approchez pour voir tout ce débris, ils virent grand nombre de corps morts sur le rivage . . . la terre sur ce rivage y [étoit] couverte de corps morts en divers endroits, ceux qui les ont vus font état qu'il y a plus de trois mille morts. Mais ce qu'il y a de lamentable dans ce naufrage, c'est qu'étant tous morts dans l'hérésie, c'est autant d'âmes damnées. . . . Tout le monde est si persuadé que c'est un coup du ciel et que cette défaite de nos ennemis est un coup extraordinaire et miraculeux de la divine providence sur nous, qu'en action de grâces le dimanche d'après cette nouvelle . . . on chanta solennellement le *Te Deum* dans la cathédrale à Québec et le soir on fit un beau Feu de joie, durant lequel les soldats firent plusieurs décharges . . . à la vue de 50 Anglois prisonniers, qui avoient été pris en divers partis par nos sauvages." Letter by R. P. Joseph Germain, 1711, in *Jesuit Relations* . . . (Cleveland, Ohio: The Burroughs Co., 1900), LXVI, 196–201.

CHAPTER III

Growth of Self-Esteem
Among Commoners

THE INCREASING SOCIAL and political importance of a middle class has often marked the transition from authoritarian to liberal government. In most European nations the growth of that segment of the population has been possible because of the increase in commerce and foreign trade.

When overseas trade dwindled in Spain and Portugal before a middle class had had an opportunity to become firmly established, the change from authoritarian and Christian monarchies was accomplished at the cost of alternating revolutions and new absolutisms. In Switzerland, small landowners and artisans were represented in the legislative assembly of Schwyz in 1294, at a time when government by "unimportant people" was not being suggested in either England or France. In the Low Countries, the middle class had already gained an enviable status by the seventeenth century, and the solid burghers, in large numbers, had had themselves registered for posterity in portraits by Rembrandt, Nikolas Maes, and others. French portrait painters of the same period had had only noble clients, for in France esteem, or self-esteem, of commoners was not openly or frequently expressed. It was very rare for a man to be an authentic bourgeois without being apologetic about the fact in society.

These social values did not disappear with the death of Louis XIV. Indeed, several years after 1715, a young man of decent and responsible middle-class family gave up his father's and his own name, Arouet, to be known as "Voltaire." There is no doubt that he did this "in order to avoid the scorn of society," as one peasant hero in the literature of the 1730's put it. But a distinct change had taken place in French society by that time, and Jacob, the peasant hero of Marivaux's novel, could represent a commoner without shame.

I

The pride of English commoners in their useful occupations, often observed by French visitors, and the close relations between the two countries invite quotation from a few authors, both known and obscure in literary history, who were writing in England between 1700 and 1735.

Many Englishmen shared the opinion of Bishop Gilbert Burnet, who died in 1715 after a long and busy life as a churchman and author. The text of his *History of His Own Time,* not published during Burnet's life in accordance with his request, appeared in parts between 1724 and 1734, and in French translation at The Hague in 1735. In the first volume of the French edition, the following opinion appears: "Manufacturers and Merchants generally make up the soundest part of our Nation and the part in which the most Generosity, Regularity of Manners and Charity are to be found."[1] Praise of the moral conduct of the middle class in the Bishop's statement is an indirect criticism of the morals of noblemen. This attitude was not entirely due to the ecclesiastical profession of the author, for just such moralizing statements are found in the words of other English authors of the same period who were laymen.

It will be remembered that Sir Roger de Coverley said on one occa-

[1] "Les Manufacturiers, et les Négocians forment, en général, le Corps le plus sain de notre Nation, et celui dans lequel il y a le plus de Générosité, de Régularité dans les Mœurs, et de la Charité." Gilbert Burnet, *Histoire de ce qui s'est passé . . . en Angleterre pendant la vie de Gilbert Burnet, Evêque de Salisbury* (2 vols.; The Hague: Jean Néaulme, 1735), I, 271.

sion: "Gain is the chief end of traders. They never pursue any other. . . . What can there great and noble be expected of him whose attention is forever fixed upon balancing his books, and watching over his expenses?"

The answer which this gentleman gets, and which he does not refute, is in the spirit of much of the *Spectator* and doubtless represents the belief of many Englishmen in September, 1711. It would, however, have been far less frequently expressed by the "best people" in France at that date.

> Now what is there of scandal in this skill? What has the merchant done, that he should be so little in the good graces of Sir Roger? He throws down no man's inclosures, and tramples upon no man's corn; he takes nothing from the industrious labourer; he pays the poor man for his work . . . he furnishes employment and subsistence to greater numbers than the richest nobleman; and even the nobleman is obliged to him for finding out foreign markets for the produce of his estate. . . . It is the misfortune of many other gentlemen to turn out of the seats of their ancestors, to make way for such new masters as have been more exact in their accounts than themselves; and certainly he deserves the estate a great deal better who has got it by his industry, than he who has lost it by his negligence.[2]

Very early in the anonymous tale, *The Matchless Rogue*, printed in London in 1725, it is stated that the scandalous hero who "Stiled himself Baron of Bridewell and Marquis of Newgate" was given every chance to be a good boy. At the age of sixteen, he was "apprenticed to a Mercer on *Ludgate Hill:* A trade so reputed that it has been honored with the sons of Noblemen, who, in former Ages, thought it no Disgrace to bring up their younger Children to that Business."[3]

In 1728, Daniel Defoe's *A Plan of the English Commerce* contains the following definition of trade: "Trade, like Religion, is what every Body talks of, but few understand. . . . When 'tis particular to a Place, 'tis *Trade;* when 'tis general, 'tis *Commerce.*"[4] Being occupied with trade or commerce was clearly considered no disgrace by Defoe or his readers.

George Lillo's melodramatic play, *George Barnwell, or The London Merchant,* was popular in the London of 1731, not because of its drab

---

2 Richard Steele, *Spectator,* No. 174, Sept. 19, 1711.

3 *The Matchless Rogue: or an Account of the Contrivances, Cheats, Stratagems, and Amours of Tom Merryman, commonly called Newgate Tom, who stiled [sic] himself Baron of Bridewell . . . Marquis of Newgate* (London: A. Moore, 1725), p. 3.

4 Daniel Defoe, *A Plan of the English Commerce* (London: Charles Rivington, 1728), chap i.

title certainly, but in all likelihood because of its extreme sentimentality. Some of its scenes strike us as very bad Shakespeare: "A dismal gloom obscures the face of day. Either the sun has slipped behind a cloud, or journeys down the west of heaven with more than common speed to avoid the sight of what I am doomed to act. . . . Murder my uncle!"[5] Such an example of horror and of the pathetic fallacy, followed in the final act by a moral speech about the hero (after he has been condemned to be hanged) apparently moved an emotional, middle-class audience very deeply then, although reading the play today may make sophisticated people laugh aloud: "Let his ruin teach us diffidence, humanity, and circumspection; for we, who wonder at his fate—perhaps, had we like him been tryed, like him perhaps, we had fallen too."[6] Lillo's London audiences undoubtedly welcomed a moralizing statement such as that "Few men recover reputation lost, a merchant never."[7]

By reading the issues of the *Gentleman's Magazine* for 1731, 1732, and 1733, one gets the impression of a society very different from that of gentlemen in contemporary France, who were still scornful of men "in trade."[8]

II

It seems appropriate to give some indications here regarding the use of middle-class characters who could be admired by French audiences before the time of Lillo's drama. The great French author of tragedies, Pierre Corneille, in the period before he founded the French classical tragedy, suggested that it was possible to compose a play which would make the audience laugh without using ridiculous characters.[9] In 1630 *La Galerie du Palais*, composed in conformity with that theory, was successfully performed, and its characters behaved as normal contemporary people did. A bookseller, a linen draper, and a cloth merchant held the stage, and commonplace speeches were frequent.

During the glorious period of French literature that followed, ridiculous characters continued to hold the comic stage. Yet Molière, while making sport of the vagaries of commoners, had more than one of them

[5] George Lillo, *The London Merchant, or the History of George Barnwell* (London: John Gray, 1734), Act III, scene 3 (in some editions, Act III, scene 5).
[6] *Ibid.*, Act V, scene 1.
[7] *Ibid.*, Act III, scene 1 (in some editions, Act III, scene 3).
[8] See chap. iv.
[9] Corneille, *Examen de "Mélite."*

utter sententious statements based on common sense. Monsieur Jourdain was ridiculous, not because he was a commoner, but because he refused to accept the fact that he was.

Twenty years after Molière's death, Dancourt created a manservant who foreshadowed in 1692 the famous character of Figaro a century later. Dancourt's Frontin abetted the love affairs, both of the husband who was unfaithful to his wife and of the wife who was unfaithful to her husband; and the rascal explained that "he was only trying to give them both pleasure."

In 1696, in his comedy *Le Moulin de Javelle,* another openly immoral play, scene 25 of the single act contains passages of sardonic humor spoken by a servant at the expense of a countess. When his master, a *chevalier* and therefore a young nobleman, is in a quandary, his servant, Lolive, makes a suggestion:

> LOLIVE: Oh, Sir, if only my unfortunate cousin, poor girl, had not been hanged last year. . . . The fact is we need somebody with real talent, you know. Ah, what a shame that my aunt and my sister are still in prison at the Chatelet!
> LE CHEVALIER: Well! And what can your wretched family have to do with all this?
> LOLIVE: You are right, Sir, and I am wrong. You are expecting to meet Madame the Countess here. And she is a match for those nice people, my relatives.
> LE CHEVALIER: Yes truly, she is.[10]

By 1700, Dancourt apparently felt free to entitle a play *Les Bourgeoises de Qualité.* A woman of petty nobility who has married a Parisian lawyer is portrayed as being so ridiculous that noblemen and commoners alike may have been amused by her for different reasons. Madame Blandineau, the snob, loses heavily at cards while spending some time with her husband in the country. The commoner, her husband,

---

10 LOLIVE: Ah! Monsieur, si feu ma pauvre cousine n'avoit pas été pendue l'année passée. . . . C'est qu'il nous faudroit une personne de mérite, voyez-vous. Hom! que c'est bien dommage que ma tante et ma sœur soient encore au Châtelet.
LE CHEVALIER: Et qu'a de commun toute ta malheureuse famille?
LOLIVE: J'ai tort et vous avez raison, Monsieur. Vous avez ici rendez-vous avec Madame la Comtesse, elle vaut bien ces honnêtes personnes-là.
LE CHEVALIER: Oui, vraiment.
Dancourt, *Le Moulin De Javelle* (1696), in *Choix de Pièces du théâtre françois* (2 vols.; Paris, 1783), scène 25.

has a perfect right to ask her for an explanation. But the pretentious woman answers him:

> Why play cards? I think you're extraordinary! What can you expect a person to do that's any better, especially off here in the country? I am willing to come with you to a thatched-roof, commoner's house, with your boring relatives: there happen to be some witty ladies in the village, persons with social experience. . . . well, gambling is the very soul of such gatherings.[11]

In *Le Double Veuvage* ("Double Widowhood") by Charles Dufresny, which dates from 1702, the humor of a middle-class widow and her serving-woman is tinged with bad-tempered jibes at the nobility—obviously intended for an audience of commoners:

> THE WIDOW: Those people of quality!
> FROSINE: The way they talk to you!
> THE WIDOW: They think their requests . . .
> FROSINE: Are orders. A nobleman of standing who begs a middle-class person to do him a favor, it's as if a member of the police force asked you to pay up a promissory note.[12]

A play by Alexis Piron was presented at the Comédie Française in 1728. It is called *L'Ecole des Pères,* and has a second title under which it is better known, *Les Fils ingrats* ("Ungrateful Sons"). Years before Nivelle de la Chaussée began to put "Tearful Comedies" on the French stage, Piron presented this emotional drama of a good and overindulgent father who is scorned and even mocked by three avaricious sons. It would be an oversimplification to say that this sentimental play is in all ways the reverse of Molière's *Miser.* What is of significance here is not a comparison of Piron's play to the plays of Molière, which are incomparably better written and in every way superior. It is, however, important that in 1728 both the public and the official theater in Paris

---

11 "Pourquoi jouer? je vous trouve admirable. Que voulez-vous donc qu'on fasse de mieux, et à la campagne surtout? J'ai la complaisance de venir avec vous dans une chaumière bourgeoise, avec votre ennuyeuse famille: il se trouve par hasard dans le village des femmes d'esprit, des personnes du monde . . . c'est le jeu qui est l'âme de toutes les parties." Dancourt, *Les Bourgeoises de qualité* (1700), in *ibid.,* Acte I, scène 5.

12 LA VEUVE: Ces gens de qualité. . . . FROSINE: Le prennent sur un ton. . . . LA VEUVE: Croient que leurs prières. . . . FROSINE: Sont des commandements. Un grand seigneur qui prie un bourgeois de lui faire une grâce, c'est comme un sergent qui prie de payer une lettre de change. Charles Dufresny, *Le Double Veuvage* (1702), in *Chefs-d'œuvres des Auteurs comiques* (2 vols.; Paris: F. Didot, Frères, 1845), Vol. II.

welcomed a play in which a father required sympathy, because of the outrageous selfishness of his sons.

Géronte, the father, wants to leave the corruption of the city and live in relative poverty "beneath the thatch of virtue"—a desire that was to be a standard literary theme some years later in France. The good man has divested himself of most of his fortune, which his sons soon squander. He has adopted an orphaned girl and would be happy if one of the sons married her. They scorn her, until at the end of the play it suddenly becomes known to all that she has had a fortune left to her. Their immediate interest in a virtuous girl at that point undeceives their father.

Minor characters supply some humor: peasants and servants are more clever in speech than Géronte and his grasping sons. The dullard of those rascals recites a poem he has written, containing two of the most wretched lines in the history of French poetry:

> Fortunate Myrtil awaits you on the grass and the moss.
> Sweet moment! Moment sweet! How sweet is your sweetness![13]

The sentimental and moral tone of the play as a whole could only have been acceptable in 1728 to a predominantly middle-class audience. The praise of gratitude and the moral condemnation of ingratitude expressed in the final speech by Géronte, the father, after his eyes have been opened, appear throughout the play. The following speech by Crisalde, delivered for the benefit of middle-class fathers and mothers in the audience, is typical:

> Fathers who are infatuated with children like these,
> See what those objects of your indulgence are like,
> Whose bringing-up cost you such trouble
> And whom you now count upon for easing your old age!
> Their way of thinking is proportionate to your means.
> Respectful and crawling, as long as they hope for money,
> They are against you, when their father's funds are gone.[14]

---

13 "L'heureux Myrthil t'attend sur l'herbe et la mousse./ Doux moment! Moment doux! Que ta douceur est douce!" Alexis Piron, *L'école des pères,* in *Œuvres choisies* (Paris, 1823).

14 "Pères enfatués d'enfans tels que ceux-ci!/ Voilà donc ces objets de votre complaisance,/ Dont, avec tant de soins, vous élevez l'enfance,/ Et que de vos vieux ans vous croyez les soutiens!/ Leur façon de penser se mesure à vos biens./ Respecteux, rampans, tant qu'un espoir les flatte;/ Mais du Père épuisé la plainte à peine éclate." *Ibid.,* Acte III, scène 9.

Despite the sensitive Archbishop Fénelon's sympathy for suffering around him in a year of famine and the logical and patriotic protests by a soldier like Vauban and a few others of the gentry, most of those in dominating positions continued, even after the eighteenth century, to hold much the same opinions and prejudices as their seventeenth-century ancestors. Some of the descendants of eighteenth-century aristocrats similarly looked down on the "upstart" Napoleon and on the new nobility he created as Emperor.

The peasants, who formed a much larger group, for years after the death of Louis XIV retained their loyalty to the throne and their belief that France was the greatest of military powers. The Swiss writer, Muralt, expressed astonishment at their attitude as early as the 1690's (his book was not published until 1725), and there is no doubt that other Frenchmen exploited such peasant sentiment for their own benefit.

It was otherwise with the middle class, or with some considerable part of it. When the cohesive and logical set of concepts of the French Golden Age became clearly opposed to the facts of middle-class life, discordant voices arose in Paris, and many critical words were published, even by men of the petty nobility who had been financially ruined by 1721 or 1722 and thereby "demoted to the ranks."

Protestants abroad, as early as 1709, the year of famine, wondered why there was no general uprising and revolution in France. The sheer momentum of a system, which much of the French public continued to find tolerable because it had obtained in the glorious times, may account in part for the durability of a monarchy that made but a few minor concessions here and there to dissatisfied public opinion. For instance, when the Regent confiscated the millions of some outstandingly rapacious taxgatherers and moneylenders, he delighted both the noble and middle class in Paris.

It is worth remembering, with regard to the growing self-esteem of commoners in France, that merchants and shopkeepers in Paris could not look back a generation or more, like the nobles, to the "great days" and to the exploits of their ancestors. Commoners had to look forward, with what hope they could muster, to possibly increased social standing. Financial disasters like the Mississippi affair, loss of foreign markets, and that most horrifying of events to such men—mob violence in the streets—necessarily affected the middle class deeply.

In the years from 1690 to 1740, one would expect to find in middle-class writings expressions of commercial pride comparable in number to similar statements in England. But, reading the French books and pamphlets of that period, without any strongly preconceived ideas, one is surprised to find so few examples of a mercantile spirit. Even making allowance for the unequal preservation of various categories of books and pamphlets, it appears likely that the praise of trade or of the commercial classes was less frequent in the early 1700's than high-minded protests against cruelty, immorality, and the overbearing manners of noblemen or of the very wealthy.

One explanation of this fact may be found in the large number of sons of well-to-do merchants, lawyers, and other bourgeois families who attended the best *collèges* in Paris. The influence of a Jesuit education in particular upon these young men must have accounted for the breadth of view, the superior literary taste, and the ability to write shown by the large number of middle-class boys.

A few examples of mercantile pride may be found in the early 1700's and deserve mention here. For instance, six years before the patriotic nobleman, Vauban, suggested a single tax and acknowledged the financial importance of the commoners (who were considered "low" but who paid almost all the taxes in France), a book was surreptitiously printed "at Rouen," bearing the doubtless false authorship of "Jean Le Pelletier, a former Judge" on its title page. This author makes a narrower claim than Vauban was to make in his *Dixme royale* (1707). The middle class and, in particular, those who bought and sold goods, are considered in this book as the one essential group in France:

> Everyone's interest is served by fostering the one calling which is the necessary bond between all others. . . . This profession, which is so useful and so necessary to the happiness of men is that of commerce; it is scorned today because people are not aware of its importance.[15]

The curious remedy proposed in this book of 1701 for all the national troubles is very simple: "Syndics" or Trustees, named by merchants, to serve and advise the authorities of the kingdom!

15 "Mais parce qu'entre ces Professions, il s'en trouve une qui est la liaison des autres . . . tout le monde a interest de veiller principalement à sa conservation. . . .
Cette Profession si utile et si necessaire au bonheur des hommes est celle de Negociant, qu'on laisse aujourd'hui dans le mépris, parce qu'on en ignore la valeur." *Mémoires pour le rétablissement du commerce en France. Rédigez par Le Sr. Jean Le Pelletier, ancien Juge Consul* . . . (Rouen [?], 1701), pp. 4–5.

These Trustees would be particularly necessary for the glory and good of France, because there are no states in Europe which are not apprehensive of seeing French commerce reestablished . . . the French people pay some two hundred millions each year for their rights and for the expenses of administration, as well as for the profit of the tax-collectors. . . . France has no mines which produce that exorbitant sum. . . . It must necessarily come from the trade of its excess commodities and from the industry of its population.[16]

Like Vauban and others who suggested reforms in France up to, and including, the middle of the eighteenth century, Le Pelletier urged innovations within the framework of the existing monarchy. But his supreme confidence that merchants could guide the authorities of the kingdom is unusual.

In 1707, when Vauban's *Dixme royale* was published, shortly before his death, two unsigned volumes appeared at Rouen, attributed to Le Pesant de Boisguilbert, Lieutenant General of Police at Rouen: *Le Testament Politique de Monsieur de Vauban* (Vol. I), and *Le Detail de la France* (Vol. II).

Vauban is hailed in the second volume as "the advocate of all farmers and merchants in the Realm, which is to say of all those who are the source and vital principle of all the wealth of the state."[17] It is to be noted, however, that in writing which shows strong commercial prejudice and in the many theoretical discussions regarding luxury not quoted here, the self-esteem of commoners was the driving emotion involved, rather than the penury of gold-pieces. Class pride, which appears to have been primary, was easily extended to include criticism of the nobility, as will appear in a later chapter.

Only a few of the complaints and laments written by French Protestants will be mentioned in this chapter. Their inflammatory statements and emotions, which enlarge our understanding of the exaggerated

---

[16] "Ces Syndics seroient d'autant plus necessaires pour la gloire et le bien de la France, qu'il n'y a point d'Etats dans l'Europe qui n'appréhendent le rétablissement de son Commerce . . . le Peuple de France paye tous les ans autour de deux cens millions, tant pour les droits, pour les frais de régis, que pour le profit des Gens d'affaires [fermiers de rentes]. . . . La France n'a point de Mines qui lui produisent cette somme exhorbitante. . . . Il faut de necessité qu'elle lui vienne du Commerce qu'elle fait de ses denrées surabondantes et de l'industrie de ses peuples." *Ibid.,* pp. 16–17.

[17] "Avocat de tout ce qu'il y a de Laboureurs et de Commerçants dans le Royaume, c'est-à-dire, de tous ceux qui sont la source et principe de toutes les richesses de l'Etat." Vauban, Sébastien Le Prestre de, *Projet d'une dixme royale* (2 vols.; Rouen [?], 1707), II, 7; hereafter cited as Vauban, *Dixme royale.*

sentiment found in novels, plays, memoirs, and confessions, and which provided material for the *philosophes,* will be examined later.

A religious attitude prevailed among others than the Protestant exiles which was Christian in essence rather than Protestant. It formed one of the bases of the equalitarian attitude in politics that was pleasing to commoners, although not to the nobles nor to officials of the monarchical system. It was the emotionally charged subject of all men's equality before divine judgment. In a book of sermons by François Turrettini, a Protestant pastor in Geneva, we read:

> It would not matter much to lose all one's possessions at death, if we did not have to expect judgment, if we did not all have to appear before the awful Tribunal of the Judge of the Universe, there to be rewarded according to whether we have done good or evil. All must appear there, the great as well as the small, the rich as well as the poor. And the highest kings and princes in the world, who have made the earth tremble with their great power, must appear just as the least of their subjects, to give an account of their administration and to hear the sovereign sentence of the Divine Judge, who determines the bliss or the eternal suffering of men.[18]

Robert Chasles, a realistic novelist, for years a supercargo on merchant vessels and a man given at times to accounts of lascivious evenings ashore, was far removed from the attitudes of a Protestant pastor. In his *Voyage to the East Indies* (written in 1690 but not published until 1721), there appears the following: "In fact, it is a certainty that the salvation of the soul of an ordinary man is as precious in God's eyes as that of a great nobleman. They are equal in God's sight; the truth of this is doubted by no one."[19] This Christian conviction was to serve as a basis both for ideas of political justice and for the commoners' criticism

18 "Ce seroit encore peu de choses de perdre tous ses biens par la mort, si après la mort il n'y avoit point de jugement à attendre, et s'il ne faloit [*sic*] pas tous comparoître devant le Tribunal épouvantable du Juge de l'Univers, pour recevoir chacun en son corps, selon qu'on aura fait soit bien soit mal. C'est là où il faut que les Grands aussi bien que les petits, les riches de même que les povres, les Rois et les Princes les plus relevés du monde, qui ont fait trembler toute la terre sous leur empire, se presentent comme le moindre de leurs sujets, pour rendre comte de leur administration, et pour entendre la sentence souveraine de ce divin Juge, qui doit decider du bonheur ou du malheur éternel des hommes." François Turrettini, *Recueil de Sermons* (Geneva: Samuel de Tournes, 1687), pp. 445–46.

19 "En effet, il est certain que le salut de l'âme d'un simple particulier est aussi précieux devant Dieu, que celui d'un gros Seigneur: tous deux sont égaux devant lui; c'est une vérité dont qui que ce soit ne doute." Chasles, *Journal d'un voyage,* III, 39.

of their social superiors. It justified the moral condemnation in which they engaged, as well as their growing sense of worth and dignity.

III

Jean Marteilhe, a young Protestant from Bergerac who served for years as a galley slave and went to Bern in Switzerland after his release in 1713, comparing conditions in France with another, apparently more enlightened country, made the following illuminating comment:

> Being alighted [at Bern] we were accosted by the Secretary of State, who there expected our arrival. He received us with all the Politeness and Humanity in his Power. He was obliged, however, to let us know his Dignity, for we would otherwise never have guessed it from his Appearance; neither his dress nor Equipage testifying to any thing above the common Rank. In this Country the Governors only differ from the Governed by superior Talents, and not superior Fortune.[20]

Not far different in tone is Gueudeville's *Le Censeur, ou Moeurs de La Haye* (1715), a criticism of the morals and manners of the Dutch at The Hague, and much more besides. Gueudeville wanted, like Theophrastus, "to understand the manners of men."[21] The following has a fine, middle-class flavor:

> There are no men who ought not *to be busy,* some of them in one way, others in another; our self-interest and the very preservation of our health require this of us, not to speak of the Law of the Creator, "Thou shalt eat thy bread in the sweat of thy face."[22]

Gueudeville was very serious indeed in condemning frivolous amusements. And yet, answering a girl who had asked him how to choose among a young man giving promise for the future, a foreigner of

---

[20] Jean Marteilhe, *Mémoires d'un Protestant, condamné aux galères pour cause de religion . . . depuis 1700 jusqu'en 1713,* edited by Daniel de Superville (Rotterdam: J. et D. Beman, 1757). The translation used here is by Oliver Goldsmith, *The Memoirs of a Protestant Condemned to the Galleys of France* (2 vols.; London: J. M. Dent, 1895), II, 159; hereafter cited as Marteilhe, *Mémoires.*

[21] "Il ne faut pas être Octogénaire comme Théophraste pour connoître aujourd'hui les mœurs des Hommes." Nicolas de Gueudeville, *Le Censeur, ou Mœurs de La Haye* (The Hague: H. Scheuleer, 1715), p. 1.

[22] "Il n'y a pas d'Homme qui ne doive *s'occuper,* les uns d'une manière, les autres d'une autre; notre intérêt, la conservation même de notre santé exige cela de nous: sans parler de la Loi du Créateur, *Tu mangeras ton Pain à la sueur de ton Corps." Ibid.,* p. 105.

pleasant manners, and a wealthy man three times her age, this author shows that the sentimental attitude of his period with regard to "love" extended even to men of his cast of mind:

> It seems to me that in such an important matter as this, one should consult only one's heart and one's reason; parents are very wrong to extend their rights to this moment of their children's lives. Their children's choice [at age twenty-three] concerns them alone, not their parents.[23]

Middle-class authors in France were to express the same emotional attitude as this a few years later, with regard to younger girls.

The dignity of poor girls was stated in heartfelt fashion by Chasles, in more than one of the tales of *Les Illustres Françoises* (1720, with succeeding editions until 1737):

> "My fortune is not sufficient for me to marry you," said Angélique, "but I am not of low birth, and I have too much feeling and too much virtue, ever to be your mistress. You asked me to give you an answer, after thinking this over seriously. There you are. I believe I have done so."[24]

Honorable young men, whether commoners or members of the quite undistinguished petty nobility in Paris, also speak in Chasles' book:

> "I am, thank the Lord, rich enough for both of us and will probably be even richer some day. So I give you my solemn word here and now never to bother you on that score and to leave your sister in untroubled possession of all her property, even if there were twenty times as much."[25]

Such an attitude on the part of a young man was (and is still) quite rare, in a society in which dowries are a vital consideration.

In the same year as Chasles' book (1720), there appeared in Amsterdam a book entitled *Historical Dissertation on Duels,* condemning these contests as contrary to reason and to the duty of a Christian and a good

---

23 "Il me semble que dans une affaire aussi importante que celle-ci, on ne devroit consulter que son cœur et sa raison; et les Parens ont très mauvaise grâce d'étendre leurs droits jusques sur ce moment de la vie de leurs Enfans qui les regarde uniquement et non leurs Pères et Meres." *Ibid.,* p. 165.

24 "Je ne suis point de fortune à vous épouser; mais je ne suis point de basse Naissance, et j'ai trop de cœur et de vertu, pour être jamais votre Maîtresse. Vous m'avez priée de vous répondre sérieusement, voilà; je crois l'avoir fait. . . ." "Hist. de M. de Contamine et d'Angélique" in Robert Chasles, *Les Illustres Françoises, Histoires véritables,* N'lle éd. (Utrecht: E. Néaulme, 1737), I, 87.

25 "Je suis, grâce à Dieu, assez riche pour elle et pour moi, et je dois l'être encore un jour davantage: ainsi je vous jure dès à present de ne jamais vous faire de peine de ce côté-là, et de vous laisser la possession tranquille de tout le bien, y en eût-il vingt fois plus." Chasles, "Hist. de Terny et de Mlle de Bernay," in *ibid.,* I, 147.

citizen. The author, who appeared as "M. B." on the title page, was identified by the editor of the *Journal des Sçavans* (Holland, May, 1721) as Monsieur Basnage, the prolific Protestant writer and a moralist of strict views.

Between 1722, when the *Spectateur français* by Marivaux began, and 1736, when the fifth part of his novel, *Le Paysan parvenu*, appeared, there are many examples of this nobleman's appreciation of the moral stature of commoners. Ten years after he had lost everything in the financial crash of 1720–21, Marivaux put into the mouth of Marianne, as she tells her life story, the following "declaration of the rights of commoners in literature":

> There are people whose vanity is involved in everything they do, even in their reading . . . it is only the actions of lords, princes and kings, or at least of those who have been very prominent, that such people care to read about. That is all that satisfies their noble taste. Forget about the rest of humanity! Let them live, but let us not discuss them! Nature might well have omitted bringing them to birth, such readers will tell you; commoners are a dishonor to Nature.[26]

The moral and political point of view of the novel, *La Vie de Marianne*, is epitomized in a brief passage of the fourth part of her story. The psychology of upright and self-respecting commoners is skilfully represented when she says:

> I was of no importance whatever. I had nothing which would cause people to show me consideration; but those who have neither rank nor wealth to impress others have a soul nonetheless, and that is a great deal. Sometimes, it is more important than rank or wealth, for a soul can face no matter what circumstances.[27]

In the same vein, commoners who were reading the Abbé Prévost's magazine, *Le Pour et Contre,* which featured items for every taste, must

[26] "Il y a des gens dont la vanité se mêle de tout ce qu'ils font, même de leurs lectures . . . ils ne veulent voir agir que des seigneurs, des princes, des rois, ou du moins des personnes qui aient fait une grande figure. Il n'y a que cela qui existe pour la noblesse de leur goût. Laissez là le reste des hommes: qu'ils vivent; mais qu'il n'en soit pas question: ils vous diraient volontiers que la nature aurait bien pu se passer de les faire naître, et que les bourgeois la déshonorent." Pierre de Chamblain de Marivaux, *La Vie de Marianne* (1728–34, here quoted from ed. of Paris: Charpentier, 1842), 2e partie, p. 43.

[27] "Je n'étais rien, je n'avais rien qui pût me faire considérer; mais à ceux qui n'ont ni rang ni richesse qui en imposent, il leur reste une âme, et c'est beaucoup; c'est quelquefois plus que le rang et la richesse, elle peut faire face à tout." *Ibid.,* 4e partie, p. 147.

have approved of the following sentences from one of Prévost's book reviews:

> It is not surprising that services of such importance [to the Queen] raised the status of Merchant to the degree of honor and consideration which it enjoys in England. This is carried to the length that persons of the highest lineage do not hesitate to become Merchants and to limit their ambition to that station. The brother of the last Count [Earl?] of Oxford died at Aleppo, where he was manager of a trading company. The brother of the Duke of Townshend [Viscount?] is at present a London Merchant. . . .[28]

In the same year (1734), a novel by Madame Meheust appeared in Paris, with Approbation and Privilege of the King: *The Memoirs of Chevalier de ——*. In this wild tale of adventure, the following expresses an awareness of the worth of the hero's manservant, Tournai:

> I was greatly indebted to him and ever since then I have respected him. The most abject lot in society must not efface the impression of an admirable action. A man's merits raise him above his social class, and the intelligent person respects him whatever his status.[29]

The Up-to-date Guide to Manners by Charles de Fieux, Chevaliér de Mouhy (1735) was supposed to make any young man capable of comporting himself with dignity in Paris by reading it. The author, without shame, in a passage typical of the anti-aristocratic values which were developing, urges a young man to watch his expenses and not to waste money, advising as follows:

> I wish to point out to you that you save a good quarter of the price, if you go to a used-clothing dealer rather than to a tailor. The reason for this is that the former gets his goods [to remake costumes from secondhand clothing] much more cheaply than the custom tailor does. . . . Thus a suit for which the tailor would charge you 200 livres will cost only 140.[30]

28 "Il n'est pas surprenant que des services de cette importance [à la Reine] ayant élevé la Condition de Marchand au degré d'honneur et de considération où elle est en Angleterre; jusques-là que les personnes de la plus haute naissance ne font point difficulté de s'y engager, et d'y borner toute leur ambition. Le frère du dernier Comte d'Oxford est mort Facteur à Alep. Celui du Duc de Townshend est actuellement Marchand de Londres. . . ." Prévost, *Le Pour et Contre*, No. 46 (1734), t. IV, pp. 5–6.

29 "Je lui devois beaucoup, aussi depuis ce tems je l'ai toujours considéré, le sort le plus abjet ne doit point effacer l'éclat d'une belle action, le mérite élève au-dessus de l'état, et l'homme sensé le révère en quelque lieu qu'il se trouve." Mme Méheust, *Les Mémoires du Chevalier de—*(Paris: Dupuis, 1734), p. 61.

30 "Je veux vous faire remarquer que vous gagnez un grand quart, à préférer le Fripier au Tailleur: la raison de cela est, que ces sortes de gens tirent leurs étoffes à bien meilleur compte que le Marchand . . . votre habit, selon ce calcul, vous coûteroit deux cens livres, et il ne revient qu'à cent quarante. . . ." [Charles de Fieux, Chevalier de Mouhy], *Paris, ou le Mentor à-la-mode*, par le Chev. de M (Paris, 1735), pp. 22–23.

Shortly before this, there appeared the Abbé Pluche's *Spectacle of Nature,* which was read and approved of by the young Rousseau. A considerable number of others before 1740 seem to have known and enjoyed this work, both in French and in an English translation which followed. The characters who converse about Nature are, as the Abbé Pluche says, "ordinary in disposition and conversation, decent people such as assemble by chance every day."[31] This statement, in the preface to the book's first volume, issued in 1732, goes on to say that commonplace characters in a book

> . . . are less enticing at first than those of illustrious names, and yet, as the reader proceeds, he finds them pleasant to hear about, because it takes no effort to listen to them and to follow their meaning. . . . We are glad to learn from those like ourselves. When we hear them speak, we think ourselves capable of thinking and acting as reasonably as they. And the secret approbation we confer on such characters somehow becomes a natural inclination to imitate them.[32]

The Abbé Pluche had a calm, unhurried view of the world and men's actions in it, and his book is of great value as an aid in appreciating the point of view of the middle class in the French provinces during the 1730's. Pluche was not angry and did not seem to feel the need to expostulate about the worthy qualities of commoners. He expected to be read calmly by others of his social status and desired, without passion, to make the "spectacle of nature" appealing to the young. The idea of crying "shame" seldom occurred.

One of Pluche's characters, "The Prior," probably speaks for its author. His observations about digging in the earth and the love of flowers, which he makes the touchstone of all humanity, reveal a kindly judgment about all classes in France in the 1730's, a rare thing in the writing of that period.

> Man in his innocence was from the earliest time destined to cultivate the earth, and we have not lost the feeling of our pristine nobility. On the

---

[31] ". . . d'un caractère et d'une conversation ordinaire, d'honnêtes gens, telles que le hazard les assemble tous les jours." Abbé Pluche, *Le Spectacle de la nature* (9 vols.; Paris: Frères Etienne, 1764) (1st ed., 1732–33), Preface.

[32] ". . . préviennent d'abord moins favorablement que des noms illustres, cependant par la suite on s'en accommode mieux, parce qu'il ne faut point d'effort pour les entendre et pour les suivre. . . . Nous sommes flattés d'apprendre de nos semblables: en les entendant on se croit capable de penser et de s'occuper aussi raisonnablement qu'eux: et l'approbation secrète qu'on leur donne, devient, je ne sais comment, une amorce naturelle à les imiter." *Ibid.*

contrary, it seems that any other occupation enslaves us or degrades us. As soon as we can be free and breathe a few moments at liberty, a hidden inclination brings us all back to gardening. The merchant thinks himself fortunate to move from his counter to his flowers. The artisan, constantly tied to the same spot by harsh necessity, decorates his window with a box of greenery. The gentlemanly soldier and the magistrate sigh for life in the country.[33]

An opinion about the advantage of being born a commoner was expressed by the Abbé de Saint-Pierre in his *Project to Make Honorable Titles More Useful to the State,* a treatise published several times before the edition of his *Works* (Rotterdam, 1733):

> Regarding the title of Duke . . . those who possess it by virtue of their birth do not have the urge to outdistance their fellows by hard work or by the exercise of talents, which could serve the Nation . . . for, when you consider the matter, who takes pains when there is no reward to be hoped for?[34]

IV

The clearest proof of the sense of dignity on the part of commoners is the freedom with which they criticized men who scorned them. Some middle-class writers bitterly reproached aristocrats who looked down on them and turned these reproaches into effective statements against the nobility. All such statements quoted here were found in works of 1730 and later. Throughout the 1730's, other heartfelt emotions also occurred more frequently than before.

No writer exceeded the passion of a woman author who, in 1730, published *La Spectatrice.* Enough of her text was reprinted in a seventeen-page review in the *Journal des Sçavans* (June, 1731) to give the

---

33 "L'homme innocent avoit été destiné dès le commencement à cultiver la terre: nous n'avons point perdu le sentiment de notre ancienne noblesse. Il semble au contraire que tout autre état nous asservisse ou nous dégrade. Dès que nous pouvons nous affranchir, ou respirer quelque moment en liberté, une pente secrette nous ramène tous au jardinage. Le marchand se croit heureux de pouvoir passer du comptoir à ses fleurs. L'artisan qu'une dure nécessité attache toujours au même endroit, orne sa fenêtre d'une caisse de verdure. L'homme d'épée et le magistrat soupirent après la vie champêtre." *Ibid.,* 2ᵉ partie, t. II, Entretien V.

34 "Le titre de duc . . . Ceux qui le possèdent par leur naissance n'ont pas l'aiguillon qui les presse de surpasser leurs pareils par leur application et par des talents utiles à la Nation . . . car enfin qui est-ce qui prend de la peine quand il n'y a aucune récompense à espérer pour cette peine?" Abbé Castel de Saint-Pierre, "Projet pour rendre les titres honorables plus utiles à l'Etat," in *Ouvrages* . . . (ed. of 1735), II, 127–28.

flavor of this now very rare book. The review begins: "This author mingles moral considerations with her narratives, as she does everywhere else, whenever she feels so inclined." There follows verbatim this corrosive attack upon noblemen's prejudice:

> . . . some are beguiled and stubborn regarding their noble birth. They almost deny the possibility of nobility of soul and merit. They are impossible to deal with on that subject, for they look upon *Bourgeois* as a race of very inferior men, and, when all is said and done, they are unable to agree that greatness of soul may surpass that which one obtains by ancestry. They cannot agree that an intelligent and sensitive man without noble blood or fortune may be a thousand times more noble than the greatest lord, whose entire grandeur consists of the distinction of his blood and of the racket made by his carriages.[35]

There can be little doubt that the idea contained in the statement above was influenced by Marivaux's similar passages about "nobility of soul," quoted earlier. *The Woman Spectator* also excoriated another group in French society which looked down upon useful members of the middle class. This attack too was reproduced verbatim in the review:

> A so-called first-rate Scholar looks upon himself, even if he is penniless, as the Monarch of the Republic of Letters. He considers as completely worthless a man who has no pretension of learning, who knows only the necessary things like earning enough to eat, to dress decently and fittingly, to establish his children in society, and so forth.[36]

In 1733, the Abbé Prévost put a downright condemnation of the majority of nobles and rich men into his periodical *Le Pour et Contre:*

> With some experience in society, one cannot fail to realize that the majority of the Great and Wealthy are hard, scornful, without compassion for the

---

[35] ". . . ces entêtés de la noblesse du sang, qui donnent presque l'exclusion à celle de l'âme et du mérite; gens intraitables sur cet article, lesquels, dit-elle, regardent les Bourgeois comme une espèce d'hommes fort subalternes; gens enfin incapables de convenir que la grandeur de l'âme surpasse celle qu'on peut tirer de ses ancêtres et qu'un homme d'esprit et de cœur, sans naissance et sans fortune, est plus noble mille fois, que le plus grand Seigneur, quand toute sa grandeur est réduite à la noblesse de son sang, et aux fracas de ses équipages." *Journal des Sçavans* (Holland), juin 1731, review of *La Spectatrice* (1730), pp. 171–72.

[36] "Un Sçavant qu'on appelle du premier ordre, fût-il dans l'indigence, se regarde comme le Monarque de la République des Lettres. Un homme sensé, qui ne se pique pas de science, qui ne sait que les choses nécessaires à la vie, comme gagner de quoi se nourrir et se vêtir honnêtement et commodément, de quoi établir ses enfans, et le reste, est un gueux pour le Sçavant." *Ibid.*

misfortunes of others, and occupied solely with their own advantage, by which they judge everything.[37]

In the year following, Madame Meheust said in her novel, *Memoirs of Chevalier de ——*, that ancestry was of little account.

> If a long series of ancestors, all of them honored by high positions, gave a person some degree of merit, I should not fail to display here the collection of ancestors from whom I have the honor to be descended . . . but I condemn the vanity which infatuates most nobles with the prejudice in favor of their origin. . . . Those fine titles which cast some brilliance on us, far from making us haughty and proud, should rather make us blush by revealing our own defects more clearly.[38]

In Chapter V of that curious work previously mentioned, Mouhy's *The Up-to-date Guide to Manners* (1735), a lady has written a "City Councillor" asking him to advance her ten thousand francs against her jewelry. "That letter caused me great embarrassment," he said, "and what I should do about it troubled me more still. I was not much inclined to take the risk of lending money to people of quality."[39]

Jacob, the peasant who has risen to wealth in Marivaux's novel, *Le Paysan parvenu* (1735), recounts in the third part of his life story the harsh treatment he received at the hands of a prosecutor who hated him. A worthy bystander, seeing the roughness of the arrest of an innocent man, exclaimed:

> "They have him arrested as if he were a criminal . . . but he is a subject of the King like everyone else, and it is not allowable to maltreat the King's subjects, or to push them around like that because one is a judicial officer

---

37 "Avec un peu d'usage du monde, on ne sçauroit ignorer que la plûpart des Grands et des Riches sont durs, méprisans, sans compassion pour le mal d'autrui, uniquement occupez de leur intérêt auquel ils rapportent tout." Abbé Prévost, *Le Pour et Contre, Ouvrage d'un Goût nouveau, par l'Auteur des Mémoires d'un Homme de Qualité* (Paris: Didot, 1733–35), No. 14 (1733), p. 317; hereafter cited as Prévost, *Le Pour et Contre*.

38 "Si une longue suite d'ayeux, tous honorés de dignités . . . donnoit quelques degrés de mérite, je ne manquerois pas d'étaler ici ce fatras d'ancêtres dont j'ai l'honneur d'être issu; mais . . . je condamne la vanité dont la plûpart des Nobles sont entichez sur la prévention de leur origine. . . . Ces belles qualités dont l'éclat rejaillit sur nous, loin de nous rendre orgüeilleux, devroient plutôt nous faire rougir, puisqu'elles mettent nos défauts dans un plus grand jour." Mme Méheust, *Les Mémoires du Chevalier de —*, first page.

39 "Cette lettre m'embarrassa beaucoup, dit-il, et encore plus le parti que je devois prendre. Le risque qu'on court à prêter de l'argent à des gens de qualité, ne me convioit pas beaucoup à le faire." Mouhy, *Paris, ou le Mentor à-la-mode*, chap. v.

of high standing and they are naught. In my opinion the man should remain here!"[40]

In the fourth part of the novel, Jacob protests, years after the fact, against the scornful treatment he had received in the office of important persons at Versailles:

> I have never forgotten that scene. I have become rich too, at least as much so as any of those gentlemen who were there. And yet I still do not understand that there can exist men whose spirit can become as overbearing toward any man whatsoever as I have described them.[41]

Resentment against supercilious treatment, particularly by those who were newly arrived, is evident also in Crébillon *fils'* description of a nobleman, as seen by middle-class individuals. In his *Aberrations of the Heart and of the Mind* (1735), there occurs this description:

> He was a man who, being just barely a noble, showed that fatuous attitude toward his birth which is unbearable even in persons of the highest rank. He wore people out on all occasions with details of what was probably the shortest genealogy at the Court.[42]

Monsieur de Moncrif was one of the "Forty Immortals" of the *Académie française*. His *Essays on the Necessity and Means of Pleasing Others* was published in 1738. On certain pages of this volume of essays, it might seem that the author had the Duke of Saint-Simon in mind:

> Does a person have the advantages attaching to lofty birth and to brilliant rank? If he does, then he is not exempt from the necessity of pleasing others. When lesser men have shown attentive and serious respect, they have acquitted themselves of all obligations toward the Great.[43]

That excessive opinion of the advantages a man has over others less often delights men born in the midst of honors, than those who are suddenly

---

[40] "C'est comme criminel qu'on envoie le prendre . . . mais c'est un sujet du roi comme un autre; et il n'est pas permis de maltraiter les sujets du roi, ni de les faire marcher comme cela sous prétexte qu'on est président et qu'ils ne sont rien; mon sentiment est qu'il reste." Marivaux, *Le Paysan parvenu*, IIIe Partie, p. 133.

[41] Original unobtainable (ed.). *Ibid.*, IVe Partie, p. 230.

[42] "C'était un homme qui, noble à peine, avait sur sa naissance cette fatuité insupportable même dans les personnes du plus haut rang, et qui fatiguait sans cesse de la généalogie la moins longue que l'on connût à la cour." Crébillon *fils*, "Portrait de M. de Pranzi," in *Les Egarements du cœur et de l'esprit* (Paris, 1736–38).

[43] "Possède-t-on les avantages attachés à la haute naissance et à l'éclat du rang? On n'est point affranchi de la nécessité de plaire. Les inférieurs avec un respect bien attentif et bien sérieux, sont quittes de tout ce qu'ils doivent aux Grands." Moncrif, *Essais sur la Nécessité et sur les moyens de plaire* (Geneva: Pellissari, 1738), p. 6.

placed in a social stratum which they have long observed only by looking upward.[44]

Among the many "Letters" published by Frenchmen in the first half of the eighteenth century purporting to be written by Persians, Chinese, Peruvians, and other foreigners, there appeared in 1738 at Amsterdam the *Lettres d'un Sauvage Depaysé, contenant une Critique des Mœurs du Siècle, et des Réflexions sur des Matières de Religion et de Politique.* For obvious reasons, Joubert de la Rue, who is supposed to be the author of those letters, found it advantageous to publish his "reflections on religious and political matters" in Holland rather than in France. The opinions of his imaginary "savage" are of less concern here than the fact that the author begins his first letter "To The Lord Public" instead of to "Lord This" or "Lord That," in clear recognition of the existing middle-class self-respect, which felt more free by 1738 to criticize the nobility.

In the same year *The Gentleman Peasant* appeared—a novel of adventure by "Catalde," of whom little is known. The hero, Monsieur Ransau, is the grandson of a ruined gentleman, but the son of a peasant who provides the boy with an adequate allowance and sends him to a good school at the age of nineteen.[45] Instead of the single story of the hero, as in the case of Marivaux's Jacob, the reader finds the lives and adventures of other characters as well. Freely intermingled with tales of bandits, abductions, and swordplay are a substantial number of moralizing statements in speeches made by the characters. One of these may serve as an example:

> "I think highly of the Great, when they are obliging and when they recognize merit by the benefits which they bestow. If, on the contrary, lacking in virtue, their sole advantage over others is their rank, I have little respect for them."[46]

In this period, theoretical statements about the advantages of trade to a nation and to merchants are lacking or lost in the emotional fervor of

---

44 "Cette opinion outrée des avantages qu'on a sur les autres, séduit moins communément les gens nés dans le sein des honneurs, que ceux qui se trouvent transportés subitement dans une région qu'il n'avoient long-temps considérée qu'en élevant leurs regards." *Ibid.,* p. 7.

45 "Catalde," *Le Paysan Gentilhomme, ou Aventures de M. Ransau* (The Hague: De Hondt, 1738).

46 "Je considère les Grands, lui répondis-je, quand ils sont obligeants et que par des bienfaits, il reconnoissent le mérite: si au contraire, dépourvus de vertu, ils n'ont pour tout avantage que la grandeur, j'en fais peu de cas." *Ibid.,* p. 36.

declarations on the virtue of commoners and the shortcomings of nobles. Passages like those quoted above must have provided much more emotional satisfaction than such statements as: "Commerce is the exchange of the superfluous for the necessary."[47]

[47] "Le commerce est l'échange du superflu pour le nécessaire." [J. F. Melon], *Essai Politique sur le Commerce* (n.p., 1734), p. 10. (Voltaire, in *Le Mondain*, 1737, altered this to "the superfluous, which is so necessary.")

CHAPTER IV

Growth of Compassion

THOSE FAMILIAR with the French literature of the seventeenth century think first, perhaps, of the metaphysical pity expressed by the mystic and scientist, Blaise Pascal. Rarely has pity for man and his fate been more cogently stated than it was by this author in the middle of the century, though many readers since the days of Jansenism have been repelled, or appalled, by Pascal's theological concept of the human race—"like a group of condemned prisoners awaiting execution and eternal damnation," seeing one after another disappear from their number.

That passage by Pascal, like his statement concerning "the terror inspired in me by the contemplation of infinite space," is frequently quoted because of its lyric despair. However, expressions of intimate personal emotion became very rare in the best French literature in the years following the accession to power of Louis XIV, for the tenet that the "ego" was hateful appears to have dominated the spirit of French high society and literature between 1660 and 1690.

I

Even the lovable, lyric poet La Fontaine found it wise by the 1670's to conceal his personal feelings of pity by expressing them in fables with animal characters. The great tragedies of Racine demonstrated the doctrine that high drama must expound the fateful and sublime suffering of ancient heroes. The feelings of his audience were directed toward the lofty and the universal, to the exclusion of national heroes of the recent past. On the tragic stage anything resembling pity for contemporaries was unthinkable.

Even in the novel, which was still in the experimental stage, the most gifted author of the period, Madame de La Fayette, chose a heroine dating from a century earlier and thereby concealed whatever personal feelings she may have had, in *La Princesse de Clèves* (1677).

Sympathetic treatment of the misery of a contemporary is conspicuously absent from the forms of literature so brilliantly produced in the French classic period. For aesthetic reasons, valid to the restricted public concentrated in Paris and at the court, it was the universal and not the particular that was considered a proper subject for art. Whatever was looked upon as vulgar or "unreasonable" was treated in comic vein, as an aberration from "common sense." Middle-class and peasant characters appeared in farces, in comedies, and in satires. But they were represented as ridiculous, not as fellow-beings worthy of respect or deserving of pity. The analogy of the Negro in minstrel shows until fifty years ago in the United States is perhaps not far-fetched. Like him, those of middle- and lower-class status during the great days of Louis XIV were treated in literature as clowns, whose possible suffering was never considered.

The gentlemanly tradition of *noblesse oblige* did continue to teach noblemen the virtue of aiding those of inferior ranks: household servants, if not tailors and merchants. But this ancient doctrine by no means implied that the lower orders deserved pity or help, unless their needs were considered to be "in accordance with law and order." In the comedies of the period and in the brilliantly witty *Caractères* of La Bruyère (1688), there are indications that the manner of asking for help by an inferior was extremely important to the nobility. On the other hand, there is almost no indication of kindliness in noble society itself, as analyzed by La Bruyère. It is, in fact, even debatable whether this clear-sighted author himself had any pity for the unintelligent wretches who necessarily made up a very large segment of the French people.

It did seem illogical to La Bruyère, and doubtless to many of his noble contemporaries, that peasants who raised the food for all should lack food themselves because of the requirements laid upon them from above. But part of a page devoted to peasants, among hundreds of pages about the manners of high society, does not show great interest in tillers of the soil. There is far too much cruelty and unconscious hardness of heart in La Bruyère's writing to allow one to conclude that he felt keen pity for peasants. His single, bitter paragraph about the peasantry might better be interpreted as a clever and veiled criticism of the maladministration of public affairs in France than as an expression of sympathy for the lowly.

If we select among the undeniably gifted French authors of the period from 1660 to 1690 one man who was not witty, but who wrote with deep seriousness at all times, we find another excellent example typical of the general lack of pity for living men. In January, 1686, a few months after the revocation of the Edict of Nantes which had been in force since 1598, the celebrated Bossuet preached the funeral sermon of Michel le Tellier, and there is little doubt that in this sermon the great orator spoke not only for himself, but for many of those who heard him. He knew, and they knew, that from the time when Louvois had succeeded Colbert as Prime Minister, thousands of French men, women, and children had begun to be persecuted by royal troops in their villages for their Protestant faith, while the Edict which protected them was still legally in force. Here are Bossuet's words, from the sermon of January, 1686:

> Let us pour forth our gratitude for Louis' piety. Let us make our acclamations resound to Heaven and say to this latter-day Constantine, to this modern Theodosius: "You have strengthened the Faith, you have exterminated the Heretics. This is worthy of your reign; it is its distinguishing characteristic. Through your agency, Heresy no longer exists: God alone has wrought this marvel."[1]

---

[1] "Epanchons nos cœurs sur la piété de Louis. Poussons jusqu'au ciel nos acclamations; et disons à ce nouveau Constantin, à ce nouveau Théodose: . . . 'Vous avez affermi la foi; vous avez exterminé les hérétiques! c'est le digne ouvrage de votre règne; c'en est le propre caractère. Par vous l'hérésie n'est plus: Dieu seul a pu faire cette merveille.'" Bossuet, "Oraison funèbre de Michel le Tellier," 25 janvier 1686, in Bossuet, *Œuvres complètes* (Paris: Lachat, 1863), XII, 595.

This opinion was not necessarily shared by all the pious minor clergy in France, nor by those in monastic orders who held less political convictions about Christian charity. But it is hard to find French churchmen before 1700 expressing any feeling of pity for persecuted Protestants who were "heretics." Such feelings would obviously have been thought disloyal to the monarch and dangerously contrary to what was considered "law and order."

Protestants had been characterized, even by some charitable Catholics, as disloyal, as traitors and as revolutionaries, ever since the disastrous Religious Wars of 1562–89. This feeling seems to have become intensified in the general progress of conformism and absolutism after 1660. The absence of expressions of pity for the "heretics" who had been coerced by force before 1685 and were sent to row in the royal galleys after that date is explainable—even in the case of the great preacher Bossuet—by very strong political and patriotic convictions. The Protestants' complaints about their harsh treatment will be dealt with elsewhere in this study. The significant observation here is the general absence of expressions of pity for contemporaries on the part of the outstanding authors from 1660 to 1690.

II

It would be unfair to belabor the great authors of the time of Louis XIV for exhibiting less compassion toward their contemporaries than we find in authors of a later period. However, in their attitude toward the lowly and downtrodden, these classic authors differed also from some of the best authors of earlier periods. The ideal of a beneficent lord or king runs all through the medieval literature about Alexander, or Alexander as the Christians thought of him. A monarch who was merciful and quick to forgive his erring subjects, even for major crimes, continued to be admired by François Villon in the fifteenth century and by the many sixteenth-century readers of Plutarch's *Lives* in the brilliant translation by Amyot.

Of course before, during, and after the Religious Wars of the sixteenth century, Protestant writers emphasized principles of mercy, toleration, and kindliness. The best known of French humanists, Montaigne, stated several times in his *Essays* the pity he felt for the lowly and the unfortunate, although he remained an adherent of the Catholic cause during the Religious Wars. He was, as he said, "more inclined toward those who extended their hands to him from below" in society. Clearly, in his time it was possible to have such sentiments without offending public taste, or being considered disloyal to the monarch. Detesting cruelty in any form, Montaigne disliked Protestants who wanted drastic changes, for these led to public disorder and violence, in which men's worst passions found free scope.

As literature sometimes reflects the mentality of a society, literary evidence in the years between 1660 and 1690 indicates an acceptance of absolute opinions. Nicolas Boileau doubtless spoke for a good part of the restricted public in Paris and at the court when he announced that the expression of personal emotion was intolerable. And it is more striking still that in his *Caractères,* La Bruyère stated flatly that there are no such things as "good taste" and "bad taste." For him, one had taste, or one did not. Absolutism was, therefore, proclaimed not only as a political doctrine, but also in a quite different domain by the most noted literary critics.

These limitations brought different responses. A genius like Racine worked easily within the limitations. A gifted lyric poet, La Fontaine, found it possible to conform rather rapidly to these tightly defined requirements against personal expression and confession. Lesser authors, as one might expect, began with an understanding of the rules laid down and created what they thought the homogeneous reading public or theater audiences would enjoy. As a result, to put it briefly, in one of the outstanding literary periods in Western culture—the years from 1660 to 1690—cases of unashamed confessions of pity are very rare. Examples do exist, however, and two outstanding instances are of such merit that they are still remembered today. Curiously enough, both are personal outpourings of self-pity on the part of contemporary women: a girl in love, and a madly devoted mother.

The *Letters from a Portuguese Nun,* published in 1669 and frequently reprinted during the years which followed, constitute a series of laments by a girl in a Portuguese convent over the departure of a potential lover and husband. The heartfelt self-pity of these letters is not only passionate; it is psychologically realistic, and the emotional anguish seems convincing, even to modern readers.

Some of the many passionate letters written by Madame de Sévigné to her daughter, who was living far away, must also be mentioned:

> It seems to me that I wrong my feelings by trying to explain them in words; you would have to see what is going on in my heart about you.[2]

> . . . I started to write to you at the end of that little shaded lane that you love. I was seated on that mossy place where I have sometimes seen you lying. . . . There is no spot, either in the house, or in the church, or in the country about, or in the garden, where I have not seen you. . . . I do not know what may be your state of mind when you read this letter. . . . Still, it helps to comfort me for the moment. That is all I expect from writing it.[3]

These outpourings of feeling are in sharp contrast to the usual restrained expressions of the classic period, when the elegant letters by Voiture, Guez de Balzac, Chapelain, and other "perfect" writers of letters set the tone, though obviously not for the two women mentioned above.

The new epistolary and sentimental novels by Samuel Richardson and Jean-Jacques Rousseau in mid-eighteenth century were possible in France only after a great change had taken place in the reading public. Richardson, in translations by the Abbé Prévost, was immediately accepted, and Rousseau's *Nouvelle Héloïse* (1761) was widely acclaimed.

Human emotions like self-pity may be banned from a literature in one period but regain the right to appear later. Thus, during the decline of classicism in France and the progressive weakening of aesthetic standards, it is natural to expect a resurgence, not only of self-pity, but of pity for contemporary individuals who were poor, or suffering from the woes of adolescence, or from still other causes. The present study shows the specific evidence of this change in attitude as mirrored by the growing frequency of written expressions of such pity.

[2] "Il me semble que je fais tort à mes sentiments de vouloir les expliquer avec des paroles: il faudroit voir ce qui se passe dans mon cœur sur votre sujet." A Mme de Grignan, 25 février 1671, in Mme de Sévigné, *Lettres* (The Hague: P. Gosse, J. Néaulme et Cⁱᵉ, 1726).

[3] ". . . je me suis mise à vous écrire au bout de cette petite allée sombre que vous aimez, assise sur ce siège de mousse où je vous ai vue quelquefois couchée. Mais, Mon Dieu, où ne vous ai-je point vue ici? et de quelle façon toutes ces pensées me traversent-elles le cœur? Il n'y a point d'endroit, point de lieu, ni dans la maison, ni dans l'église, ni dans le pays, ni dans le jardin, où je ne vous ai vue. . . . Je ne sais en quelle disposition vous serez en lisant cette lettre . . . elle sert toujours à me soulager présentement; c'est tout ce que je lui demande." A Mme de Grignan, 24 mars 1671, *ibid.*

III

The increasing expression of sympathy for the woes of the destitute had become popular with the public by the 1750's and 1760's. Some critics have suggested that this sympathy was augmented by the acquaintance with English writers in the first part of the eighteenth century, who are known to have influenced political thought in France. But broad comparisons between English and French affairs can seldom be made with certainty. Frenchmen and others who visited England were impressed by the general prosperity, as well as by the individual's liberty to differ from the majority in that country, where the royal power had already been attenuated by revolution and even by the execution of a king. Certain French visitors were also impressed by the fact that the multiplicity of sects made religious toleration not only possible, but a matter of necessity in daily living and business dealings. Observations such as these were of more importance to rationalistic authors like Voltaire and Montesquieu than to sentimental writers like the Abbé Prévost —and Prévost did much to explain the ways of the English to more sentimental French people in the 1730's. A few examples from the stream of literature by which he was affected will illustrate the point.

In 1961, Moses Pitt, a bookseller in London, wrote and published *The Cry of the Oppressed*, the preface of which was intended to be read and wept over, as the following shows:

> I have put into thy Hand a small Book, as full of Tragedies as Pages, which are not Romances but Truths, they are not Acted in Foreign Nations among Turks and Infidels, Papists and Idolaters, but in this our own Countrey-men and Relations each to the other, not Acted time out of mind by Men many Thousands, or Hundred years agone, but now at this very day by Men now living in Prosperity, Health and Grandeur.[4]

Details of the main body of this book need not be repeated here, but the author plainly assumed that his fellow-Englishmen would be revolted by a report of those "who lie Starving, Rotting with Soars and Carbuncles, Devour'd with Vermin, Poison'd with Nasty Stinks. . . ."

An English Translation of the Frenchman François Froger's *Relation*

---

4 Moses Pitt, *The Cry of the Oppressed, Being a True and Tragical Account of the Unparalleled Sufferings of Multitudes of Poor Imprisoned Debtors, in Most Gaols in England, under the Tyranny of Gaolers* (London: for Moses Pitt, 1691), "To the Reader."

of a Voyage . . . commanded by M. de Gennes appeared in London, at the print-shop of one Gillyflower, in 1698. The fierce competition between France and England for overseas trade may have recommended this book to Britain's merchants. The text, and particularly the illustrations of pages 116–20, are striking evidence of the censuring of cruelty, as are the passages about Dutch colonial slaveowners in Voltaire's *Candide,* written more than a half century later. Froger describes the cruelty of Portuguese colonists in the New World: a slave's leg cut off in punishment for trying to run away, an ankle of one slave chained to another slave's neck until his leg stiffened so that the poor Negro could only walk with a cane. Froger's tale of Portuguese cruelty has an unmistakable eyewitness quality.

It is possible that less sympathy could have been expected from the public in 1706 by Quaker authors, whose laments about their treatment in the West Indies were detailed by Jonas Langford. It may even be that both Catholic and Protestant readers in Great Britain were still indifferent to the persecution of Quakers on the Island of Antigua, who were whipped until blood was drawn and then fined five hundred pounds of tobacco each for refusing to bear arms, or to take an oath, as related in Langford's *Brief Account.*[5]

A Short History of the Birth and Progress of Quakerism, published in 1692, in French, by Philippe Naudé, a Protestant Frenchman "who had lived some time in London," was one of the first books in French about "KOUAKERISME."[6] In Naudé's book, Quakers are accused of being like Baptists in Germany and Deists in England, even of permitting atheism! In his chapter 22, this rock-ribbed Protestant avers that toleration has recently been extended to Quakers in England, although withheld from Catholics, "because these latter obey a Foreign Prince, the Sovereign Pontiff at Rome!"

The importance of religious doctrines and the political history of competition between different sects, in both England and France, are sufficient to preclude flat statements about the development of widespread feeling of pity among those of divergent sects. At this time, many more Englishmen read French than Frenchmen read English, and it is

---

[5] Jonas Langford, *A Brief Account of the Sufferings of the Servants of the Lord called Quakers: From their first Arrival in the Island of Antegoa . . . from 1660 to 1695* (London: T. Sowle, 1706).

[6] Philippe Naudé, *Histoire abrégée de la naissance et du progrès du Kouakerisme, avec celle de ses dogmes* (Cologne: P. Marteau, 1692).

possible that the increasing number of expressions of compassion in French may have had some influence on Protestants in England. While the French translation in 1720 of *Robinson Crusoe* was an immediate success, translations of Addison, Steele, Pope, and Milton did not instantly follow.

There is no reason to assume that the emotional preaching of compassion in works by laymen had to be influenced from abroad. Yet it is hard to resist the temptation to mention the novel, *The Compleat Mendicant, or Unhappy Beggar,* by "Peregrine," which was published in English in 1699.[7] Copies of it are extremely rare now. No attempt is made here to attribute either great popularity or influence to it, for it is principally a harbinger; the time had not yet come when great success could be expected for such a novel.

In "To the Reader," the author says: "I can see no reason why the fabulous Life of a Vertuous [*sic*] Mendicant should not be as acceptable to the world as an *English* Rogue, a Gusman Lazerillo, or any other Romantick History of Villanous [*sic*] Tricks, &c." The virtuous beggar, a lad of good family and education who has been reduced to begging, moralizes as follows in the first chapter:

> It must necessarily be allowed, that the greater part and generality of Mankind are but one bare remove at best from flat and substantial Misery . . . but my own woeful Experience shall not urge me into complaints, or a long Introduction.[8]

> Indeed I have been amazed to see with what indifference and satisfaction some of our wealthy Cormorants have beheld their own humane Nature pining and starving in the person of their poor Brother, tho' at the same time perhaps they have been burthen'd with an excess of another kind, and might be relieved against both by a more equal distribution.[9]

It will be obvious, even from the brief texts quoted in this study, that the emotion of pity for their contemporaries was expressed more and more frequently by French authors in this fifty-year period. With some notable exceptions, authors who contributed most to this "movement" were middle-class men who had been reduced from lives of comfort and decent standing to poverty and disgrace among their fellows. In

---

[7] Peregrine (pseud.), *The Compleat Mendicant: or, Unhappy Beggar, Being the Life of an Unfortunate Gentleman* (London: E. Harris, 1699).

[8] *Ibid.*, pp. 2–3.

[9] *Ibid.*, pp. 4–5.

fact, we remember best today names like Defoe in England, or Prévost and Pierre Bayle in France, who had also suffered loss of standing in society.

One striking indication of difference between the status of the middle class in England and in France is revealed: there was no periodical like the *Gentleman's Magazine* of London published in Paris. No Parisian periodical which we know listed deaths of actors, merchants, and baronets side by side. Nor, in the best-known and most widely read Parisian periodicals until after 1730, did bankrupt wool-jobbers, drapers, silk weavers, innkeepers, or milliners see their names listed in a magazine whose title suggested that it was read by "gentlemen"!

IV

Martial glory was pictured in many books and periodicals in both England and France during their long struggle for supremacy on land and at sea. But feelings of compassion moved at least one French writer, remembered as a historian of heresies, to condemn the cruelty of the new ways of waging war. Pierre Bayle had withdrawn to Holland from a learned career in his native France because of the persecution of Protestants. Those who have studied his career remember that Bayle quarreled with his fellow Protestants in exile and ended by holding no position, and devoting himself to the then-scandalous *Dictionnaire*, which was to go through numerous editions in both French and English and to serve as a storehouse of antireligious material for the French *philosophes*.

There are two antiwar articles in his *Nouvelles de la République des Lettres* of 1684, published in June and July, which may be quoted here under the heading of compassion, or pity.

Article VII for June contains the review of a book published in French at The Hague in that year, entitled *New Manner of Fortifying Cities*. Part of the review reads:

> . . . the art of hurling bombs. But it would be still more desirable for all Christians by agreement to give up such a harsh manner of warfare. Such an action would be the more just because this invention causes great distress, without gaining any decisive advantage in war, for although the French have raised this Art to an extraordinary degree of perfection, and although they practice it in the most terrible manner that can be imagined,

they still do not achieve anything by it. . . . [The town of] Oudenarde did not change masters for having been bombed. Luxembourg was none the easier to conquer because of being bombed.[10]

Article III in the July number invokes the essence of the Christian doctrine of charity:

> If, in these corrupt times, there were as much virtue as obtained among Christians of the Early Church, decisions in such cases would have been quickly arrived at: people would never take up arms, even if they were to perish to the last man by the harshness of tortures inflicted upon them.[11]

This expatriate Frenchman was not a Quaker. But more than ten years before William Penn published his project for universal peace in Europe, Bayle, like the Quakers, was distressed by the killing and torturing of Christians by one another. In this he was among the first of the French, during the reign of Louis XIV and before the revocation of the Edict of Nantes, to emphasize for the learned public the fundamental and compassionate Christian doctrine in defiance of a glorious military tradition.

Another gentleman by birth, and author of the best-selling *Adventures of Telemachus*, Archbishop Fénelon, composed a set of *Directions for a King's Conscience* (probably written 1697, published 1709 in Holland). Two of the Directions—which were written for the instruction of the Duke of Burgundy—are quoted:

> You have imagined, have you not, that the New Testament is not supposed to be the rule for kings as it is for their subjects? You have imagined that politics excuses kings from being humble, just, sincere, moderate, compassionate, ready to pardon insults. Has some subservient and corrupt

10 ". . . l'art de jeter des Bombes. Mais il seroit encore plus à souhaiter, que tous les Chrétiens renonçassent de concert à une manière si rigoureuse de faire la guerre. Cela seroit d'autant plus juste qu'on fait de grands désordres par cette invention, sans remporter aucun avantage décisif, car encore que les François ayent porté cet Art à un degré de perfection extraordinaire, et qu'ils l'exercent de la plus terrible manière qui puisse se concevoir, ils n'achèvent pourtant quoi que ce soit par cette voye. . . . Oudenarde n'a point changé de Maître pour avoir été bombardée. Luxembourg, n'en a pas été pour cela plus aisé à conquérir." Pierre Bayle, *Nouvelles de la République des Lettres*, Vol. I (juin 1684), Art. VII, review of *Nouvelle Manière de fortifier les places*, par M. Blondel, maréchal. (The Hague, 1684).

11 "Si l'on avoit dans ces siècles de corruption autant de vertu que les Chrétiens de la Primitive Eglise, on auroit bien-tôt pris son parti dans des occasions comme celles-là, car on ne prendroit jamais les armes, dût-on tous périr sous la rigueur des supplices." *Ibid.* (juillet 1684), Art. III.

flatterer not told you . . . that kings must, for the good of their realms, conduct themselves by certain maxims of pride, hardness of heart, dissimulation, and that they are forced to rise above the ordinary rules of justice and humanity?[12]

Have you not acted unjustly at times toward foreign nations? A poor wretch is hanged for stealing a coin on the highway, in his extreme need; a man who makes a conquest, that is to say who unjustly subjugates regions of a neighboring state, is called a hero![13]

Fénelon's political disgrace after certain actions of his had displeased the intransigent Bishop Bossuet is a matter of historical record. Both men agreed, of course, that it was "contrary to law and order" to steal on the highway, even if a man suffered from extreme hunger. But Louis XIV had long acted on the conviction that it was quite "according to law and order" for his government to unite all Frenchmen in the Catholic faith, even though this violated the Edict of Nantes before it was officially revoked. The immediate cause of Fénelon's banishment by the king and his life exile to Cambrai was a theological punishment sanctioned by the king. The good man had been led into a mystical and therefore "dangerous" kind of Christianity, and he had refused to condemn the person who had influenced him in the path of "Quietism." What is important today, when Quietism is dead and gone, is that nothing mystical could have been condoned, or even tolerated by Boussuet, whose position in the Church at the end of the seventeenth century in France was not only official, but pre-eminent. All forms of mysticism will probably continue to be anathema to partisans of "law and order" or conformity in Church matters, for it is impossible to regulate them.

The ills and misery besetting France at the end of the seventeenth

---

[12] "Ne vous êtes-vous point imaginé que l'Evangile ne doit point être la règle des rois comme celle de leurs sujets; que la politique les dispense d'être humbles, justes, sincères, modérés, compatissants, prêts à pardonner les injures? Quelque lâche et corrumpu flatteur ne vous a-t-il point dit . . . que les rois ont besoin de se gouverner pour leurs états par certaines maximes de hauteur, de dureté, de dissimulation, en s'élevant au-dessus des règles communes de justice et de l'humanité?" Fénelon, *Directions pour la conscience des rois et des princes souverains, composées pour l'instruction de Louis de France, duc de Bourgogne* (The Hague: J. Néaulme, 1747), Direction II, p. 163.

[13] "N'avez-vous point fait quelque injustice aux nations étrangères? On pend un pauvre malheureux pour avoir volé une pistole sur le grand chemin dans son besoin extrême, et on traite de héros un homme qui fait la conquête, c'est-à-dire qui subjugue injustement les pays d'un état voisin!" *Ibid.*, Direction XXV, p. 188.

and the beginning of the eighteenth centuries were openly and directly criticized by Vauban, whereas Fénelon had only criticized the king's policies indirectly and by appealing to abstract principles. Vauban was held in high esteem as the most brilliant military architect of his time. His presence at more than twoscore sieges had taught him the realities of fortifying strong points. What is of interest here, however, is that Vauban time and again endangered his own interests for the sake of his nation, in opposition to an absolute monarch. It took an exceptional man to resist being made a Marshal of France, for the reason, which seemed valid to him, that he had "been at too many sieges and too many times wounded" to serve his King usefully in that exalted rank.

None of his suggested reforms for the good of the country was heeded. Only four years after the revocation of the Edict of Nantes, Vauban had been bold enough to suggest that Protestants be recalled from abroad, because their absence was ruining French manufacturing and trade! A careful reading of his work on *The Conduct of Sieges,* and his most celebrated *Dixme royale* will convince anyone of the selfless patriotism of their author.[14] Eighteenth-century French writers, intent on destroying the Christian-monarchical tradition, did his memory a marked disservice by labeling him as one of their own who had been working "against Louis XIV." Anyone who reads him without bias is impressed by Vauban's unfailing loyalty to the deluded and ambitious king whom he tried persistently to help by patriotic statements based on experience and common sense. It was Vauban's misfortune that Louis XIV, in the 1690's and early 1700's, was proof against either of those considerations. Vauban's often quoted statements about not wasting the lives of soldiers unnecessarily are logically the result of his patriotism, not the effects of heartfelt pity for individuals of inferior station. He was not a tender-hearted man, except for his unashamed tenderness for France.

> Emulation between generals often leads them to expose their soldiers to no purpose, asking them to do what is beyond their power and not hesitating to cause the death of a hundred men to advance four steps farther than their comrades. . . . In fact, if Nations only perish for lack of good soldiers to defend them, I know of no punishment severe enough for those who cause

[14] Sébastien le Prestre de Vauban, *Mémoire pour servir à l'instruction dans la conduite des sièges* ([written 1669], Leiden, 1740); *Dixme royale* (Paris, 1707).

such soldiers to die uselessly. However, there is nothing as frequent among us as this brutality, which depopulates our troops of experienced soldiers and allows a ten years' war to exhaust a whole kingdom.[15]

Years after the foregoing was composed, Vauban, in his *Dixme royale*, made the following statement regarding the importance of the common people:

> It is the lower orders of the people who, by their labor and their trade, as well as by what they pay to the King, enrich both him and all his kingdom. It is they who furnish all the soldiers and sailors of his armies and navies and a great number of officers, all the merchants and the lesser judiciary . . . to put it briefly, it is they who carry out all the large and small enterprises in town and country. That is what this part of our population consists of, a part which is so useful and so scorned, which has suffered and continues to suffer so greatly at the moment I am writing these words. . . . It is a fact that the greatness of kings is measured by the number of their subjects; it is this that constitutes kings' property, happiness, riches, strength, and fortune, and determines the respect they enjoy in the world.[16]

It obviously required angry political prejudice to regard such statements as a series of antimonarchical outbursts. On the other hand, only considerable sentimental prejudice could read into these lines any similarity to the pity for the poor that is found in the writings of Fénelon. Vauban, who remained a loyal soldier of the king all his life, had values very different from those of the Archbishop and does not represent the

[15] "L'émulation qu'il y a entre les officiers généraux fait souvent qu'ils exposent les soldats mal à propos, leur faisant faire au-delà de leur possible et ne se souciant d'en faire périr une centaine pour avancer quatre pas plus que leurs camarades. . . . En vérité, si les Etats ne périssent que faute de bons hommes pour les défendre, je ne sais pas de châtiment assez rude pour ceux qui les font périr mal à propos. Cependant il n'est rien de si commun parmi nous que cette brutalité qui dépeuple nos troupes de vieux soldats et fait qu'une guerre de dix années épuise tout un royaume." Vauban, *Mémoire . . . la conduite des sièges.*

[16] "C'est encore la partie basse du peuple qui, par son travail et son commerce, et par ce qu'elle paie au Roi, l'enrichit et tout son royaume; c'est elle qui fournit tous les soldats et matelots de ses armées de terre et de mer, et grand nombre d'officiers, tous les marchands et les petits officiers de judicature . . . et pour achever de le dire en peu de mots, c'est elle qui fait tous les gros et menus ouvrages de la campagne et des villes.

"Voilà en quoi consiste cette partie du peuple si utile et si méprisée, qui a tant souffert, et qui souffre tant de l'heure que j'écris ceci. . . .

"Il est constant que la grandeur des rois se mesure par le nombre de leurs sujets; c'est en quoi consiste leur bien, leur bonheur, leurs richesses et leurs forces, leur fortune, et toute la considération qu'ils ont dans le monde." Vauban, *Dixme royale*, Preface.

genuine expressions of pity in the writings of Frenchmen around 1700. The time for such expression had apparently not yet arrived.

V

To indicate the flowering of a sense of pity, there is perhaps no more striking way than to quote two writers of verse, separated in time by a little over fifty years. The first, Edme Boursault, published in 1698 a poem on an earthquake in Southern Italy; the second, Voltaire, published his meditation on the earthquake in Lisbon in 1755.

The sprightly, almost gay verse of Boursault, writing at the end of the seventeenth century, reflects his lack of compassion toward unfortunates, especially when not witnessed close at hand. The prose translation which follows does little damage to the wretched verse of this author:

> I have been informed that in Calabria, which the wrath of Heaven is demolishing, a loud racket has occurred, causing an unusual stir. . . . Amongst fourteen or fifteen families, seven oldsters, nine unmarried chaps, ten girls, two coquettes who were primping, four old women who were gossiping, a dying man being exhorted by a priest, a lackey who was stealing from his master, all these together were suddenly crushed by the same fate. Then, having finished their course, they went off in a group so as not to get bored. A few went on high and many went down yonder, where those of evil actions wear garlands of snakes.[17]

By the time of the earthquake at Lisbon in 1755, sympathy for the unfortunate had been frequently expressed for a growingly sentimental French public. Those who, like Voltaire, had been born in the 1690's, had lived through that period of change. In *Le Désastre de Lisbonne* (1755), which is too well known to require quotation here, Voltaire gives, especially toward the end, evidence of unashamed personal emotion much like what we have encountered elsewhere. He confessed his inability to do anything but "suffer and not complain" of the ways of

---

[17] "On m'a dit que dans la Calabre/ Que le courroux du Ciel délabre,/ Il est arrivé du fracas/ Qui cause un étrange tracas. . . ./ De quatorze ou quinze familles/ Sept Vieillards, neuf Garçons, dix Filles,/ Deux Coquettes qui s'habilloient,/ Quatre Vieilles qui babilloient,/ Un mourant qu'exhortoit un Prestre,/ Un Laquais qui voloit son Maistre,/ Tous ensemble écrasez d'abord/ Eprouvèrent le mesme sort;/ Puis ayant leur trame finie/ S'en allèrent de compagnie/ Afin de ne s'ennuyer pas,/ Peu là haut, et beaucoup là bas,/ Où les gens à damnables œuvres/ Ont des guirlandes de couleuvres." E. Boursault, "Tremblement de Terre," in his *Lettres de respect, d'obligation, et d'amour* (Paris: Guignard, 1698), pp. 282–83.

an inscrutable Providence, in which he still believed, although he could not explain the evil in the world.[18]

Pity for animals was even more rarely expressed during the reign of Louis XIV than pity for the poor and unfortunate. An expression not only of interest in animals but of pity for them does appear, however, in Baron Lahontan's book on Canada, read in its many editions after its publication in 1703 for reasons other than those which were sentimental. His corrosive remarks about European civilization were what made his reputation in his own time and after. The following appears in his description of the lucrative trade in beaver skins:

> When the pond is frozen, the Savages make holes in the ice near the beaver houses and pass nets from one of these holes to the next. When the nets are properly stretched, the Savages chop off the tops of the houses of these poor creatures with axes, and the beavers, taking to the water, come to the holes in the ice to breathe, there becoming entangled in the nets. Not a single one escapes, but as the Savages do not wish to destroy them utterly, they throw an equal number of males and females back into the holes.[19]

A little Capucin monk, Martin de Nantes, in his otherwise undistinguished book, *Account of His Mission in Brazil* (1707), exemplifies the continuing, gentle tradition among various monastic orders in the New World, already expressed in the early 1500's in the writings of the great humanitarian, Bartolomé de Las Casas. The tradition of pity for the American savages appears in passages like the following: "These poor Indians, having neither Faith, nor Laws, nor King, nor Arts . . . had fallen into disorders which such a general lack can cause."[20]

The notion of primitivism, in the sense of admiration for men not yet

[18] It must be added that some students of Voltaire, in contrast to this interpretation, refuse to take the concluding lines of the poem literally, preferring to see them as a safety measure vis-à-vis the authorities. See G. R. Havens, "The Conclusion of Voltaire's *Poème sur le désastre de Lisbonne*," *Modern Language Notes*, LVI (1941), 422–26.

[19] "Lorsque l'étang est glacé, ils font des trous aux environs de la loge des Castors, dans lesquels ils passent des rets de l'un à l'autre, et lorsqu'ils sont tendus comme il faut, ils découvrent à coups de hache la Cabane de ces pauvres Animaux qui se jettant à l'eau et venant prendre l'haleine à ces trous, ils s'enveloppent dans les filets: il n'en échappe pas un seul, mais comme les Sauvages ne veulent pas les détruire, ils rejettent dans les trous le même nombre de mâles et de femelles." Louis Armand, baron de Lahontan, *Dialogues curieux entre l'auteur et un sauvage de bon sens qui a voyagé . . .* ed. G. Chinard (Baltimore, Md.: Johns Hopkins University Press and Oxford University Press, 1931), p. 135.

[20] "Ces pauvres Indiens, n'ayant ny Foy, ny loix, ny Roi, ny arts . . . étoient tombés dans tous les désordres que peut causer ce défaut général." Révérend Père Capucin: Martin de Nantes, *Relation Succinte [sic] et Sincère de la Mission du Père Martin de Nantes, Prédicateur Capucin . . . dans le Brézil* (Quimper: Jean Perier, 1707), p. 7.

"afflicted with the ills of civilized life," obviously did not exist in the mind of this missionary. But his notions of law and order, being shocked by the society he had found in Brazil, did cause him to pity the savages.

Mention has already been made of the suffering in France during the famine of 1709. The editors of periodicals published in Holland who were Protestant refugees were quick to make known the contents of letters received from their former homeland. In January, 1709, such a letter appeared in the *Mercure historique et politique:* "All this region [the Dauphiné], which was so highly cultivated and so fertile . . . is now nothing more than a frightful wasteland in the midst of which a few decrepit oldsters are dying of hunger."[21] In the issue of the same periodical for April, 1709, the following appeared: "Letters we receive from the Provinces in France are filled with the wretched poverty suffered there because of the shortage of food and the great damage caused by this long and harsh winter. Money is still very scarce."[22]

One of the most distinguished proponents of ideas for improving society in France and in Europe generally was the Abbé de Saint-Pierre. This indefatigable reformer's *Project for Perpetual Peace* was first published in 1716; a first form, entitled *Memoires pour rendre la paix perpetuelle,* dates from 1712. The author's desire to defend the weak against the encroachments of the strong and the acceptance of this idea by the public further indicates the growing concept of pity and the increasing frequency of its expression in the first part of the eighteenth century. The popularity of this idea is indicated by a short review published in the *Journal des Sçavans* for February, 1732: "Although we reviewed this work in January and February, 1717, and although the present book is only an abridgment of that work, we nevertheless give an extract from the 1729 summary."[23]

The extract quoted from the short form of Saint-Pierre's *Project* emphasizes the following: "What makes for peace among citizens and

---

21 "Tout ce pays, qui étoit si bien cultivé ou si fertile . . . n'est plus maintenant qu'un affreux désert, au milieu duquel quelques Vieillards décrépits meurent de faim." *Mercure historique et politique* (The Hague), Vol. XLVI (janvier 1709).

22 See chap. i, note 33.

23 "Quoiqu'en 1717 (dans les mois de janvier et février) nous ayons rendu compte de l'Ouvrage dont ce morceau n'est que l'abrégé, nous en donnerons cependant l'Extrait." Abbé de St. Pierre: *Abrégé du projet de paix perpétuelle, inventé par le Roi Henri le Grand, approuvée par la Reine Elisabeth, par le Roi Jacques son Successeur, par les républiques et par divers autres potentats . . .* par M. L'abbé de S. Pierre, de l'Académie Françoise (Rotterdam: Jean-Daniel Beman, Paris: Briasson, 1729), compte-rendu in *Journal des Sçavans,* février 1732.

keeps them from having recourse to violence, is the existence of a court whose authority protects the weak from the enterprises of the stronger."[24] This sentence, especially used to justify a comity of nations, would have seemed rank heresy and treason to many in 1660 or 1680. But in the French society of 1716, recognition that the strong did oppress the weak and a general opinion that this was deplorable must have existed or Saint-Pierre's assertions would assuredly have fallen flat. The appearance of a condensed form of the original *Project* indicates that publishers in Holland still expected a market in 1732 as well.

Yet loyalty to the king was still too strong for any concerted and general uprising to develop against those who were powerful in society in the 1720's. Localized revolts of farmers in France between 1716 and 1729 had been put down by the use of troops.

Jean Buvat, looking out from the Royal Library upon the rue Vivienne during the time of Law's financial débacle, or walking the streets when men and women were trying frantically to exchange paper for valid money, observed and listened. His *Journal,* covering the period of 1715 to 1723, showing us how history looked to an ordinary man, remained unpublished until 1865. But his reporting of street scenes, rain, lightning bolts, and accidents is as informative as the memoirs containing personal affairs at court and quarrels among the nobility.

A single example of Jean Buvat's power to picture events, as well as of his compassion for the unfortunate, is given here:

> . . . the ice, having broken free . . . between the bridges in the city, crushed several boats. Several washerwomen on laundry barges moored to the banks perished and were cut in two. The heads of some appeared on top of the ice and their bodies were submerged, without anyone being able to give help. This was a sad sight.[25]

It was some years before such macabre happenings were used in imaginative literature. But the appearance of the melodramatic in the

---

[24] "Ce qui fait la paix des Citoyens, et ce qui empêche d'avoir recours aux voyes de fait, c'est l'érection d'une tribunal dont l'autorité met le plus faible à l'abri des entreprises du plus fort." *Ibid.*

[25] ". . . les glaces s'étant détachées . . . entre les ponts de cette ville, fracassèrent plusieurs bateaux, dont plusieurs blanchisseuses périrent et furent coupées en deux; les têtes de quelques-unes paraissaient sur des glaçons et leurs corps étaient enfoncées en dessous, sans pouvoir leur donner aucun secours, ce qui faisait un triste spectacle." Jean Buvat, Ecrivain de la Bibliothèque du Roi, *Journal de la Régence* (1715–1723). Publié pour la première fois . . . par Emile Camparadon, Archiviste aux Archives de l'Empire (2 vols.; Paris: H. Plon, 1865), I, 119, 6 février 1716.

writings of the Abbé Prévost and of other novelists after 1730 can be partially explained by the existence of an audience of literate Frenchmen who, like Jean Buvat, had already developed a taste for accounts of contemporary violence. Without such a public, sentimental novels like those of Prévost might have remained unpublished.

Edmond-Jean-François Barbier's account of the great fire of 1718—written at the time although not published until 1847—again is a report of suffering among the lowest class. Fire on boats in the Seine had caused them to be cut loose from their moorings. They drifted with the current, then became fixed to a bridge. Dwellings on that bridge caught the flames and were destroyed:

> It was heart-rending to see people from all the neighborhood of the Petit-Pont moving their effects into the Marché-Neuf and into the rue de la Huchette. Everybody that one saw was carrying furniture, and servant-girls in nightshirts could be seen carrying away their own clothing.[26]

As his name indicates, Barbier was middle class, but he came from a much more fortunate family than his contemporary Buvat, his father having been close to some great families. The cast of mind of the son inclined him toward political and economic affairs without, however, depriving him of his humane sympathy for the afflicted. The above excerpt shows Barbier's feeling for individual terror and misfortune, a sort of writing very difficult to find in the accounts of the time by noblemen. The latter were to be preoccupied for many decades with questions of high policy, intrigues at court, and who was present at social or diplomatic events.

VI

There is another object of compassion in French writing, even before 1720, which is in clear contrast to what authors of the preceding century had thought proper to discuss or describe. Although Molière had portrayed the budding young girl with masterly touches in his *École des Femmes* a half century earlier, no treatment of the trials of an adolescent boy appears to exist in French classical literature. Unless the boy in

---

[26] "C'était une désolation de voir tous les environs du Petit-Pont déménager sur le Marché-Neuf et dans la rue de la Huchette; on n'apercevait que des gens qui portaient des meubles, jusqu'à des servantes en chemise qui emportaient leurs hardes." E.-J.-F. Barbier, *Journal historique et anecdotique du règne de Louis XV* (Paris: Jules Renard, 1874), I, 4.

question were of noble family and had lived long ago, for example in the time of Theseus, he was of only very minor interest to the literate French public of the 1660's and 1670's. That an author, nowadays relatively unknown, was able to publish his confessional remembrance of his sufferings as a schoolboy in 1719 therefore suggests real significance.

Vallange's *New System for Gaining Knowledge of the Arts and Sciences* is a long diatribe against the unnecessarily hard and unpleasant methods of teaching boys in school. The emotional and compassionate statement of the author's personal experience is of special interest here. In one long paragraph in particular, his outburst against the traditional system of teaching and its horrors is as bold and forthright as Montaigne's criticisms more than a century earlier:

> They are taught *singulariter nominativo haec Musa,* the Muse; *genitivo hujius Musae,* of the Muse, etc. Beautiful notions surely of Latin culture! How clear those notions are! How distinct! I still remember those days of martyrdom with indignation. I did not know whether the teacher took me for insane, or whether he was insane himself. . . . Poor youngsters, how you are to be pitied in such a wretched situation! It pains me deeply to see them destroy your reason.[27]

Making sport of pedants had long been a venerable tradition in France, even before the scathing treatment by Rabelais and Montaigne in the sixteenth century. But it was not the custom, in the era of Louis XIV, to consider seriously and emotionally the sufferings of boy scholars. Latin and other difficult subjects were then generally supposed to be learned with some agony; as a necessary part of an education, they were calmly accepted by grown people as painful to youth, in much the same way as the use of the rod. The anger and passionate outbursts of Vallange in 1719 were to be far more cogently stated forty years later, in the *Emile* by Rousseau, who had greater genius of expression and was equally devoid of humor on the subject of education.

Professor Roddier of the University of Lyons is probably as well in-

---

[27] "On leur apprend *singulariter nominativo haec Musa,* la Muse; *genitivo hujius Musae,* de la Muse, etc. Belles idées de latinité! Je me ressouviens toujours de ces tems de martyre avec indignation. Je ne sçavois si l'on me prenoit pour un fou, ou si le Maître l'étoit lui-même. . . . Pauvres Enfans, que vous êtes à plaindre dans ce triste état! Je vois avec un déplaisir sensible que l'on commence à immoler votre raison." De Vallange, *Nouveaux Systèmes ou Nouveaux Plans de Méthodes . . . pour parvenir en peu de tems et facilement à la connoissance des Langues et des Sciences* (Paris: Cl. Jombert, J.-B. Lamesle, 1719), I, 311–12.

formed as anyone of our time concerning the curious case of Robert Chasles (or Challes), whose writing has been too long ignored in the history of French realism.[28] It is of interest here, with regard to the sentiment of pity, that *Les Illustres Françoises* by Chasles appeared in a number of editions between 1720 and 1737. Chasles' writings reveal a gift for realistic description of contemporary people and scenes, as well as a real sense of pity for the poor which we have already encountered. *Les Illustres Françoises* was first published in 1720, the same year as the French translation of *Robinson Crusoe*, and only one year after publication of the original of that great novel. The stories contained in *Les Illustres Françoises* are presented by various characters. The one who tells the "Tale of Frans and Sylvie" says:

> Even if I were to be the poorest and most unfortunate Gentleman in all France, I should never lower myself to becoming the Persecutor of the people and of the peasants. . . . My sense of honor was too strong, and my feelings as well, to allow me to participate in the cruelties which were inflicted upon them under the pretext of collecting what was due to the King. . . . I was too humane to look with indifference upon the harsh treatment they suffered. Far from ruining them and persecuting them, as one was obliged to do when serving as a collector, I would have given all I had to deliver them. . . . I was not born to become a defrauder, or a tax gatherer; those ways of dealing were not at all in accord with my conscience, or with my sense of honor.[29]

Such a moral statement by a fictional character of the petty nobility in the presence of his friends who were of his rank or of the higher middle class is an indication of one facet of Chasles' writing. Elsewhere there are examples of rather coarse immorality, anticlericalism, remarkably realistic description and, most curious of all perhaps, a kind of mysticism. In his *Account of a Voyage to the East Indies*, published after 1730,

---

28 See Henri Roddier, *L'Abbé Prévost* (Paris: Hatier-Boivin, 1955); *J.-J. Rousseau en Angleterre au XVIII*e *siècle; l'œuvre et l'homme* (Paris: Boivin, 1950).

29 "Quand je devrois être le plus pauvre et le plus malheureux Gentilhomme de France, je ne m'abaisserois jamais à devenir le Persécuteur du Peuple et des Païsans. . . . J'avois trop de cœur et d'honneur pour prêter la main aux cruautez qu'on exerçoit contr'eux sous prétexte de lever les Droits du Roi. . . . J'étois trop humain pour voir d'un oeil tranquille les duretez qu'ils essuyoient, et bien loin de les ruiner et les persécuter comme on étoit obligé de le faire dans les Commissions, je donnerois tout le mien pour les en déliverer. . . . Je n'étois pas né non plus que lui pour devenir Maltotier, ni Partisan; ce qui ne s'accordoit point ni avec ma conscience ni avec mon Honneur." Robert Chasles, "Histoire de Frans et de Silvie," in *Les illustres Françoises, Histoires véritables* (Utrecht: E. Néaulme, 1737), II, 88.

but presumably written many years before as a diary, there is another statement of pity for the poor which deserves quotation. Instead of the self-righteous statement of an imaginary gentleman who would not oppress the poor, Chasles expresses his own sentiment of sympathy for the wretched life of common seamen on merchant vessels:

> One of our sailors died during the night. I have already said that one fell from a yard-arm into the sea this morning. These men work and labor greatly, day and night, at the risk of their lives. They are poorly fed, compared to what workmen have to eat on land. They are not cared for, and added to that, are sometimes soundly beaten! Are they any the less men than others? How grateful to God we should be, when we are born with the gifts of fortune! *Non fecit taliter omni Nationi.* I now look upon poverty with much more compassion than ever before, although I may state that I never did look upon it with scorn.[30]

Loss of his own fortune in Canada, followed by his imprisonment by the English in the New World, had impelled Chasles to take work as a supercargo on merchant vessels. As in the case of Defoe, Marivaux, the Abbé Prévost, and other sympathetic novelists, it was apparently his own destitute state which made this writer more compassionate. Even for one who has read a great many accounts of ocean voyages by Frenchmen of the sixteenth and seventeenth centuries, it is difficult to recall any such pity for the common sailors as Chasles discloses. Jean de Léry (1570), Marc Lescarbot (1609), both kindly Protestants, and the benign priest, Father Du Tertre (1667), were all distinguished by their sympathy for the savages of the New World. But they are not remembered as men who appreciated the hard lives that their sailor companions on board were forced to lead. Yet conditions for common sailors were hardly less dangerous or unpleasant in those earlier times than when Chasles sailed to the East Indies with Admiral du Quesne.

A much better-known author, writing from 1722 until 1736, is an excellent example of the growth of the expression of pity in France. Marivaux's fame as a dramatist is sufficiently indicated by the fact that

---

[30] "Il est mort un de nos Matelots cette nuit: je l'ai déjà dit; il en est tombé un ce matin de l'Amiral à la Mer. Ils travaillent et fatiguent beaucoup nuit et jour, au hazard de leur vie; ils sont mal nouris, en comparaison de ce que les ouvriers mangent à terre; peu soignez, et avec cela quelquefois bien battus! Sont-ils moins hommes que les autres? Que ceux qui sont nez avec des biens de fortune ont de grâces à rendre à Dieu! *Non fecit taliter omni Nationi.* Je regarde à présent la pauvreté, avec bien plus de compassion que jamais; quoique je puisse dire, que je l'ai toujours regardé sans mépris." Chasles, *Journal d'un voyage*, II, 118.

the word *marivaudage* is still used to mean clever and brilliant, sometimes affected and excessively subtle, dialogue about tender feelings.[31] What is more important here than his reputation in comedy is his talent as a reporter of the contemporary scene. His definitely expressed feelings are plain enough in the two novels and in the various periodicals which he wrote.

As in the case of Chasles, whatever fortune Marivaux had previously possessed disappeared suddenly. The financial crisis and debacle of Law's schemes in 1720–21 reduced this dramatist to destitution. Poverty and the loss of a wife who left him with a young child to support forced him into association with others of the poor and the disinherited. Little wonder that he should have reported the woes of the poor in his *Spectateur françois* in 1722!

Here is a tale told the *Spectateur* by a young girl, along with a moralizing statement about her lot:

"I am a girl of good family; my father held a rather important post in the provinces. He died three years ago . . . and left my mother a widow with three daughters to care for, of whom I am the eldest. After selling what we had left, my mother and I came to Paris to hasten the settlement of a lawsuit which, if successful, would re-establish us. . . . Those who should be expediting it neglect to do so, because we have no funds with which to pay. Finally, Sir, the poverty-stricken state into which we have fallen, added to the grief, the foul air and darkness of our quarters . . . have made my mother despair . . . a rich townsman offers me all possible help. But what help, Sir! It would save my mother's life; it would everlastingly dishonor mine. This is my present state; can any be more terrible?"

Every decent man will feel how the words of this girl affected me. . . . [says *the Spectateur*]. Just Heaven! What are the designs of Providence in the mysterious distribution it makes of wealth! Why does Providence seem prodigal of riches with men who are devoid of feeling, born hard and pitiless, whereas it is sparing of riches with those who are generous and compassionate, hardly according them the absolute necessities? Since this is the way it is, what is to become of poor wretches who find no help either in the abundance of the former or in the compassion of the latter?[32]

---

31 Voltaire's characterization of Marivaux as a man who spent his life weighing fly-eggs on a spider-web scale ("un homme qui passe sa vie à peser des œufs de mouche dans des balances de toile d'araignée"), is too hostile to be useful but states one tendency of *marivaudage*.

32 "Je suis une fille de famille; man père avait une charge assez considérable en province; il mourut, il y a trois ans . . . et ma mère est restée veuve, chargée de trois filles, dont je suis l'aînée. Nous sommes venues à Paris, ma mère et moi, après avoir vendu ce qui nous restait, pour hâter la décision d'un procès dont le gain nous rétablirait. . . . On néglige de travailler pour nous, parce que nous n'avons point de

Other examples exist, here and there, in his *Spectateur:*

There is no person more out of favor among men, more abandoned by them, than a man who is both poor and virtuous. All hearts are icy toward him; he is like a stranger in Nature. An indigent scamp is perhaps more scorned, but he is better treated and less often rebuffed . . . for he is subservient toward men. It flatters them and they have the pleasant feeling of being better than he is, when they help him. But a virtuous man who is shamefaced, yet worthy of respect, disgusts them.[33]

I was then nothing but an unknown wretch upon this earth. I had none but enemies in the world, for not having anyone to depend on means having to defend oneself against everyone, means being in the way everywhere.[34]

La Vie de Marianne (1731–41) by Marivaux is often listed among the best of French novels. A few quotations from its pages will suffice to show how deeply this author pitied the unfortunate. The heroine tells the story of her own life, in this confession-type of sentimental novel which flourished during the 1730's in France.

When, early in the story, Marianne is offered charity by a self-consciously virtuous benefactor, she expresses her revulsion:

Charity was never displayed more conspicuously as a duty than by this person; my heart was drowned in shame . . . it is cruel indeed to be abandoned to the help of certain people, for what is such kindness when it

---

quoi payer; enfin, monsieur, la misère où nous sommes tombées, le chagrin, le mauvais air et l'obscurité du lieu où nous logeons . . . ont entièrement abattu ma mère . . . un riche bourgeois m'offre tous les secours possibles. Mais quels secours, monsieur! Ils sauveraient la vie à ma mère; ils déshonoreraient éternellement la mienne. Voilà mon état; en est-il de plus terrible?
Tout honnête homme sentira combien les discours de cette fille ont dû me toucher. . . .
Juste ciel! quels sont donc les desseins de la Providence dans le partage mystérieux qu'elle fait des richesses! pourquoi les prodigue-t-elle à des hommes sans sentiment, nés durs et impitoyables? pendant qu'elle en est avare pour les hommes généreux et compatissants, et qu'à peine leur a-t-elle accordé le nécessaire. Que peuvent, après cela, devenir les malheureux, qui par là n'ont de ressource, ni dans l'abondance des uns, ni dans la compassion des autres?" *Le Spectateur françois* (1722–23), 4e feuille, pp. 58–61.
[33] "Il n'y a point d'objet plus disgracié parmi les hommes, plus abandonné d'eux, que l'homme pauvre et vertueux tout ensemble; tous les cœurs sont glacés pour lui; il est comme un étranger dans la nature. Un fripon indigent est peut-être plus méprisé mais mieux servi, moins rebuté . . . il est rampant avec eux; cela les flatte; ils ont le plaisir de primer sur lui quand ils le servent, au lieu que l'homme vertueux est honteux et respectable, et cela les dégoûte." *Ibid.*, 24e feuille, pp. 300–01.
[34] "Je n'étais plus sur la terre qu'un malheureux inconnu; je n'avais plus que des ennemis dans le monde, car n'y tenir à qui que ce soit, c'est avoir à y combattre tous les hommes, c'est être de trop partout." *Ibid.*, 25e feuille, p. 311.

shows no consideration for the feelings of the poor and begins by crushing a poor person's self-esteem, before trying to help?[35]

Again, in Part III, the self-respect of those who are poverty-stricken flares up in indignation: "I did not come here to ask for alms. I think that, if one has real feelings, one must not resort to that except to keep from dying of hunger. And I shall wait until I reach that extremity, thank you."[36]

The self-pity of a once pretty older woman is convincing. In a statement which she makes to Marianne, the down-to-earth quality of her French has the same poignancy of regret which is found in the similarly direct words of François Villon's fifteenth-century crones, "crouched on their hams about a little fire, soon lighted and soon extinguished," who confessed that "we were once so cute and pretty." Says Marivaux's former beauty: "I got into plenty of scrapes with my cunning little face, although you wouldn't think so to see me today. My face makes me sad now, when I look at it. And I don't look at it except by chance."[37]

The Widow and the Magician is one of the tales, all of which appeared in 1734, in *The Philosopher's Study*, a periodical written by Marivaux. The joys of generosity to those of lesser fortune are explained by the author in the following analytical sentences:

> This girl was not rich and brought him as her dowry very little besides her personal charms. Sometimes, this is so much the better, for it makes a young and beautiful girl the cause of tender feelings in a man. In addition to the love he feels for her, it is a further pleasure for him to be generous to her by thus increasing her fortune. And this pleasure has a great attraction for sensitive souls.[38]

35 "Jamais la charité n'étala ses tristes devoirs avec tant d'appareil; j'avais le cœur noyé dans la honte . . . c'est quelque chose de bien cruel d'être abondonné au secours de certaines gens: car qu'est-ce qu'une charité qui n'a point de pudeur avec le misérable, et qui, avant que de le soulager, commence par écraser son amour-propre?" Marivaux, *La Vie de Marianne* (1731–41), 1ère partie, p. 21.

36 "Je ne venais pas demander l'aumône. Je crois que, lorsqu'on a du cœur, il n'en faut venir à cela que pour s'empêcher de mourir, et j'attendrai jusqu'à cette extrémité, je vous remercie." *Ibid.*, 3e partie, p. 128.

37 "J'ai eu un petit minois qui ne m'a pas mal coûté de folies, quoiqu'il ne paraisse guère les avoir méritées à la mine qu'il fait aujourd'hui: aussi il me fait pitié quand je le regarde, et je ne le regarde que par hasard." *Ibid.*, 1ère partie, p. 40.

38 "Celle-ci n'était pas riche, et n'apportait presque pour toute dot que ses charmes. Quelquefois c'est tant mieux; cela attendrit pour une jeune et belle personne. Avec l'amour qu'on prend pour elle, on a encore le plaisir de pouvoir être généreux avec elle, de lui faire sa fortune; et c'est un grand attrait que ce plaisir-là pour les âmes délicates." *La Veuve et le Magicien* (dixième feuille du *Cabinet du Philosophe*, 1734), p. 968.

It might seem that for many years it was Marivaux the reporter and novelist who frankly expressed his pity for suffering humanity, whereas as a playwright for a more restricted and refined public more traditional in taste, he gained high reputation by his light and brilliant comedies. This generalization is, however, too broad to be accurate and complete. One of his best plays, produced in 1736, late in Marivaux's career, showed the same preoccupation with undeserved riches and the wretchedness of the poor which he had displayed as early as 1722 and 1723 in the *Spectateur françois.*

In the first act of his play, *Les Fausses Confidences,* the heroine says: "It always disturbs me to see decent people without money, while an endless number of scoundrels with no worth possess outstanding fortunes. This state of affairs gives me pain."[39]

Preoccupation with money characterized society in France in the 1720's and 1730's to a degree that is not evident in earlier and more upper-class literature. As the growing middle class came into greater social prominence, talk of riches and property became more respectable. It is perhaps less generally emphasized that other feelings of these people were also frequently expressed: a delight in reading about outraged justice, melodramatic events, and great passion characterized this period in which the middle class was becoming a larger portion of the reading public.

At this point in our chronological series of examples of pity, it may be appropriate to pause for a moment to deny the oversimplified notion that French writing in the period following 1700 can be significantly divided into works which were, on the one hand, either witty or critical of tradition, and on the other, which dealt sentimentally with the passion of love. This neat division does not appear meaningful if we consider Chasles, who had been forgotten until recently, or Marivaux. No such simple statement has meaning when applied to a few score of authors.

The ascertainable fact is that in the first part of the eighteenth century there was a rapidly increasing production of printed works of many sorts, and it is obvious that there were many more readers in 1740 than in 1690. Writers of philosophic, theological, and metaphysical taste counted on the interest of a part of this increased public. Those who wrote

---

[39] "Je suis toujours fâchée de voir d'honnêtes gens sans fortune, tandis qu'une infinité de gens de rien et sans mérite en ont une éclatante: c'est une chose qui me blesse." Marivaux, *Les fausses confidences* (1736), Acte I, scène 7.

on mathematical and physical sciences also found it possible to see their works printed. A considerable group of readers evidently continued to admire the more traditional literary forms: tragedy, lyric poetry, fables, and fairy tales. Still others must have liked sentimental stories which resembled what they witnessed about them, but in which interest was sustained by the pains and sorrows of the characters.

VII

A man who clearly changed his own attitude toward the unfortunate and the poverty-stricken after 1725 was René-Louis d'Argenson. He was born in 1694, the same year as Voltaire, but of very different family background. René-Louis' father was the celebrated chief of police, and young D'Argenson himself held positions of responsibility at an early age, when his contemporary Voltaire was getting in and out of trouble.

In his *Journal* for the year 1725, D'Argenson wrote of his duties in the provinces, at Sézanne, with guarded sympathy for the peasantry. He was then very outspoken about the difficulty of carrying out the work ordered by royal decree in a time of crop failure:

Imagine the extraordinary poverty of the rural regions. The matter of prime importance then was harvesting the ripe grain and the other crops of all kinds. This had not been accomplished earlier, on account of the continuous rains. The unfortunate farmers were watching for a dry moment to gather these, but the district had other troubles as well. . . . His Majesty's horses being quite worn out, orders had been given to collect all the horses of the peasants from ten leagues around to carry the royal baggage. These were paid for but not fed. . . . I spoke to some of the poor peasants. Their horses were there but had eaten nothing for three days. . . . In addition to these levies on the district, there came orders to furnish Paris with a certain quantity of wheat from twenty leagues around. . . . There had been dangerous uprisings in Paris, and bread there cost even more than it had in 1709 [year of famine].[40]

40 "Cependant qu'on se représente la misère inouïe des campagnes: en ce moment il s'agissait des moissons et récoltes de toutes sortes qu'on n'avait pu encore ramasser par les pluies continuelles; le pauvre laboureur guettait un moment de sec pour les ramasser, cependant tout le canton était battu de plusieurs verges. . . .

Les chevaux des équipages [de Sa Majesté] étant sur les dents, on avait commandé tous les chevaux des paysans à dix lieues à la ronde pour tirer ses bagages . . . on les payait et on ne les nourrissait point. . . .

Je parlai à de pauvres paysans; ils avaient là leurs chevaux . . . leurs chevaux n'avaient rien mangé depuis trois jours. . . .

Par-dessus toutes ces corvées pour la campagne, il arriva des ordres de fournir à Paris une certaine quantité de blé à vingt lieues à la ronde. . . . Il y avait eu à Paris des séditions dangereuses; le pain y avait monté plus cher qu'en 1709." René-Louis d'Argen-

Because D'Argenson had received the same sort of education as Voltaire, he could create a striking, firsthand picture of difficulties in the year 1725. Still, his diary for that year does not show a true *bienfaisance* —deep feeling for *kindliness through sympathy*—a French term first used in that period. Nine years later, after he had associated with the Abbé de Saint-Pierre and other idealists at the club called the *Entresol*,[41] his entry contains the following: "We exist here on earth only to be happy and to make our compatriots happy as well, to the extent of our ability. In that way, we honor the Creator, of whom we do not lose sight."[42]

The conception that we exist on earth to be happy is perhaps as far as the human mind can move from the dismal picture of humanity as "condemned prisoners," which Pascal had painted less than a century before. But although D'Argenson's work, like that of Buvat and Barbier already quoted, was not published until much later, his view was shared by a number of publicists. The writings of the *philosophes* in France in the 1730's are filled with this "new" concept of man's happiness— which was, of course, already as old as the work of Epicurus and his disciple Lucretius. More examples of the joyous emotion felt in altruistic action, as recorded in documents of the period, will be adduced later.

In the same year as D'Argenson's entry in his diary about the agricultural catastrophe in the provinces, there appeared the Swiss author Muralt's *Letters concerning the English and the French* (1725), based on a stay in England in 1694 and probably written shortly thereafter. This book, published nearly a decade before the *Philosophic Letters* (*Lettres sur les Anglais*) of Voltaire, was widely read, perhaps because of the acute observations of a genuine foreign visitor so soon after the imaginary *Persian Letters* (1721), produced by the young Montesquieu.

Unlike Voltaire and Montesquieu, Muralt was by training and nature averse to wit and light humor. His observation of men and manners in

---

son, *Journal et Mémoires du Marquis d'Argenson* (Paris: Société de l'histoire de France, 1859), Sézanne, 1725.

[41] The dates of the club are 1724–31.

[42] "Nous ne sommes ici-bas que pour nous rendre heureux, et nos compatriotes avec nous, autant qu'il est en nous; par là, nous honorons le créateur, que nous ne perdons point de vue." *Ibid.*, année 1734.

England and France is very keen, frequently unfavorable, but never lighthearted or devil-may-care. It is easy to understand the astonishment of a serious Swiss, accustomed to the many self-respecting small farmers in his own country, when observing the French peasantry.

[The peasant in France is] completely wretched. He is badly housed, badly dressed, badly nourished and lives only from one day to the next. Yet . . . the greatest poverty cannot cast him down completely nor lead him to revolt. . . . What is curious about it is that he has a feeling for the greatness of the Monarch by whom he appears to be reduced to naught. You would think that his black bread tastes better to him each time he hears of the winning of a battle, or the capture of a town.[43]

VIII

In 1728, a book of sermons in French by Pastor Lenfant was published in Holland. Like other serious Protestants of the period, this minister of the gospel apparently thought it wrong to take any pleasure in doing good to the unfortunate. Christian charity was to him a matter of serious duty, laid upon him and his congregation as an obligation. The title of one of these sermons is *Les Devoirs de la miséricorde* (The Duty of Showing Mercy) and his text gives the impression that anything done without a grave and solemn face might border on sin. It would be highly unfair to berate anyone who preached kindness, with whatever countenance, at a time when there was a great deal of cruelty and hardness of heart in European society, and Pastor Lenfant is mentioned as a variation of the sentimental attitude according to which it was considered a duty to please others in order to be happy oneself.

The Triumph of Poverty and Humiliations, or the Life of Mademoiselle de Bellere du Tronchay, commonly called Sister Louise, with her letters, which experts in anonymous books attribute to the Jesuit Jean Maillard, appeared in 1732. It is possible that the review of this volume which appeared in the *Journal des Sçavans* for January, 1733, had as many readers as the book itself and helped spread the story of this

---

43 [Le paysan est] "tout à fait misérable: il est mal logé, mal vêtu, mal nourri et ne vit qu'au jour la journée. Cependant . . . la plus grande misère ne sçauroit ni l'abbatre entièrement, ni le porter à se soulever. . . . Ce qu'il y a de singulier, c'est que le Païsan est sensible à la Grandeur du Prince sous laquelle il paroît accablé; il semble qu'il trouve son Pain noir plus savoureux toutes les fois qu'il apprend le gain d'une Bataille, ou la prise d'une ville." Béat de Muralt, *Lettres sur les Anglois et sur les François* (Cologne, 1725), p. 173.

beneficent lady among those who had not seen her, or heard of her work before. A paragraph of the review describes her as:

> . . . a girl of excellent family in the Province of Anjou, whose virtues and great piety have edified, not only her region and the neighboring Provinces, but even the city of Paris, where the outstanding evidence of her love for the poor and her devotion to the service of the poor have shone brilliantly in the public institutions for their care.[44]

All those who have a knowledge of the history of France are familiar with the picture of the 1720's and 1730's which emphasizes the immoral, licentious, and hypercritical nature of high society and of many intellectuals. "Sister Louise" also lived and labored at that time, however, and the impression one receives of her is that she attempted single-handed to do what Saint François de Sales had done more than a century before, and what humble "Abbé Pierre" has attempted to do more than two centuries later, in our own time. Recorded history often fails to mention this outstandingly humane sort of person. Unless self-sacrifice is organized and becomes a political force, this is perhaps bound to be the case. But the fact remains that destitute people who were aided by "Sister Louise" were comforted, and that some of her contemporaries had the sentimental imagination to admire her.

Much of the overdrawn and lachrymose pity expressed by the Abbé Prévost in his novels will be considered elsewhere. It will be sufficient here to quote a moralizing statement from his popular novel, *The Dean of Killerine* (1735–40), and a piece of sympathetic reporting which appeared in 1735 in his periodical *Le Pour et Contre*. The whole novel is told in the words of the benevolent hunchback, the Dean himself. It is, nevertheless, often difficult to ascertain whether it is the character or the author who speaks. Prévost's habit of writing a certain number of pages of copy each day for the printer made him fill those pages with whatever came to mind, with a resulting subjectivism which anticipated the work of many of his more celebrated followers. Thus, Rousseau and the

---

[44] ". . . une fille de condition de la Province d'Anjou dont les vertus et la grande piété ont édifié, non seulement sa Patrie et les Provinces voisines, mais encore la Ville de Paris, où les caractères singuliers de son amour pour la Pauvreté, et de son dévouëment au service des Pauvres, ont éclaté dans les Hôpitaux." [Le P. Jean Maillard], *Le Triomphe de la pauvreté et des humiliations, ou la Vie de Mademoiselle de Bellere du Tronchay, appellée communément, Sœur Louïse, avec ses Lettres* (Paris: G. Martin, 1732), reviewed in *Journal des Sçavans*, janvier 1733.

French romantic novelists often allowed their characters to speak as they would have spoken themselves, and later, in Balzac, the line between moralizing by characters and moralizing by author is often difficult to discern.[45]

In Book V of the *Doyen de Killerine,* that gentle moralist (or Prévost himself) says:

> It being our constant duty as men to assuage the weakness of women by taking the larger part of the burden ourselves, I consoled her by vague maxims of firmness and patience and by the promise of divine help which never fails, sooner or later, to come to the innocent.[46]

Two years later, in his *Pro and Con,* Prévost tells the story of an Englishman condemned to be hanged and praises the humane manner in which the English treated even the most severely punished among felons:

> He obtained permission to be taken [to the execution] in a coach which was curtained. The English treat all those wretches condemned to death by Justice with great humanity. No matter what be the crimes of which they are guilty, the English always consider them to be pitied.[47]

In the year 1735, a novel of philosophic travel was printed with its title page bearing "Paris, printed by Claude Simon and Pierre de Batz." Whether it actually appeared in Paris or not, the book was for sale in Amsterdam and was reviewed at length in the *Journal des Sçavans* for June, 1736. The title, translated, is: *The Military Women, Historical Account of a Newly Discovered Island.* This book of more than 300 pages is one of a series of utopian novels which had long been appearing in France and which continued at least until Voltaire's descriptions of

---

45 See G. Atkinson, *Les Idées de Balzac, d'après la Comédie humaine* (5 vols.; Geneva: E. Droz, 1949–50).

46 "Cependant le devoir de notre sexe étant toujours de soulager la foiblesse des femmes en nous chargeant de la plus grande partie du fardeau, je la consolois par des maximes vagues de fermeté et de patience, et par la promesse du secours céleste qui ne manque point tôt ou tard à l'innocence." Prévost, *Le Doyen de Killerine* [1735], in *Œuvres choisies* (Paris, 1823), Livre V, p. 18.

47 "Il obtint la permission de se faire conduire [à l'exécution] dans un carosse drappé. Les Anglois traitent avec beaucoup d'humanité tous les malheureux que la Justice condamne à la mort. De quelques crimes qu'il soient coupables, ils les croient toûjours à plaindre." Prévost, *Le Pour et Contre,* No. 7.

El Dorado in *Candide* (1759).[48] The author, "L. C. D.," preached kindness and pity on many pages of his novel, in which the ideal community was reported to exist "a few hundred leagues beyond the Bermudas."

As the book itself has become almost impossible to find in our time, the long review in the *Journal des Sçavans* is summarized here: The hero, named Frédéric, tells his own story. When he had lost his fortune, those in high positions in Paris promised to make strong recommendations in his favor. Not one of them kept his word. This led Frédéric to give his opinions of the rich and the powerful. Later, when walking in the Tuileries Gardens, he was recognized by a former servant of his father, now comfortably established as a merchant in the rue des Petits-Champs, and this good man befriended him. Having received gratuities from Frédéric in days long past, the now prosperous merchant gave him back "his own money, with interest" and enabled him to set forth on a voyage to make a fortune in the New World. Thus the hero, so he says, "was lucky enough to put his hand upon a beautiful flower growing on a dunghill."[49]

Shipwreck threw him later upon an unknown shore (a traditional feature of many such utopian tales), among people who had none of the civilization of Europe: ". . . all the use of their reason amounts to obtaining the things necessary for life by the most pleasant means possible, to amassing nothing for a future which they may possibly not enjoy, and to keeping themselves in good health, without which no other possession has meaning."[50]

Praise of the virtue and simplicity of "primitive man" was nothing new in French letters in 1735. Montaigne and other humanists of the sixteenth century had expressed much the same sentiment.[51]

---

[48] See G. Atkinson, *The Extraordinary Voyage in French Literature from 1700 to 1720* (2 vols.; Paris: Librairie ancienne Honoré Champion, 1922).

[49] ". . . eut le bonheur . . . de mettre la main sur une belle fleur plantée dans un fumier." *Journal des Sçavans*, juin 1736, rev. of *Les Femmes militaires, Relation historiques d'une Isle nouvellement découverte*, par L.C.D. (Paris: Claude Simon, Pierre de Batz, 1735, et Amsterdam: Compagnie des Libraires).

[50] ". . . tout l'office de leur raison se réduit à se procurer par les voyes les plus douces, les choses nécessaires à la vie, à ne point amasser pour un avenir dont on ne jouïra peut-être pas, et à se conserver une bonne santé, sans laquelle on ne possède rien." *Ibid.*

[51] See G. Atkinson, *Les Nouveaux Horizons de la Renaissance* (Paris: E. Droz, 1935), *passim*.

L. C. D.'s moral preaching is very Biblical in tone: "The seventh day after their children are born, they engrave on each one's left arm these two words in letters which cannot be effaced: 'Worship God,' and on the right arm these words: 'Love your fellow man.' These are their only laws. A hundred-thousand volumes on ethics contain more sentences without containing more substance."[52] It is noteworthy that this book was reviewed at great length by a journal in Holland in 1736, when Voltaire's poems on "the Worldling" ("Le Mondain") were about to appear—poems which delighted the partisans of luxury and scandalized some people on religious grounds.

Many of the novels of the 1730's, a period in which there was a distinct increase of such books, expressed pity; there must, therefore, have been a growing sentimental public to read them. Life stories written in the first person gave free scope for recounting the woes of youth, even of adolescents. The following appeared in the *Mémoires de Comminville* by Du Castre d'Auvigny, in the year 1735:

> In my youth, I kept wishing for a somewhat more advanced age, in order to be more free. . . . Sometimes even, being deprived of freedom, of money, of mistresses, I complained of my fate and found life unbearable. . . . I often envied those whom age has made cold and weak, in whom the wornout passions appear to slumber in the depths of their hearts. How silly I was! Would to Heaven that I might exchange the insipid repose of the passions in which I now languish for the anxieties and worries of those early days! I thought I was to be pitied then, but now I really am.[53]

A few pages later in the introspective and sentimental confession of this hero, the following description of adolescent misery and indecision occurs:

> There are enough warriors to defend our frontiers. Is there any lack of magistrates to sustain the widow and the orphan? It must be our hearts

---

[52] "Le septième jour après que leurs enfans sont nés, on leur grave sur le bras gauche, en lettres ineffaçables ces deux mots: "Adore Dieu": et sur le bras droit, ceux-ci: "Aime ton semblable." Voilà toutes leurs Loix, cent mille Volumes de Morale contiennent plus de phrases, et ne renferment pas plus ce choses." *Journal des Sçavans,* juin 1736.

[53] "Dans ma jeuneuse, je souhaitois toujours un âge un peu plus avancé, pour être plus libre. . . . Quelquefois même privé de liberté, d'argent, et de Maîtresse, je me plaignois du sort, je trouvois la vie insupportable . . . j'enviois souvent l'âge froid et débile, où ces passions fatiguées semblent dormir au fond du cœur. Insensé que j'étois! plût au Ciel que je pusse changer ces tems d'inquiétudes et de troubles, contre l'insipide repos où je languis maintenant. . . . Alors je me croyois à plaindre; c'est à présent que je le suis en effet." Du Castre d'Auvigny, *Mémoires du Comte de Comminville* (1735), pp. 2–3.

which determine what career we must follow—and I am inclined to idleness. Furthermore, I can be of use in the nation without embracing any employment. There are so many people to feel sorry for—and I can relieve some of them. Is the work of destroying an enemy of the nation, or of punishing a man who is guilty of crime, as worthwhile as succoring the unfortunate?[54]

This picture of the hero as a young nobleman is a far cry indeed from the ideal of such a person in contemporary French society. The kinship is much closer to the romantic heroes of the early nineteenth century, when Chateaubriand's and Alfred de Musset's bewildered and uncertain adolescent characters stirred the sympathy of the reading public. Of course it is not certain that French readers of the 1680's would have laughed aloud at such a confession by a man, grown old, if not wise, still thinking of his tortured youth; but it is quite certain that they would have considered it childish.

The wretched taste and form of D'Auvigny's novel are best not dwelt upon. The story does serve, however, to show that a sentimental literature existed in the work of mediocre authors, who wrote without waiting for the leadership of the great.

Among novels written in the form of memoirs, it seems fitting to quote from the *Memoirs of the Count of Claize,* which appeared in Amsterdam in 1738. The author is shown in catalogues only as "Catalde," which may very well be a pseudonym. What is important in this search for pity is not the identity of the authors, but the willingness of a sentimental segment of the public to buy and read their works. At the beginning of this novel the hero confesses: "It is only since I have suffered misfortune myself, that I have become truly sensitive to the misfortunes of others."[55] The hero's self-pity is equally clear on the page following:

I was the only fruit of their union. My birth caused them extreme joy, but that joy was upset by the death of my mother, two days after she had given me birth. My father, unable to bear the loss of so dear a wife, succumbed

54 "Il est assez de guerriers pour défendre nos Frontières; manque-t-il de Magistrats, pour soutenir la veuve et l'orphelin? Le cœur doit décider de notre état, et je me sens porté à l'oisiveté. Je puis d'ailleurs servir la République, sans me charger d'aucun emploi. Il est tant de gens à plaindre, je puis en soulager quelques-uns. Le soin d'immoler un ennemi ou de punir un coupable, vaut-il celui de soulager un malheureux?" *Ibid.,* pp. 8–9.

55 "Ce n'est qu'après avoir essuyé des disgrâces, que je suis devenu vraiment sensible aux malheurs d'autrui." "Catalde," *Mémoires de Monsieur le Comte de Claise* (Amsterdam: n.p., 1738), p. 2.

the weight of the grief which carried him to his grave. Thus, I had arcely seen the light of day, before I remained an orphan.[56]

Once again, it would be useless to attempt to defend the form or the excruciating self-pity of passages reproduced from sentimental novels. Many authors of such creations have been deservedly forgotten. Awareness of the existence of such writing at this period is necessary, however, for by forgetting it, critics and historians have tended also to forget that there was a French public which read those books. As a result, after two centuries the clever works in superb French style stand out as the majority of literary productions from 1690 until 1740 and are judged to be a valid barometer of the preferences of the French reading public— which they probably were not. Certainly there were many far from clever or witty readers of French, such as the Swiss writer, Muralt, who not only did not appreciate clever writing, but were repelled by it.

Moncrif, a member of the French Academy and author of *Essays on the Necessity for Pleasing Others and on the Means of Doing So* (1738), is another case in point:

> The kind of caustic wit which I have just depicted is as scorned as it is hateful in those who do not possess such wit naturally but try to make themselves known by using it. Nothing is as displeasing as people who bring up as ridiculous what is not ridiculous at all, or who announce to you as a discovery some worn-out bit of ridicule, which it is no longer customary to poke fun at.[57]

This attitude of Moncrif is connected with his admiration of those who are "gentle, sensitive and indulgent," as he says in another passage of the same serious-minded book:

> When spirits which rise above the ordinary weakness of men are also gentle, sensitive and indulgent, you are drawn to them, and it is their virtue which particularly attracts you. But when you come upon persons who look down

---

[56] "Je fus l'unique fruit de leur union: ma naissance leur causa une joye extrême, mais elle fut troublée par la mort de ma Mère deux jours après m'avoir mis au monde. Mon Père, ne pouvant supporter la perte d'une Epouse si chère, succomba sous le poids de sa douleur qui le conduisit au tombeau; de sorte qu'à peine j'avois vû la lumière que je restai orphelin." *Ibid.,* p. 3.

[57] "Le genre d'esprit caustique que je viens de dépeindre, est aussi méprisé que haïssable, dans ceux qui, ne le tenant point de la nature, veulent s'en faire un caractère; rien ne déplaît tant que les gens qui vous proposent à titre de ridicule, ce qui ne l'est pas, ou qui vous annoncent comme une découverte, des ridicules usés, et dont ce n'est plus l'usage de se moquer." Moncrif, *Essais sur la Nécessité et sur les moyens de plaire* (Geneva: Pellissari, 1738), p. 23.

upon you from the height of their merits, show you a kind of imperious kindness, a sort of pity which points out to you your smallness and their superiority . . . you feel little esteem for their virtues, and a good deal of aversion for their persons.[58]

According to this admirer of those who set out to please others, even the young and the naïve can be pleasing, and do so without intending to. They please others, he says, by their very naïveté—a quality which was the butt of much wit in France from the time of Lesage's *Gil Blas* in the second decade of the eighteenth century to the publication of Voltaire's uproarious and caustic *Candide* in 1759.

Sentimental approval of the charms of youthful innocence is apparent in the following words of Moncrif, who presumably spoke for some proportion of the public in 1738:

> I know of only one way to please without intending to do so. This is one of the strange phenomena almost inseparable from youth. . . . I refer to the extreme sensitivity with which young people entering society are struck by everything, because everything seems new to them. Their delight, their naïveté in speaking of their pleasant impressions as if the pleasure were a discovery which only they had made—those first agitations of the soul, which they find so marvelous, make young people appear lovable, it is true, for the reason that they reveal an openness, a simplicity, which is explained by lack of experience.[59]

Witty people continued to mock the unself-conscious ways of innocence, of course, and notable examples of this fact exist. But through sentimental outpourings in novels of the 1720's and 1730's for a very different part of the French public, the picture of lovable innocence and

[58] "Quand les âmes, au-dessus des foiblesses ordinaires, sont en même temps douces, sensibles, indulgentes, vous les aimez, et c'est leur vertu même qui vous attire encore plus à elles; mais quand vous trouvez ces personnages vertueux qui vous regardent du haut de leur mérite, vous marquent une certaine bonté impérieuse, une certaine pitié qui vous annonce leur supériorité et votre petitesse . . . vous sentez peu d'estime pour leur vertu, et beaucoup d'éloignement pour leur personne." *Ibid.*, pp. 3–4.

[59] "Je ne connois qu'une sorte de moyen de réussir à plaire, sans que nous en ayons le désir; il fait partie de ces erreurs presque inséparables de la jeunesse. . . . C'est cette extrême sensibilité avec laquelle les jeunes gens qui entrent dans le monde, sont frappés de tout, parce que tout leur paroît nouveau; leur ravissement, et cette naïveté avec laquelle ils parlent des impressions agréables qu'ils reçoivent; comme si le plaisir étoit une découverte qui n'eût été faite que par eux: ces premières agitations de l'âme, qu'ils croyent si merveilleuses, les font, il est vrai, paroître aimables, parce qu'elles marquent une franchise, une certaine simplicité, que le manque d'expérience justifie." *Ibid.*, p. 36.

naïveté was being created for another sort of reader. Those novels would have been meaningless if that sort of reader had considered these "lovable characteristics" to be ridiculous.[60]

Increasingly numerous expressions of pity for the young, for the recently impoverished, and even in one case quoted above for common sailors, seem indicative of a growing emotional attitude long before mid-century. One wonders whether the writing of rationalistic authors who were intellectual and clever could have appealed with as much force to their sentimental contemporaries as the writings of emotional authors who were quite comprehensible to ordinary men and women who knew poverty at first hand. Long before 1740, *bienfaisance* had become a new word in the French language, meaning "doing good to one's fellows in difficulty." With many literate Frenchmen, even among the intellectuals, this word became quickly known and admired. What had been for centuries called "Christian charity" was understood, by those who used the new word *bienfaisance* with admiration, to mean a *social virtue* of humanitarian significance, rather than a religious virtue.

[60] As a sample of the political implications, we offer the following passage, a little after our period: "Les malheureux sont déjà assez humiliés par l'éclat seul de la prospérité; faut-il les outrager par l'ostentation qu'on en fait? Il est pour le moins imprudent de fortifier un préjugé peut-être trop légitime contre les fortunes immenses et rapides." Charles Pinot Duclos, *Considérations sur les Mœurs* (1750); edition quoted here is by F. C. Green (London: Cambridge University Press, 1939), pp. 123–24.

Hallward Library - Issue Receipt

Customer name: Ahmed, Sara Yasmin

Title: Morality and social class in eighteenth-century French literature and painting / Warren Roberts.
ID: 6000109980
Due: 12/01/2011 23:59

Title: The sentimental revolution : French writers of 1690-1740 / by Geoffroy Atkinson ; edited by Abraham
ID: 6001044714
Due: 12/01/2011 23:59

Total items: 2
16/11/2010 13:18

All items must be returned before the due date and time.
The Loan period may be shortened if the item is requested.

WWW.nottingham.ac.uk/is

CHAPTER V

Praise of Lay Benevolence

THE WORD *bienfaisance* was apparently coined by the Abbé Castel de Saint-Pierre[1] and rapidly became a favorite term during the first half of the eighteenth century in France. No single English word translates *bienfaisance*. *Bienveillance* is rendered by "benevolence" but does not necessarily imply any action, whereas action is essential in the meaning of *bienfaisance*; those who spoke or wrote admiringly of the *bienfaisance* of an individual were praising his "doing good" to others.

If the Abbé de Saint-Pierre invented the French word, he did not, of course, invent the idea of "doing good" as a social virtue rather than as a pious action. He had, however, a strong and old tradition to combat. Before the birth of Christ, man's nature had already been defined by the pagan Plautus, in his comedy *Asinaria*, by three words: *Homo homini lupus*. The English philosophers, Bacon and Hobbes, had both accepted this definition of man as a ravening wolf to his fellows, and Christian

---

[1] Littré's dictionary gives the form "beneficence" as appearing in Calvin and Amyot.

99

doctrine for many centuries had insisted that man, having fallen in Adam, is essentially evil. Kindly actions toward one's fellows were therefore thought of as acts of piety, not in line with man's natural urges. A writer like Pierre Charron, who wrote the words "Man is naturally good" in 1601 in his *De la Sagesse,* was not publicly reviled. He was simply ignored.

I

No one could ignore the Abbé de Saint-Pierre in Paris. He was a stormy petrel of a man, full of projects and hope for the reformation of everything which was wrong both in his country and in Europe. His expulsion from the French Academy for having written a relatively harmless work only added to his celebrity among other optimists. It was doubtless compassion for Europeans in general which caused the Abbé to publish his most celebrated *Projet de paix perpétuelle* (1713),[2] which many people regard as the first significant plan for a League of Nations. Without attempting to judge, we may quote from an earlier proposal which presented an equally emotional appeal. In 1695, William Penn, a Quaker, published in London *An Essay towards the Present and Future Peace of Europe.* On the first page of that document there occurs the following passage:

> He must not be a Man but a Statue of Brass or Stone, whose Bowels do not melt when he beholds the Bloody Tragedys [*sic*] of this War, in Hungary, Germany, Flanders, Ireland and at Sea: The Mortality of sickly and languishing Camps and Navys and the mighty Prey the Devouring Winds and Waves have made upon Ships and Men since 88.[3]

The solution offered by this English Quaker is the same as that later suggested by the Abbé de Saint-Pierre: "Now if the Soveraign [*sic*] Princes of Europe . . . would for the same reason that engaged Men first into Society, viz. *Love of Peace and Order,* agree to meet by their stated Deputies in a General Diet. . . ."[4]

The tenets of the Society of Friends were not welcome in France

---

[2] Quotations from Saint-Pierre are here given from *Ouvrages de Politique par M. l'abbé de Saint-Pierre, de l'académie Françoise* (3 vols.; Rotterdam: J. D. Beman, 1733).

[3] William Penn, *An Essay towards the Present and Future Peace of Europe, by the Establishment of an European Dyet, Parliament or Estates* (London: n.p., 1695).

[4] *Ibid.,* pp. 16–17.

during the Abbé's youth. Many years after the *Projet de paix perpétuelle,* Voltaire, in spite of a deep respect for the basic goodness of the Quakers, was to write some of his most amusing prose about them in his *Letters on the English.* Quakers are few among the French to this day. Another and far less distinguished member of this sect was George Keith, who published in New York in 1693 a six-page pamphlet which repeated the same belief with regard to enslaving American Indians for which Bartolomé de las Casas had fought in Catholic Spain of the 1500's. The following religious criticism of Negro slavery occurs on the first page: *"Negroes, Blacks and Taunies* are a real part of Mankind, for whom Christ hath shed his precious Blood, and are capable of Salvation, as well as *White Men."*[5]

The altruism and calls to action in the Abbé de Saint-Pierre's many *Projects* are summed up in the large edition of his *Works:* "There is no one who will not agree that, if all men in a Society were just and *bienfaisants* [inclined to do good], all the citizens would be incomparably happier."[6]

It should be emphasized that neither William Penn nor Saint-Pierre was a revolutionary in the political sense. Neither intended to upset the regular functioning of order in a kingdom; the goal of both these sentimental men was moral reformation in society. That Saint-Pierre did not imagine his country, nor any European country of importance, without a monarch is implicit in the following argument for perpetual peace:

> Can a man ever be tempted to conspire against his Sovereign, to put a crown upon his own head, if he sees even ten Sovereigns near by and powerful, bound together for their natural security and ready to protect the unfortunate scion of a royal family who has escaped a conspiracy, and to punish the Conspirator?[7]

Applying "bienfaisant" to the Deity, Saint-Pierre wrote as follows in the preface to his project for *Making the Bestowing of Honors Useful*

[5] George Keith, *An Exhortation and Caution to FRIENDS Concerning Buying or Keeping of Negroes* (New York: n.p., 1693).

[6] "Il n'y a personne, qui ne convienne que si tous les hommes d'une Société étaient justes et bienfaisants, tous les Citoyens n'en fussent incomparablement plus heureux." Saint-Pierre, *Ouvrages,* I, 119.

[7] "Or, un Homme peut-il jamais être tenté de conspirer contre son Souverain pour se mettre une Couronne sur la tête, s'il voit qu'il y a seulement dix Souverains voisins, et puissants, ligués pour leur conservation naturelle, et pour protéger les malheureux restes d'une Famille Royale échapée d'une Conspiration, et à poursuivre vivement la punition du Conspirateur?" *Ibid.,* I, 89–90.

to the State: "The 'good-doing' Being who causes men pleasure in satisfying a great hunger or a great thirst, also makes them enjoy another pleasure of another kind in feeling themselves distinguished among their fellows."[8] Those who continued to believe in a vengeful, not to say irascible, Deity and in the doctrine of the fall of man could scarcely share Saint-Pierre's optimism for the future of mankind or his concept of a benevolent Providence.

The word *bienfaisance* for a social action which gave pleasure to the one helping his neighbor was rapidly adopted in France; a word to express kindliness to one's fellow man with no implication of religious cant was needed. The use of the new word was no doubt further encouraged by reviews of the Abbé de Saint-Pierre's various projects and of his *Works* published in periodicals. For instance, the *Journal des Sçavans* for January, 1729, printed an approval of his project to make children more *bienfaisants*.[9] In the following year, this periodical gave notice of two of his *projects:*

> The Third Project: that it is in the public interest for girls to be well educated . . . to give them the habit of Christian prudence, of avoiding injustice, of good works (*œuvres bienfaisantes*) and of reasoning correctly from evident principles.[10]

The editors gave the following direct quotation: "There are Orders of Knighthood given to men distinguished by public service in major positions . . . there ought to be one to honor gentlemen for justice and kindliness (*bienfaisance*) toward other individuals."[11]

II

It would be a mistake to believe that all Edicts which at first glance appear to be motivated by kindness were so in reality. The Decree of

8 "L'Etre bienfaisant qui fait goûter aux hommes un grand plaisir à satisfaire à une grande faim et à une grande soif leur fait encore goûter un autre grand plaisir d'une autre espèce à se sentir distingués entre leurs pareils." "Projet pour rendre les titres honorables plus utiles à l'Etat," in *ibid.,* II, 121.

9 *Journal des Sçavans* (Amsterdam, janvier 1729), review of *Ouvrages de M. l'abbé de S.-P. sur divers sujets* (Paris: Briasson, 1728).

10 "Le Troisième Projet: qu'il est de l'intérêt publique que les filles soient bien élevées . . . leur donner l'habitude à la prudence chrétienne, à éviter les injustices, aux œuvres de *bienfaisance,* à raisonner juste sur des principes évidens." *Journal des Sçavans,* juin 1730, p. 240.

11 "Il y a des Ordres de Chevaliers, pour se distinguer par le service dans les grands Emplois . . . il en faudroit un où les Gentilshommes fussent distingués par la justice et par la *bienfaisance* envers les particuliers." *Ibid.,* p. 245.

May 9, 1720, for instance, forbade the sending of any more criminals or vagabonds to Louisiana—a practice wept over by Prévost in his *Manon Lescaut*. The fact is that the Mississippi Company refused to take any more useless laborers and that the Regent did everything possible to foster Mr. Law's Company. Negro slaves had been found much more profitable in Louisiana than exiles from French jails, and the *Black Code*, which became law for the colony in March, 1724, obviously intended to preserve the utility of Negro slaves there, while men from French jails continued to be sent to other colonies in the Antilles. Article XXI of the Code decreed that slaves unable to work because of old age, sickness, or some other reason, were to be fed and cared for by their masters.[12] Slaves were also required by this Code to be instructed in the Catholic faith and to be baptized (Article II).

It may be added here that the first Article of the Code ordered the expulsion of all Jews, on pain of "confiscation of bodies" and possessions. "Confiscation of bodies" may have been interpreted to mean "becoming the property" of the Company, in which case Jews might have been liable to be treated as the Natchez Indians were, who had been captured after a rebellion and sold "for the profit of the Company" to the Spanish in the West Indies. In many ways, French colonial policy in the first part of the eighteenth century was as little influenced by Christian charity as that of the "Catholic Monarchs," Ferdinand and Isabella in 1500. Frenchmen of the early 1700's who were either irreligious or inclined to "doing good" were out of sympathy with official policy. Such men praised their fellows who, being also tenderhearted, provided examples of "doing good" to others.

The following statement about a friend in Paris, who had been kind and helpful, occurs in Chasles' *Voyage aux Indes Orientales*, his diary written on shipboard in the early 1690's, but not published until 1721:

> . . . I shall feel sincere gratitude to him, as long as I live. He is beyond doubt one of the most decent men in the world and one of the most given to "doing good." His probity is equal to that of Monsieur Ceberet. I can say nothing stronger to praise him.[13]

[12] *Le Code Noir, ou Edit du Roy servant de Règlement pour le gouvernement et l'Administration de la Justice . . . le commerce des Esclaves Nègres dans la Louisiane* (donné à Versailles au mois de mars, 1724).

[13] ". . . j'en conserverai toute ma vie une sincère reconnoissance. Il est sans contredit un des plus honnêtes hommes du monde, et des mieux faisans. Sa probité égale celle de Monsieur Ceberet; je ne puis rien dire de plus fort pour en faire l'Apologie." Chasles, *Journal d'un voyage*, I, 52.

A number of passages in the *Spectateur françois* by Marivaux, which appeared in 1722 and 1723, stand out for their emotionalism, as in the following street scene:

> The King passed by. As they usually do, the people shouted, "Long Live the King!" and I found that their acclamations excited my own tender feelings. He was more than a King, more than a Master, appearing there. . . . He was their protector, their hope, their loved one and their delight. . . . Princes! be gentle, kindly, high-minded, compassionate, and friendly in your speech, and you will gain those blessings—the striving for which has made men great, but which they have been able to attain only in small part.[14]

The times were hard in 1722 and 1723 for many who, like Marivaux, had lost whatever wealth they had possessed. The twenty-fifth and final number of the *Spectateur* shows, however, that he was not any more of a revolutionary than his contemporary of the many *Projects,* the Abbé de Saint-Pierre. Both men, seeing the misery about them, pleaded for more kindliness as a solution to social problems. The acceptance of social facts and the hope for something better are worth remembering in the following sentences from the pen of a man who also wrote amusing and brilliant comedies:

> There exists a Superior Being who presides over us and whose wisdom doubtless allows the unequal distribution which we see in things of this world. It is in fact because of this inequality that men do not completely rebuff each other but come together, seek each other out and help one another. So, let the fortunate of this world peacefully enjoy their abundance and the beneficence of the laws; but let their pity for the poor, for the wretched, reach out to them and thus reduce their aversion to the observing of those laws. All the suffering is on their side.[15]

14 "Le Roi a passé. Le peuple, à son ordinaire, a crié: Vive le Roi! J'ai trouvé ses acclamations attendrissantes. C'était plus qu'un roi, plus qu'un maître, qui paraissait . . . c'était le protecteur, l'espérance, l'amour et les délices du peuple que l'on voyait passer. . . . Princes! soyez doux, affables, généreux, compatissants, caressants dans vos discours, et vous êtes possesseurs de ces biens dont l'ambition a fait les grands hommes, et dont à peine ont-ils pu s'acquérir une petite partie." Marivaux, *Le Spectateur françois* (1722-23), 5e feuille, pp. 71-73.

15 "Il est un être supérieur qui préside sur nous et dont la sagesse permet sans doute cette inégale distribution que l'on voit dans les choses de la vie; c'est même à cause qu'elle est inégale que les hommes ne se rebutent pas les uns les autres, qu'ils se rapprochent, se vont chercher et s'entr'aident. Ainsi, que les heureux de ce monde jouissent en paix de leur abondance et du bénéfice des lois; mais que leur pitié pour l'homme indigent, pour le misérable, aille au-devant de la peine qu'il pourrait sentir à observer ces lois, tout l'embarras en est de son côté." *Ibid.,* 25e feuille, pp. 317-18.

The utopian novelist, Tyssot de Patot,[16] a French Protestant in Holland who was not known for his humanitarianism, made the following remark about his early life, in a speech which he would have delivered if, as he hoped, he had been named rector of the University of Deventer. (The speech was published, instead, in the *Journal littéraire* in 1723.)[17]

> I was tempted to give myself over entirely to discovering the Philosopher's Stone, with a view to doing good to my fellow men and removing the poor from their wretchedness.[18]

Another author observed that some men in France were in the habit of being helpful to their fellows and to strangers as both a social duty and a pleasure to the one who was helpful. The Swiss, Muralt, wrote in his *Letters on the French* (1725) that gentlemen and officers whom he met felt an urge to be helpful to him.

> Foreigners . . . wish they could find themselves treated in their own country as they are by the French, whose only reason for showing courtesy to a foreigner is their kindly inclination.[19]

> I have known them to go very far in this kindly inclination, even to a sort of heroism, which is the finest of all. I am speaking of those whose strongest passion is to be useful and to please everyone, who are on the lookout for someone who may have need of them, some unfortunate person to help, or to console.[20]

---

[16] Simon Tyssot de Patot, *Le Voyage de Jacques Massé* (Bordeaux, 1710).

[17] "Discours de M. Simon Tyssot, Sr. Patot, où dans la vuë de concilier les différentes Nations au sujet de la Chronologie, il prétend démontrer Philosophiquement, et sans intéresser l'Ecriture Sainte, que le Ciel et la Terre, qu'il croit d'une ancienneté inexprimable, n'ont point été créez en six jours naturels; que les animaux ont aussi été produits depuis un tems immémorial; que le monde doit vraisemblablement encore durer des millions d'années. . . ." *Journal littéraire* (The Hague), Vol. XII (1723), Art. VI.

[18] "J'ai été tenté de me donner tout entier à la découverte de la Pierre philosophale dans la vuë de faire du bien à mon Prochain, et de tirer les Pauvres de la misère." *Ibid.*, p. 2.

[19] "Les Etrangers . . . souhaitent de trouver dans leur Païs les manières d'agir envers eux, qu'ils trouvent chez les François, qui ne sont liez à eux que par leur Inclination bien-faisante." Béat de Muralt, *Lettres sur les Anglois et sur les François* (Cologne, 1725), p. 119.

[20] "J'en ai vû pousser leur inclination bien-faisante fort loin, et même jusques à une espece de Héroïsme, de toutes les especes sans doute la plus belle. Je parle de ces gens qui n'ont pas de plus forte passion que d'être utiles, et de faire plaisir à tout le monde, cherchant quelqu'un qui ait besoin d'eux, quelque malheureux à secourir ou à consoler." *Ibid.*, p. 121.

The goodness of heart which is the basic characteristic of these Frenchmen, together with the outspoken manner which accompanies this kindliness, are the finest qualities of that nation.[21]

Some allowance must be made for the point of view of a Swiss who had been accustomed to less effusive ways in his own country. Moreover, Muralt was impressed by what seems to have been a fashion in the manners of the best French society and thought of it as a sincere virtue.

England was different from France in this respect, but whether callousness was in fact more widespread or more deeply rooted we shall probably never know. Here is one comment on attitudes toward aged relatives, in *The Protestant Monastery, or a Complaint against the Brutality of the present Age,* by "Andrew Moreton" (Defoe?). Its text begins:

> There is nothing on Earth more shocking, and withal more common in but too many Families, than to see old Age and Grey Hairs derided and ill used. The Old Man or the Old Woman, can do nothing to please . . . and is look'd upon as a Burthen to their Issue.[22]

The remedy for such heartlessness is suggested as follows: ". . . that a Joint-Stock of Twenty Thousand pounds be raised between 50 persons . . . they shall rent a convenient Hall or House . . . a Protestant Monastery for the Aged."[23] There were almshouses, both in England and in France, for the completely indigent. "Sister Louise," mentioned earlier, had succored the poor in such places. Generosity on the part of fifty well-to-do people in England of 1727, when the *Protestant Monastery* was printed, might have been a boon to some of the oldsters of the middle class, whose sons and daughters found them "a burden."

A quotation from an anonymous book, *The Charms of Christian Society* (Paris, 1730),[24] is interesting because of the mingling of Christian, equalitarian, and humane judgments in regard to servants:

> It is an error born of pride to think that some men are born to indulge the indolence and soft living of others. A Christian knows that men do not exist to be served by others, that servitude is established contrary to the plan of natural equality among men and that it is inhuman to make abusive use of a power whose only foundation is the poverty of others.

21 "La bonté du cœur qui est propre aux François, et qui fait le fond de leur Caractère, et la Franchise qui assortit cette Bonté, sont ensemble l'ornement de cette Nation." *Ibid.,* p. 125.

22 "Andrew Moreton," *The Protestant Monastery: or a Complaint against the Brutality of the present Age* (London: W. Meadows, 1727).

23 *Ibid.,* p. 24.

24 Anon., *Les Charmes de la Société du Chrétien* (Paris: J. Etienne, 1730).

Possessing these ideas, a Christian goes beyond the dictates of rigorous justice in dealing with his servants. The less education and good upbringing these have had, the more he pardons them and excuses the imperfections which annoy him in that unfortunate part of mankind. In almost all cases, such people have not had proper training and have not been set a good example.[25]

Rousseau in his *Confessions* took exactly the same point of view as that expressed by this unknown author of 1730. The difference in attitude is negligible; only the gift of expression is vastly divergent in those two men.

III

Long after Lesage had written his biting comedy *Turcaret* (1709), and had published the first part of his picaresque novel *Gil Blas* (1715), he wrote a novel of piratical adventures on the high seas, *La Vie et Aventures de M. de Beauchesne* (1732). Amid the bloodshed and licentiousness, Monneville, a foil to the often bloodthirsty hero, delivers a moralizing speech: "How great must be the joy felt by those who do good to the wretched! The consolation which such men enjoy is preferable to any other pleasure on earth."[26]

It would be hard to find a more obvious concession to the growing spirit of "doing good" in the many tales of adventure published at this period, for this moralistic statement of Monneville clashes with the whole tenor of the novel, as well as of *Turcaret* and *Gil Blas*.

Jean-Jacques Rousseau still remembered, when writing his *Confessions* many years later, how he had wept as a youngster over the novel *Cleveland* (1732) by the Abbé Prévost. The following sentimental passage about kindness and self-abnegation in the North American forest is from Prévost's novel, which appeared when Rousseau was in his twentieth year:

[My North American Indian] Iglou offered me all his clothing to protect me from the extreme cold of the night, but I stoutly refused because of my feelings of humanity. I did not see that my position as his master should

---

[25] Original unavailable (ed.).

[26] "Que la douceur que ressentent ceux qui font du bien aux malheureux doit être grande! La consolation dont ils jouissent dès cette vie est préférable à tout ce que la terre offre de plaisirs." Alain-René Lesage, *Œuvres* (Paris: A. A. Rebouard, 1821), IV, 209.

cause him to lose his status as a man, or that my superior station should take away from him the natural right to protection from the cold, when he needed that protection as much as I did.[27]

Much had, of course, been written since Jean de Léry and Montaigne had depicted the "Good Savage" of Brazil in the 1570's and 1580's. But it took the imagination of Prévost to concoct this contest in generosity between a kindly savage, the servant, and his European master for the enjoyment of sentimental French readers.

In the following year, 1733, Prévost began his *Le Pour et Contre*, a periodical of many diverse elements. Here is a passage from Number III:

> [Richard Norton, a rich man without children whose relatives are] well off, decided to choose as his heirs, those who are hungry, those who are thirsty, those who are naked, those who are strangers, those who are wounded, and those who are sick.[28]

Prévost tells us that Richard Norton's action was ostentatious: he probably wanted people to talk about him after his death. He compares Norton's kindly will and testament to the action of another Englishman, who was receiving a pension for military service but turned that pension over, during his lifetime, "to the widows and orphans of Naval Officers." This action, says Prévost, "is an example of Christian charity without self-interest."

The *Journal and Memoirs of René-Louis d'Argenson* have already been quoted, with their recommendation to "honor the Creator by making our compatriots happy." (See chap. 4.)

In the year 1735 an unsigned book, thought to be by one Jacques Ignace Latouche, was published with the imprimatur of four Paris bookshops and was reprinted in Holland, at The Hague, in 1736. *Le Militaire en Solitude,* an amorphous book of reflections by a retired soldier, contains a passage on the subject of unselfish action which particularly deserves to be noted, both because it was widely known in 1735 and

---

27 "[Mon esclave] Iglou m'offrit tous ses habits pour me garantir du moins de l'excessive fraîcheur de la nuit; mais je m'obstinai à les refuser, par un sentiment d'humanité. Je ne voyois point que ma qualité de maître lui fît perdre celle d'homme, ni qu'elle pût lui ôter par conséquent le droit naturel qu'il avait à des secours qui lui étoient aussi nécessaires qu'à moi." Prévost, *Cleveland,* II, 49.

28 [Richard Norton, riche, sans enfants, dont les parents sont] "fort à leur aise, a pris le parti de choisir pour ses Héritiers, ceux qui ont faim, ceux qui ont soif, ceux qui sont nuds, ceux qui sont étrangers, ceux qui sont blessez, et ceux qui sont malades." Prévost, *Le Pour et Contre,* No. III (1733), 65.

because it was quoted verbatim in the *Journal des Sçavans,* Dutch edition, for May, 1736:

> One day Czar Peter the Great, when inspecting the neighborhood of his camp, heard a plaintive voice nearby, like that of a person dying. Thereupon, he and his suite halted. He sent at once to find out what this sound might be and the report came that it was an officer of his troops, whose wounds were grave. The Czar was moved. He galloped to the ditch where his officer lay, unable to raise his head. Getting off his horse, Peter the Great went to the dying man, bandaged his wounds, and not finding anything with which to secure the bandages, took off his own cravat and slit it lengthwise to use for that purpose. . . . Upon learning, sometime later, that the wounded officer's colonel had been hard-hearted enough to abandon the man in that state, the Czar punished the colonel severely.[29]

The reviewer in the *Journal des Sçavans* remarks that Peter the Great, who was accused of cruelty on many occasions, on other occasions showed himself clement and compassionate, a comment which makes it appear that the medieval ideal of a compassionate ruler, epitomized in people's minds by Alexander the Great, was being revived, centuries later, in the literature praising those who "did good." At the same time, of course, the French *philosophes* were asserting the merits of a government with "an enlightened philosopher on the throne"—in other words, an intellectual.

Marivaux was, as we have noted earlier, not of political mind. But in his novels and shorter tales in magazines he was an indefatigable moralist. He pictured the idealized figure of a gentlewoman in the Fourth Part of *Le Paysan parvenu,* which appeared in 1736:

> Madame de Fécour was good company . . . she liked everyone . . . had the same attitude toward the rich as toward the poor, toward the gentleman as toward the middle-class fellow. She neither esteemed the higher rank of the one, nor scorned the lower status of the other. Her servants were not looked upon as domestics, but rather as men and women whom she had in

---

[29] "Le Czar Pierre le Grand visitant un jour les environs de son Camp, entendit à une distance peu éloignée, une vois plaintive comme d'une personne mourante. Là-dessus il s'arrête avec sa Cour, et envoie chercher en diligence sçavoir ce que ce pourroit être. Il apprend que c'étoit un Officier de ses troupes . . . ses blessures étoient considérables.

"Le Czar touché du rapport, galope vers l'officier, il le trouve dans un fossé et hors d'état de pouvoir lever la tête. Il descend aussitôt de cheval, s'approche du moribond, et le panse lui-même, après quoi voulant bander sa playe, et ne trouvant point de bande, il défait sa propre cravate, le fend en deux, et bande la playe. . . . Ayant appris quelque temps après, que le Colonel du blessé avoit eu la dureté de l'abondonner dans cet état, il l'en punit sévèrement." *Journal des Sçavans,* mai 1736, review of *Le Militaire en solitude, ou le Philosophe Crétien . . . Ouvrage nouveau par M. de xxx* (Paris: Le Gras, Cavelier, Vve Knapen, Prault, fils, 1735).

her home. They served her; she was served by them. That was all she saw in the arrangement.[30]

A series of hard years for agriculture may have some connection with D'Argenson's growing awareness of the value of mutual help among human beings. In 1737, D'Argenson's *Journal* takes note of unfortunate weather conditions:

> The year 1737 has been very strange with regard to the seasons . . . hail has ruined the best vineyards along the Loire . . . finally the season which is normally hot came along and was a veritable winter. People had to keep fires going indoors. There was rain, cold, and bad roads, and all this went on even into September. . . . This is the fourth year in which grape-harvest has been a failure in France.[31]

Noticeably less sensitive to the wretchedness of peasants earlier—in 1725—he waxed emotional about "doing good," in 1738, after the fourth successive harvest failure in the vineyards along the Loire:

> The main thing is to have sufficient intention of doing good in one's heart, so that after having seen to one's own interests, there may be some affection left over for others. And this second affection is what is called *pure love,* an emotion whose existence it is wrong to deny, for we all have some of it. Those who have none at all are monsters. . . . It is certain that we love the poor when we help them secretly. We love our mistresses quite aside from our need for pleasure. A good coachman loves his horses beyond the requirements of his mercenary duty. At the very least, we have this feeling of affection at the moment we are moved by the presence of a person, even if that person's absence immediately leaves us with no emotion at all.[32]

---

30 "Mme de Fécour était bonne convive . . . elle aimait tout le monde . . . vivait du même air avec tous, avec le riche comme avec le pauvre, avec le seigneur comme avec le bourgeois; n'estimait ni le rang des uns, ni ne méprisait le médiocre état des autres. Ses gens n'étaient point ses valets; c'étaient des hommes et des femmes qu'elle avait chez elle; ils la servaient, elle en était servie; voilà tout ce qu'elle y voyait." Marivaux, *Le Paysan parvenu,* IVᵉ partie, p. 201.

31 "L'année 1737 a été fort singulière pour les saisons . . . des grêles ont ruiné les meilleurs vignobles sur la Loire . . . enfin la canicule est venue qui a été un véritable hiver, on y a toujours fait du feu continuellement, pluie, froid, mauvais chemins, et cela a duré jusqu'en septembre . . . voilà la quatrième vendange qui manque en France." René-Louis d'Argenson, *Journal et Mémoires du Marquis d'Argenson* (Paris: Société de l'histoire de France, 1859), septembre 1737.

32 "Il s'agit d'avoir dans le cœur de la bienfaisance de reste pour, après soi, aimer encore les autres, et ce second amour est ce qu'on appelle *amour pur,* espèce d'amour qu'on a tort de nier, car nous en avons tous; ceux qui n'en ont point absolument sont des monstres. . . . Certainement nous aimons les pauvres quand nous les assistons secrètement; nous aimons notre maîtresse par delà les besoins de la volupté; un bon cocher aime ses chevaux par delà la rigueur de son mercenaire devoir; du moins, nous avons le sentiment du moment où nous sommes attendris par un objet présent, mais dont l'absence fait à l'instant cesser toute émotion chez nous." *Ibid.,* août 1738.

D'Argenson's increasing inclination to "do good" may have been influenced by the Abbé de Saint-Pierre's presentations of his Projects at the Club called "L'Entresol" in Paris in the early 1730's. Many men of distinction heard his impassioned reading of his diverse projects there, and those of like mind discussed them with friends before the general public saw them in print. In any case, D'Argenson, a faithful and loyal monarchist, became more and more sympathetic toward the poor between the time he was thirty years old and the time he was in his mid-forties.

In April, 1739, the *Journal des Sçavans* published a review of a book by Labarre de Beaumarchais which had appeared in the preceding year, supposedly at Frankfort. The translated title would read: *The Dutch, or Letters on Holland, Ancient and Modern.* Like many other authors who described the charm or the virtues of neighboring countries, De Beaumarchais wrote enthusiastically of the ways of the Dutch and was quoted at some length in the *Journal des Sçavans* published in Holland by French Protestant refugees. A quotation from that review will illustrate the author's attitude:

> The Dutch are the best husbands in the world, the most tender and indulgent fathers, the gentlest masters. Servants are nowhere as fortunate as in Holland. Mistresses particularly seem to treat their domestics only as companions who are less rich.[33]

Amid exhaustive details of taxes which the Dutch paid on servants, horses, coaches, houses, and land, and the number of persons employed in fishing, the author's repetitions about the kindly treatment of the lower class by the middle class in that country are remarkable for their emotional tone.

IV

During the quarter century between the death of Louis XIV and 1740, praise of "doing good" to unfortunate contemporaries assumed considerable proportions, both in well-written works and in books by mediocre and justly forgotten authors. Such sentiments are certainly much more

---

[33] "Les Hollandois sont les meilleurs maris du monde, les Pères les plus tendres et les plus indulgens, les maîtres les plus doux. Les domestiques ne sont nulle part aussi heureux. Les maîtresses sourtout, paroissent ne regarder leurs servantes que comme des compagnes moins riches qu'elles." *Journal des Sçavans,* avril 1739, review of M. de La Barre de Beaumarchais, *Le Hollandais, ou lettres sur la Hollande, ancienne et moderne* (2nd ed.; Frankfort: Fr. Varrentropp, 1738).

rare, if we may judge by the books and periodicals of the time, in the years immediately preceding 1700. The general absence of enthusiastic statements about "doing good" in the literature of the French classical period preceding 1690 is clear enough; not only the word *bienfaisance,* but the emotional attitude which later called for the coining of that word, had been lacking.

Continuing praise of kindly actions by unselfish men, indicated by the foregoing quotations, seems to have achieved wide acceptance by mid-century, even by some of those in positions of importance as "official authors." Thus, Pinot Duclos, from the height of his post as Royal Historiographer, expressed these feelings in words like the following, in his *Considerations on Customs and Manners:*

> Thus, politeness of the great must contain humanity; that of inferiors must contain gratitude, if the great deserve it; that of equals, esteem and mutual helpfulness.[34]

> Highly placed men who keep others at a distance by dint of politeness without kindliness deserve only to be themselves kept at a distance by respect without any kindly feelings.[35]

> A man who is prosperous makes me delight in his doing good (*bien-faisance*), if he does not forget that there are still others who are unfortunate to succor and if he anticipates their calls for assistance.[36]

On the last page of his book, Duclos wrote: "I shall add that, if everyone were to do all the good of which he is capable without prejudice to his own interests, there would not be an unfortunate man amongst us."[37]

---

[34] "Ainsi la politesse des grands doit être de l'humanité; celle des inférieurs de la reconnaissance, si les grands la méritent; celle des égaux, de l'estime et des services mutuels." Charles Pinot Duclos, *Considérations sur les mœurs* [1751], ed. F. C. Green (London: Cambridge University Press, 1939), p. 36.

[35] "Les grands qui écartent les hommes à force de politesse sans bonté, ne sont bons qu'à être écartés eux-mêmes à force de respects sans attachment." *Ibid.,* pp. 34–35.

[36] "Un homme dans la prospérité n'oublie pas qu'il y a des malheureux, les cherche et prévient leurs demandes. Je chéris sa bienfaisance." *Ibid.,* p. 55.

[37] "J'ajouterai que si chacun faisoit tout le bien qu'il peut faire, sans s'incommoder, il n'y auroit point de malheureux." *Ibid.,* p. 207.

CHAPTER VI

Moral Reprobation

THE DIFFERENCE between the emotional reprobation of immoral actions and the more familiar rational criticism of vice by the French *philosophes* is easily stated. The mocking of men and institutions by Montesquieu and Voltaire, for instance, may, in the beginning, have been caused by their feelings of displeasure with imperfections which they could not approve. But Montesquieu was a calm and judicious gentleman, who admitted that he had never known unhappiness which a half-hour's reading would not dispel. And Voltaire enjoyed using his keen wit in writing for the upper-class segment of the reading public which understood irony and satire. Accordingly, moral criticism by these two outstanding *philosophes* before 1740, despite their seriousness, gives little evidence of heartfelt emotion, but rather delights their readers by the play of wit and the fanciful juxtaposition of ideas.

On the other hand, the passages to be quoted in the following pages were written in complete seriousness, in general by laymen who did not object to being accused of moralizing. In men of this nature, evil behavior by others did not cause humorous reflections, but distress or anger. Their personal feelings, far from being restrained by the literary tradition of an already fading Golden Age, were often expressed in unashamed emotional confessions. These amateur moralists, who were either of the middle class or impoverished petty nobles, earnestly preached moral behavior during a period when many important churchmen did not do so with emotion and when the most talented authors among their contemporaries hesitated to confess deep personal feeling.

The more objective and humorous authors, who usually had greater literary talent, were, of course, the more welcome in the high society of their time. But it must be recognized that the others, the emotional moralizers, made the significant contribution to the growing sentimental literature and prepared the ground for the supreme statements of feeling about morals enunciated later by Jean-Jacques Rousseau.

I

The tendency to preach morals without appeal to Christian sanctions increased visibly between the 1690's and the 1730's. Thus, a statement like the following from Rémond des Cours' *Véritable politique des personnes de qualité* ("Proper Actions of Gentlemen and Ladies"), published in 1693 and characteristic of the period, as well as of a long period preceding, was no longer common by the 1730's.

> With regard to the advantages which we have received from Nature or from Fortune, it is a plain sign of our weakness if they make us proud; for those benefits are of no great importance in themselves and are still less important if compared to the celestial blessings to which our Faith makes us aspire. . . . Life is short and we enjoy all these advantages here for so brief a time that they must not make us proud. Sooner or later, death takes them away.[1]

By 1730 few good writers were concerned with heavenly bliss to the exclusion of earthly pleasures. The sentimental writers, surely, condemned the sins of their contemporaries without regard to the terrors

---

[1] "Au regard des avantages que nous avons receus de la nature, ou de la fortune, c'est une grande marque de nostre foiblesse s'ils nous rendent plus fiers: car ces biens sont peu de chose en eux-mesmes; ils sont encore moins étant comparez aux biens celestes ausquels la foy nous fait aspirer. . . . La vie est courte, nous jouïssons si peu de temps de tous ces avantages, qu'ils ne doivent point nous enorguiellir. Tost ou tard la mort nous les ravit." Nicolas Rémond des Cours, *La Véritable Politique des personnes de qualité* (Paris: Jean Boudot, 1693), pp. 83–84.

of a future life. Mademoiselle Aïssé, for instance, a confessed weeper,[2] treated sinful action in a hard-boiled manner, as deserving of earthly condemnation and punishment:

> There is a horrid scandal, enough to make one's hair stand on end. It is too infamous to write about, but everything which happens in this kingdom clearly foretells its destruction. How wise you are to maintain the laws and to do so severely, for innocence is preserved in that way.[3]

Enforcement of law, rather than Divine punishment, was considered by this lady the best method of combating sin, an opinion that was widespread in the worldly society of the 1730's.[4]

There is no reason to suppose that there were not a good many men and women who continued to hold fast to a religious view of life. Peasants and shopkeepers in the Provinces did not easily leave old ways behind; nor can much change be expected from the humble parishioners of little priests in unimportant churches in Paris.

Among the earliest and most articulate to denounce the evils of society were Huguenots, both pastors and laymen. The following passage will illustrate the outbursts of Calvinists, whose religious beliefs and political status—sometimes joined with pecuniary losses—combined to make them frequently vituperative. This book, first issued as *Les Voeux d'un Patriote* ("Prayers of a Patriot"), was reprinted later with the title *Les Soupirs de la France esclave* ("The Sighs of Enslaved France"). Its authorship is often assigned to the Protestant Pastor Pierre Jurieu, and the memoirs of which it consists were dated at Amsterdam from September, 1689, to August, 1690. The book was reprinted by various editors as late as 1778.

> By this same despotic and arbitrary power, the Edicts and Declarations which had been promulgated in favor of Calvinists for the good and the peace of France have been revoked. . . . The Court is Turkish, not Christian, in its maxims. . . . And what are the results of these despotic and

---

[2] Mlle de Aïssé, *Lettres à Mme C—, depuis l'année 1726 jusqu'en 1733* (Paris: La Grange, 1787), Lettre IX, p. 82.

[3] "Il y a une vilaine affaire qui fait dresser les cheveux à la tête; elle est trop infâme pour l'écrire; mais tout ce qui arrive dans cette monarchie, annonce bien sa destruction. Que vous êtes sages vous autres de maintenir les loix, et d'être sévères! Il s'ensuit de là l'innocence." *Ibid.*, Lettre IV, p. 44.

[4] In this connection, it may be mentioned that Prévost, over whose pages Mademoiselle Aïssé wept, was something of a champion of women's rights. (See his *Cleveland*, II, 136.)

arbitrary ways? Here they are. The people are not convinced that the right exists to take away from them what has been granted them. The people harbor in their hearts plans of vengeance and of shaking the yoke. And from that feeling there spring revolts. . . . Two hundred thousand subjects have been lost to the Kingdom. Commerce has been ruined. The Realm has no money left. A very great number of persons have died in prisons, or have been massacred. They have been made to suffer unimaginable sufferings. They have been sent to the galleys, or shipped off to America. And to make these acts of violence palatable, the authority of kings is preached.[5]

In 1703, the Baron Louis-Armand de Lahontan published his *Curious Conversations with a Savage of Good Sense,* which is as thoroughgoing a criticism of contemporary society as exists. The North American Indian who has traveled abroad is sorry for the Frenchman with whom he is talking:

How you are to be pitied, being exposed as you are to laws which your ignorant, unjust, and wicked judges themselves break as much in their personal conduct as in the execution of their duties, . . . who have no object but to get rich. . . .[6]

. . . just listen to this, dear Brother. Going from Paris to Versailles one day, half way I came upon a peasant who was about to be whipped for having caught partridges and hares in his snares. I saw another, between La Rochelle and Paris, who was condemned to the galleys because he was caught in possession of a small sack of salt. These two wretches were punished by your unjust laws for trying to keep their poor families alive, but at the same time a million wives conceive children in the absence of their husbands, doctors kill off three quarters of the population, and

5 "Par ce même pouvoir despotique et arbitraire, on a révoqué les Edits et les Déclarations qui avoient été accordés aux Calvinistes pour le bien et la paix du Royaume . . . la Cour est turque et non Chrétienne dans ses maximes . . . quelles sont les suites de ces manières despotiques et arbitraires? Les voici. Le peuple ne demeure pas persuadé qu'on ait le droit de lui ôter ce qui lui a été donné. Il conserve dans le cœur les desseins de se venger et de secouer le joug; et cela devient la semence des révoltes. . . . On a perdu deux cent mille sujets; on a ruiné le commerce, on a épuisé le Royaume d'argent, on a fait périr une infinité de personnes, dans des prisons, on les a massacrées, on leur a fait souffrir des maux qui ne se peuvent imaginer, on les a envoyées aux galères, on les a réléguées dans l'Amérique. . . . Pour faire goûter ces violences, on prêche l'autorité des Rois." Jurieu, *Les Vœux d'un Patriote* (also known as *Les Soupirs de la France esclave*) (Amsterdam, 1788), Troisième mémoire, pp. 41–42.
6 "Que vous estes à plaindre d'estre exposez à des Loix auxquelles vos Juges ignorans, injustes et vicieux contreviennent autant par leur conduite particulière qu'en l'administration de leurs Charges. . . . qui n'ont en veüe que de s'enrichir. . . ." Louis-Armand, Baron de Lahontan, *Dialogues curieux entre l'Auteur et un Sauvage de bon sens qui a voyagé* . . . *(1703)* (Baltimore, Md.: Johns Hopkins Univ. Press, 1931), p. 188.

gamblers reduce their families to beggary by losing everything they possess, and they do all this without being punished.[7]

In an unsigned novel, *Memoirs of Chevalier de T—*, published in 1728, a good lady advises the young hero as follows: "Young men today make a virtue of admitting all their faults. Nothing is as dangerous as that, for shame alone has the power to correct. When one confesses one's defects so easily, one does not blush for them."[8]

By 1740, when Montesquieu wrote to Monsignor Gaspard Cerati, few Parisians can have been much shocked by the statement: "In Paris, you will find a very great number of worthy people on foot, and the majority of coaches filled with scoundrels."[9]

Dissatisfaction with what they saw about them had led idealistic men for centuries before 1690, of course, to imagine that virtue had existed in reality in former times, or existed among contemporaries in other lands. These sentimental dreams of a more perfect state of society had been expressed in the times of Plato, Lucretius, and other ancients, long before Rabelais pictured old Grandgousier sitting by the fire, roasting chestnuts and telling of the "good old days" of his youth, or Montaigne, revolted by the cruelties of the Religious Wars of the sixteenth century, welcomed the picture of *Les Cannibales* living virtuously in Brazil.

The quotations below show the same idealistic yearning, the unimpaired belief that somewhere, at some time, virtue has existed, or exists still. This kind of moralizing is quite distinct from palpably sardonic fiction like Lahontan's educated and traveled "Savage," or Montesquieu's more gentle, imaginary "Persians." In many cases, the point of departure with the authors to be quoted had been personal experience of what they believed to be virtue elsewhere, or in times past, which contrasted with what they saw.

---

[7] ". . . Ecoute un peu, mon cher Frère; allant un jour de Paris à Versailles, je vis à moitié chemin un Païsan qu'on alloit foüeter pour avoir pris des perdrix et des lièvres à des lacets. J'en vis un autre entre la Rochelle et Paris qu'on condamna aux galères, parce qu'on le trouva saisi d'un petit sac de sel. Ces deux miserables hommes furent châtiez par ces injustes Loix, pour vouloir faire subsister leurs pauvres Familles; pendant qu'un million de Femmes font des enfans en l'absence de leurs maris; que des Médecins font mourir les trois Carts des hommes, et que les Joüeurs mettent leurs familles à la mendicité, en perdant tout ce qu'ils ont au Monde, sans être châtiez." *Ibid.*, pp. 198–99.

[8] "Les jeunes gens d'aprésent se font une mérite d'avoüer tous leurs défauts: rien n'est si dangereux, il n'y a que la honte qui puisse corriger. Quand on fait cet aveu si facilement, on n'en rougit pas." Anon., *Mémoires du Chevalier de T——* (The Hague: Pierre Gosse, 1738), p. 40.

[9] See chap. i, note 20.

The discovery of virtuous traits in foreign peoples who were not Christian had been related by kindly missionaries throughout the great period of exploration and colonization of the sixteenth and seventeenth centuries.[10] The *philosophes* and rationalists in France made use of such statements for their own purposes, but the reports themselves were based upon personal observation of manners abroad and were used by sincere missionaries as a means of stimulating virtue among Christians at home.

A book entitled *Du Royaume de Siam* by Simon de La Loubère appeared in Amsterdam in 1691, praising the Siamese and the Chinese:

> With regard to politeness, it is so great everywhere in the Far East, even toward strangers, that a European who has lived there for a long time finds it hard to become accustomed again to the familiar ways and the lack of consideration in our European countries.[11]

> Of course I know that the Chinese have shortcomings, but they sin less perhaps against their system of morality than we sin against ours. How greatly our morals have degenerated from those of our ancestors! But the Chinese, incomparably more ancient as a people than we are, still think it shameful to violate their moral code in public, to show less than the proper respect which they owe each other, either by some disobedience toward their parents, or by quarreling with their peers.[12]

A second edition of this book, printed at Amsterdam over twenty years later, in 1713, was favorably reviewed by the *Journal des Sçavans* in the number for July and August of that year:

> If all travel works were written with such exactitude and fidelity as those which have been published about the Kingdom of Siam, it would be wrong to call them "novels written by *philosophes*" . . . and to apply a proverb to them which tends to grant the right to prevaricate to men coming from afar.[13]

10 See G. Atkinson, *Les Nouveaux horizons de la Renaissance* (Geneva: E. Droz, 1935); Atkinson, *Les Relations de voyages du XVIIᵉ siècle et l'évolution des idées,* (Paris: Champion, 1924).

11 "Quant à la politesse, elle est si grande part tout l'Orient, même à l'égard des étrangers, qu'un Européan [*sic*] qui y a demeuré long-temps, a bien de la peine à s'accoutumer derechef aux familiaritez et au peu d'égards de ces païs-ci." De la Loubère, *Du Royaume de Siam* (2 vols., Amsterdam: A. Wolfgang, 1691), I, 164–65.

12 "Je say pourtant que les Chinois ont des vices, mais ils péchent peut-être moins contre leur Morale, que nous ne péchons contre la nôtre. Combien nos mœurs n'ont-elles pas dégeneré de celles de nos ancêtres? et les Chinois incomparablement plus anciens que nous, estiment encore que c'est une honte de violer leurs mœurs en public, et de manquer aux égards qu'ils se doivent les uns aux autres, ou par quelque désobeïssance envers leurs parents, ou par quelque querelle avec leurs égaux." *Ibid.,* II, 296.

13 Original unavailable (ed.).

This review repeats the statements about the respect which Siamese children show their parents: "Their children have great respect for parents. They are brought up to be very polite, and therefore the Siamese are very courteous."[14]

The French galley slave, Jean Marteilhe, wrote as follows, in 1714 or shortly thereafter, in his heartfelt story by a young man who had rowed on galleys with Mohammedan captives long enough to distinguish between those from Turkey and those from North Africa:

> Those from Morocco, Tripoli, and Algiers, are generally the greatest Villains alive; thievish, cruel, false, assassins and wicked to the last degree. But the Turks of Asia and Europe seem to be of a different species. . . . [These] are zealous in the observation of their Religion, tenacious of the Truth, and charitable in a supreme Degree. This last Virtue they even carry to excess. I have seen them give all they were possessed of to purchase the Freedom of a Bird in a Cage.[15]

Chasles, in his *Memoirs* which end in 1716, expressed the conviction that the corruption of contemporary France was a new thing:

> Probity and fair-dealing reigned supreme in France formerly, but today they no longer exist. Frenchmen were renowned in former times for their good faith, but now they are looked upon very differently. That virtue, which is the first and most powerful bond of civil society, has been lost among them little by little, as their leaders have shown them a bad example.[16]

It has been said earlier that Chasles detested the Jesuit missionaries in North America and accused them of many sins. But Jesuit missionaries themselves were often impatient with the immorality of French traders in Canada, who debauched the Indians. One of the many such complaints is given here from the *Jesuit Relations* of 1724:

[14] Original unavailable (ed.).

[15] "Ces derniers sont les Turcs de l'Afrique, nommément ceux des royaumes de Maroc, Alger, Tripoli, etc., qui sont en général des gens de sac et de corde, fripons, cruels, parjures, traîtres et scélérats au suprême degré. . . . Mais les Turcs de l'Asie et de l'Europe . . . sont en général . . . zélés à l'observation de leur religion, gens de parole et d'honneur et surtout charitables au suprême degré. Ils outrent même la charité. J'en ai vu qui donnaient tout l'argent qu'ils avaient, pour acheter un oiseau privé en cage. . . ." Marteilhe, *Mémoires*, pp. 256–57; Goldsmith trans., II, 10.

[16] "La probité et la droiture régnaient autrefois en France, et à présent il n'y en a plus. Les Français étaient autrefois renommés pour leur bonne foi, ils sont à présent regardés d'un autre œil. Cette vertu qui est le premier et le plus puissant lien de la société civile s'est perdue par degrés, à mesure que leurs chefs leur en ont montré l'exemple." Chasles, *Mémoires*, p. 31.

It is fortunate for the Illinois tribe that they live at a great distance from Quebec, for brandy cannot be taken to them, as is done elsewhere. This liquor is the greatest obstacle to Christianity among the Savages. . . . The disturbances and the melancholy deaths which are witnessed every day ought indeed to outweigh the profit which is obtained by trading in such fatal liquor.[17]

By the year 1735, a great deal had already been printed in French about the English nation, much of it showing admiration. It is therefore proper to include here a passage from the French translation of Bishop Gilbert Burnet's *History of His Own Time,* which appeared then. In Burnet's account of the year 1702, he wrote at length on the "Societies for the Reformation of Morals" which had become numerous.

These Societies took up considerable collections. . . . Their members resolved furthermore to inform the Magistrates of blasphemers and houses of ill fame. . . . Queen Mary published proclamations to encourage these good plans, as King William also did afterwards. Other groups were formed as well, which established Charity Schools to teach and clothe the children of the poor and to teach them trades.[18]

The notion that vice inhabited cities and that virtue was connected with country people was the basis of the "Return to the Simple Life" in France before 1740. It was already commonplace in the writings of Frenchmen by the time Marivaux's hero Jacob told his life story. When the First Part of *Le Paysan parvenu* appeared in 1734, the peasant, newly arrived in Paris, spoke as if he too knew of the wickedness of city ways. In answer to Mademoiselle Habert's statement that he seemed a trustworthy boy, clever young Jacob answered: "I only left my village

17 "C'est un bonheur pour les Illinois d'être extrêmement éloignés de Québec, car on ne peut pas leur porter de l'eau-de-vie, comme on fait ailleur; cette boisson est parmi les Sauvages le plus grand obstacle au Christianisme . . . les désordres et les morts funestes dont on est témoin chaque jour, devraient bien l'emporter sur le gain qu'on peut faire par le commerce d'une liqueur si fatale." *Jesuit Relations and Allied Documents. Travels and Explorations of the Jesuit Missionaries in New France, 1610–1791,* English translation by R. P. Jones (Cleveland: The Burroughs Bros. Co., 1900), LXVII, 176–77.

18 "Elles firent des Collectes considérables. . . . Les Membres de ces sociétés resolurent aussi d'informer les Magistrats des Jureurs, des Yvrognes, des mauvaises Maisons. . . . La Reine Marie fit publier des Proclamations pour encourager ces bons desseins; ce que fit aussi après elle le Roi Guillaume. Il se forma encore d'autres Sociétés, qui établirent des Ecoles de Charité pour faire instruire, et habiller les Enfans des Pauvres, et leur faire apprendre des Métiers." Gilbert Burnet, *Histoire de ce qui s'est passé . . . en Angleterre pendant la vie de Gilbert Burnet, Evêque de Salisbury* (2 vols.; The Hague: Neaulme, 1735), année 1702, I, 313–14.

three or four months ago and have not yet had time to go bad or to become wicked."[19] In the Fourth Part (1736), the same attitude is repeated by Madame de Fécour: "Yes indeed! Why of course, people who live in the country, farmers! Oh, I know what they're like. Yes, they are very decent people, certainly estimable. There is nothing to say against that."[20]

II

The praise of luxury, which grew rapidly in France after 1700 and was epitomized in Voltaire's poem *Le Mondain* ("The Worldling") of 1736, is well known. But, during those same years, condemnation of materialism was also expressed frequently, by the very moral critics of whom Voltaire made sport. One reason for the protest against luxury was the wealth of a number of scurrilous persons who had risen from the lowest level of society. Among the visible defects of the French government, under Louis XIV, during the Regency, and in the first years of the reign of Louis XV, was the wasteful system of farming out taxes. Envy of the taxgatherers, as well as of moneylenders and consistently fortunate speculators was often expressed in the literature of the period, even by those who were not primarily moralists. There was a widespread outcry, in which the moralists joined with enthusiasm, both against men who by devious methods had made fortunes rapidly and against those others who gave them social acceptance.

As early as 1700, anticlerical writers, both Catholic and Protestant, had begun to produce angry criticism of the love of money among Catholic ecclesiastics. A violent book, signed by "Le Noble," was published in that year. Instead of the mocking spirit with regard to the clergy which had been traditional before the time of Louis XIV and which was to reappear after his death, this book of *Worldly Schooling* is sardonic and angry. It contains sordid advice of a father to his son about getting on in society. *L'Ecole du Monde, ou Instructions d'un Père à un Fils,* was published in Paris and was reprinted among his

[19] "Il n'y a que trois ou quatre mois que je suis sorti de mon village, et je n'ai pas encore eu le temps d'empirer et de devenir méchant." Marivaux, *Le Paysan parvenu* (1735–40), Première partie, p. 45.

[20] "——Oui, certes! Comment donc, des gens qui demeurent à la campagne, des fermiers! oh! je sais ce que c'est; oui, ce sont de fort honnêtes gens, fort estimables assurément; il n'y a rien à dire à cela." *Ibid.,* IVe partie, p. 206.

works there in 1718, with royal privilege. His short novels, *Zulima* and *Mylord Courtenay,* which also are included in the 1718 edition of his works, seem to indicate that "Le Noble" was a poor devil, trying to live by his pen in Paris. The following bit of irony well represents the tone of the book:

> True friends console us in distress, help us in our needs, support us in opportunities which come to us, open doors of advancement for us, sustain us when we prosper. Finally, by spreading praise of us in Society, they establish our reputation, which is the basis of a man's fortune.[21]

Le Noble applies the same test of utility to another subject. The Ninth Interview bears the title "Specific Means of Attaining Success in the Church":

> THE FATHER: No matter what trouble a man takes, or what work he does in other professions, tell me whether there is any which can give you, overnight, twenty, thirty, or a hundred thousand *livres* income at the stroke of a pen. Yet that is what we see happening daily in the Church. A man goes to bed without a sou and is rich for the rest of his life the following morning. Another gets up as a little chaplain, or as a middling priest and goes to bed as the possessor of a rich Benefice, or as a wealthy prelate. The greatest miracles of sudden fortunes are seen in that Profession.
> THE SON: It is a fact that a young man who wears canonical collars and puts a prayer-book in his pocket can expect great things. . . . You may add . . . that the Scriptures state specifically that one who desires to become a priest desires a good work.[22]

21 "Les vrais amis nous consolent dans nos peines, nous soulagent dans nos besoins, nous soûtiennent dans les affaires qui nous arrivent, nous ouvrent les portes à l'élévation, nous appuyent dans nôtre prospérité, et enfin par des loüanges qu'ils répandent de nous dans le monde, ils établissent nôtre réputation qui est la baze [*sic*] de la fortune." Le Noble, *L'Ecole du Monde, ou instruction d'un père à son fils, touchant la manière dont il faut vivre dans le monde* (4 vols.; Paris: M. Jouvenel, 1700), 3e Entretien, I, 135.

22 "LE PÈRE: Quelques peines, quelques travaux qu'un homme se donne dans les autres Professions, dites-moi, s'il y en a une seule qui puisse du soir au matin vous donner vingt, trente, et cent mil livres de rente d'un trait de plume, et c'est ce qu'on voit tous les jours arriver dans l'Eglise. Tel se couche sans un sou, qui le lendemain est enrichi pour le reste de ses jours. Tel se lève petit Capelan ou médiocre abbé, qui se couche gros Bénéficier ou riche Prelat. Et c'est dans cette Profession qu'on voit les plus grands miracles de la Fortune. LE FILS: Il est constant qu'un jeune homme qui arbore le petit Collet, et met un Bréviaire dans sa poche peut prétendre à tout. . . . Vous pouvez ajouter . . . qu'en termes précis l'Ecriture dit que celui qui désire l'Episcopat désire un bon œuvre [*sic*]." 9e Entretien: "Des Moyens particuliers d'arriver à la Fortune, dans l'Eglise." *Ibid.,* III, 5–6.

Histories of literature always list Lesage's play, *Turcaret* (1709), which showed the despicable character of a taxgatherer, and Marivaux's *La Vie de Marianne* and *Le Paysan parvenu* of the 1730's, in which sympathetic characters suffer from the overbearing attitude of the wealthy.

Perhaps no less illustrative of this almost universal resentment are the statements of religious men who, like these authors, willingly accepted the materialistic standards of the time. Thus, the Protestant pastor, Jurieu, in *The Sighs of Enslaved France,* consisting of memoirs dating from the late 1680's, frequently judged the parlous state of France in terms of wealth, relating this, of course, with the religious persecution.

The Nobility should be both the strength and the ornament of the State. . . . Today, it is in a condition which is scorned by everyone. It is reduced to financial extremity, like the remainder of the nation. . . . The whole of the ancient Nobility in France is now in beggarly poverty.

In their place, new Nobles have appeared, whose rise is due to the favor of the Court and to financial success. These people have bought and now possess the finest estates in the realm and have a sort of despotic power over the old noblemen. When they come to spend a few months at their domains in the country, all the Nobles of the region crawl before them.[23]

Because Protestants had been forbidden to hold office, they went into wheat, wine and manufacturing. The persecution directed against them forced them to flee and, as what money there was in the Kingdom was in the hands of Huguenot merchants, these had an easier time leaving the country than others of their sect. When they left, they took immense sums with them and thereby reduced French commerce to naught.[24]

[23] "La Noblesse devroit être la force et l'ornement de l'Etat. . . . Aujourd'hui elle est dans un abattement qui la rend le mépris de toute la terre . . . elle est réduite à l'extrémité comme le reste de l'Etat. . . . Toute l'ancienne Noblesse de France est réduite à la mendicité.

A la place des anciens Nobles, il vient de nouveaux Nobles, qui tirent leur origine de la Cour et des Finances. Ces gens achètent et possèdent les plus belles terres du Royaume, et exercent sur les anciens Gentilshommes une espece d'empire despotique. Quand ils viennent à la campagne passer quelques mois, toute la Noblesse du pays rampe devant eux." Jurieu, *Les Vœux,* 1ère mémoire, p. 12.

[24] "Parce que ces gens étoient exclus des charges, ils s'étoient entièrement jetés dans le commerce de bleds, de vins, de manufactures; la persécution qu'on a exercée contr'eux, les a obligés de se retirer: et comme ce qu'il y avoit d'argent étoit entre les mains des marchands huguenots, ils ont eu beaucoup plus de facilité à se retirer que les autres. Et en se retirant ils ont tiré du Royaume des sommes immenses qui ont tari la source du commerce." *Ibid.,* p. 17.

It is curious to observe that these *Memoirs,* printed in Amsterdam at the end of the 1680's, should have contained arguments against the exiling of Protestants so nearly identical with what Vauban wrote at exactly the same period. If exiled Protestants made the same criticism of the government as a patriotic Catholic army officer, the political ineptitude of Louis XIV's ministers and of churchmen like Bossuet must have been apparent to other fellow-citizens who did not express their feelings in writing.

A purer form of moral criticism than Jurieu's occurs in the April number of the *Nouvelles de la République des Lettres* in 1709, three years after the death of its founder, Pierre Bayle. In a review of *Turcaret* in book form, the editor of this periodical criticizes Lesage for "showing so many scoundrels without virtue" on the stage. It is true that the grasping passion for money of all the characters in Turcaret is only tempered by the deeper rascality of the main personage, Turcaret, himself.

In Alexis Piron's play, *L'Ecole des Pères,* first presented in Paris in 1728, with a second title *Les Fils ingrats,* the major theme is the love of money. The good old man, Géronte, explains to his more level-headed brother in the first scene why he has been so indulgent to his three sons —and the success of the play authorizes us to believe that the audience understood whereof Piron spoke.

> I divided everything I had among my sons.
> . . . .
> The weight of riches is a burden at our age.
> For few passions little money is needed.
> The enjoyment of gold and silver, the sources of pleasure,
> Is proper for the years of youth and desire. . . .
> As for me, I want the love of my sons
> And do not wish to see them reduced to desiring my death,
> In order to see their fortunes increased.[25]

Finally, the true nature of the avaricious sons is revealed to their over-indulgent father. The heroine, whom the sons have consistently snubbed and despised as a "poor orphan" sheltered by their father, receives an

---

25 "De tout ce que j'avois, j'ai fait part à mes Fils:/ . . . Le poids de la richesse, à notre âge, importune./ A peu de passions, suffit peu de fortune./ De l'or et de l'argent, sources de tous plaisirs,/ La jouissance est due à l'âge des désirs./ . . . Je veux, moi, qu'un fils m'aime;/ Et ne soit pas réduit, pour voir changer son sort,/ Au déplorable point de désirer ma mort." Alexis Piron, *L'Ecole des Pères,* Acte I, scène 1, in *Œuvres choisies* (Paris, 1823).

unexpected inheritance and becomes desirable as an heiress. All three young men immediately find the girl, Angélique, charming and court her with a view to marriage. She gives them a punishing answer:

> What attracts you to me is wealth, and nothing more.
> Has not black ingratitude
> Been always perfidiously joined to sordid love of money?
> You have shown the first, and now the second appears;
> So I may judge the worth of your love![26]

III

Several editions of the *Jewish Letters* by the Marquis Boyer d'Argens appeared between 1730 and 1740, and the book was reissued as late as 1754 at The Hague. In this author, defeated idealism had turned to bitter enmity for a society which he abominated. One sentence from the preface will suffice to indicate its tone:

> I have done more than condemn fanaticism, hypocrisy, bad faith. I have unmasked those who skillfully use these vices to attain their own ends and who make public misfortunes and calamities serve their own private financial interests.[27]

In Letter XVIII, the feelings of impoverished nobles for the profiteers of the period are particularly venomous.

> Every day in Paris, you see men whose first claim to admiration was being household servants, but who now move about in superb private coaches and are lodged in magnificent town-houses. . . . These people who are regarded as a disgrace to our nation and the cause of the wretchedness of our population, find many persons lowering themselves to the point of trying to cultivate them. . . . Even great Lords among us seem to have kindly ways toward them. . . . Sometimes, they go so far in that weakness as to contract family relationships with these Finance fellows. . . . A noble takes his daughter out of the convent to give her in marriage,

---

[26] "Et l'opulence en moi vous tente, et rien de plus./ Ne vit-on pas toujours unis d'un nœud perfide,/ La noire ingratitude et l'intérêt sordide?/ L'une vient d'éclater, l'autre éclate à son tour:/ Et je juge par-là du prix de votre amour." *Ibid.*, Acte IV, scène 10.

[27] "J'ai plus fait que de condamner le fanatisme, l'hypocrisie, la mauvaise foi. J'ai démasqué ceux qui profitent habilement de ces vices, pour parvenir à leurs fins, et qui font servir à leur intérêt particulier les malheurs et les calamités publiques." Boyer d'Argens, *Lettres Juives* (The Hague: n.p., 1754), Preface, p. xiii.

and the young lady is quite astonished to find that her husband is the cousin of her serving-maid.[28]

In another book, *Moral and Critical Letters on the Different Ranks and Occupations of Men* (1737), the Marquis d'Argens also berated taxgatherers:

> I can pardon a writer who is close to starvation for prolonging his life by writing odes and sonnets to honor and increase the standing of several low-born scoundrels. But I cannot tolerate the praise of a Tax-Farmer, or of some other Leech who sucks blood from our people, in the works of a poet who is not beset by poverty.[29]

Another book, often attributed to a man named Barthélemi Marmont du Hautchamp, was published at The Hague in 1739, entitled *History of the Financial System . . . during the Years 1719 and 1720*. The tone of this thick book covering two catastrophic years of French history is more objective than what has been found in the preceding passages. Yet it too might stir the emotions of honest folk, even today.

> Those sprung from the gutter, who had come into possession of a million in the space of three months, felt that their situation was one of intolerable mediocrity, although before that time they had been in extreme poverty. . . . Would anyone believe that there were speculators who played a friendly game of piquet with ten thousand *livres* banknotes, just as if they were gayly using ten-sou coins? . . . In hopes of equalling the first-line millionaires, they got themselves carriages as soon as they had a hundred thousand *livres* in hand. The number of private coaches increased to such an extent that all the merchants on streets leading to the rue de Quincampoix [situation of Law's enterprises] complained of the interrup-

---

28 "On voit tous les jours à Paris des gens dont le premier mérite fut d'être Laquais, traînés dans des carosses superbes, et logés dans des palais magnifiques, ces gens qui sont regardés comme l'opprobre de la nation et l'instrument des malheurs des peuples, trouvent un grand nombre de personnes qui s'abaissent jusqu'au point de leur faire la cour. . . . Les Seigneurs même paroissent avoir des égards pour eux. . . . Ils poussent quelquefois leur foiblesse jusqu'à contracter des alliances avec ces Financiers . . . on sort la Demoiselle du Couvent et elle est tout étonnée que son mari se trouve le cousin de sa Fille-de-chambre." *Ibid.,* Lettre XVIII, pp. 182–83.

29 "Je pardonne à un Ecrivain prêt à mourir d'inanition de prolonger ses jours par un nombre d'Odes et de Sonnets, composés à l'honneur et à la gloire de plusieurs Faquins; mais je ne puis souffrir dans les Œuvres d'un Poëte, à l'abri de l'indigence, l'Eloge d'un Fermier-Général, ou de quelqu'autre Sangsue du Peuple." Boyer d'Argens, *Lettres morales et critiques sur les différens états et les diverses occupations des hommes* (Amsterdam: Michel Le Cene, 1737), p. 194.

tion of business which the congestion of Mississippi speculators' coaches caused by completely blocking the public streets.[30]

On July 31, 1720, gold and silver coins suddenly disappeared from Paris:

The avidity for coins growing steadily for five months, their circulation ceased completely, in spite of all the different means which had been tried to get them back into circulation. Misers kept them so well locked up that nothing could make them let go, no matter what was offered as an inducement to tempt their cupidity. This state of affairs was the cause of the following Decree: . . .[31]

La Nouvelle Marianne, a novel supposedly written by the Abbé Claude François Lambert, was published in 1740 as an obvious imitation of Marivaux's *Vie de Marianne.* It is filled with grandiloquent and "sublime" conversation, and with pathetic incidents, but here and there the reader comes across a passage which recalls the earlier *Marianne:* "From the first conversation I had with that woman, it was easy to see how greatly she was dominated by her love of money."[32]

A curious work published in Paris in 1740 bore the title *The Manner of Teaching and Studying Belles-Lettres, as Related to the Mind and to the Heart.* In the second volume the author, Charles Rollin, a former

---

[30] "Des gens de rien, parvenus dans l'espace de trois mois à la possession d'un million, consideroient ce changement de situation comme une médiocrité insupportable, quoiqu'avant ce temps-là ils se fussent vûs dans une extrême indigence. . . . Croiroit-on qu'il y a eu de ces Agioteurs, qui jouoient familièrement au Piquet les Billets de dix-mille livres, tout comme s'ils badinoient aux pièces de dix sols? . . . dans l'esperance d'aller de pair avec les Millionaires du premier ordre, ils prenoient équipage dès qu'ils se voyoient une centaine de mille livres entre les mains. Le nombre de Carosses augmenta tellement, que tous les Marchands des ruës aboutissantes à celle de Quinquempoix se plaignirent de l'interruption que l'embarras des équipages des Mississipiens causoit à leur commerce, en bouchant entièrement la voye publique." Du Hautchamp, *Histoire du système des finances, sous la minorité de Louis XV, pendant les années 1719 et 1720* (The Hague: Pierre de Hondt, 1739), Livre III, pp. 28–29.

[31] "L'avidité pour les especes augmentant toûjours depuis cinq mois, la circulation en étoit entièrement arrêtée, nonobstant tous les différens moyens qu'on avoit employés pour leur donner un mouvement. Les avares les tenoient si bien resserrées, que rien ne pouvoit les obliger à les relâcher, quelque séduisant que fût l'appas qu'on leur présentoit pour tenter leur cupidité. Cette conjoncture occasionna l'Arrêt suivant:" *ibid.,* Livre III, p. 202.

[32] "Dès le premier entretien que j'avois avec cette femme, il avoit été facile de connoître combien l'amour du gain la dominoit." Abbé Claude François Lambert, *La Nouvelle Marianne, ou les Mémoires de la Baronne de—— (The Hague: n.p., 1740), IVe partie, p. 52.

rector of the University of Paris, invokes the virtue of the ancients as follows:

> Gold and silver are the only or principal object of men's admiration, desires and labors. They are regarded as the source of pleasure and reputation in life, and poverty, on the contrary, as the source of shame and misfortune.
>
> And yet Antiquity tells us of an entire people (astonishing, yet true) who cried out against such sentiments. Euripides had Bellerophon utter a magnificent glorification of riches. . . . Those verses were revolting to the whole Athenian people, which rose up with a single voice against the poet.[33]

Since it was no longer "good form," in 1740, to invoke Biblical authority, Rollin condemned the love of money by using the example of a virtuous people who, so he thought, had existed in Athens. Condemnation of luxury continued in the writing of minor authors until and including the time of Jean-Jacques Rousseau's fulminations against it.

Alexis Piron, the far from gifted poet whose one successful play, *La Métromanie,* had been acclaimed in 1738, wrote a preface for it long afterwards, printed in the 1756 edition. This preface is, among other things, an autobiography, and Piron's remembrance of a time in France toward 1710 contains the following:

> A man born under a thatched roof could in that time hope to live surrounded by gilded wainscoting some day, if he took a very short, very easy and very well-worn path. Million by million, he could hope to rise, bit by bit, until he died the son-in-law or the father-in-law of persons in the highest society. I was not attracted to that way. Two things repelled me about that sort of elevation: going up that way and getting back—the manner of getting there and the drawbacks of having arrived.[34]

---

[33] "L'or et l'argent sont l'unique ou le principal objet de l'admiration des hommes, de leurs désirs, de leurs travaux. On les regarde comme ce qui fait toute la douceur et la gloire de la vie, et la pauvreté au contraire comme ce qui en fait la honte et le malheur.
Cependant l'antiquité nous fournit un peuple entier (chose étonnante!) qui se récrie contre de tels sentiments. Euripide avoit mis dans la bouche de Bellérophon un éloge magnifique des richesses. . . . Ces vers révoltèrent tout le peuple d'Athènes. Il s'éleva d'une voix commune contre le Poète." Rollin, *De la Manière d'enseigner et d'étudier les belles-lettres, Par rapport à l'esprit et au cœur* (Paris: Vve Estienne, 1740), pp. 11–12.
[34] "Né sous le chaume, on pouvoit en ce temps-là [1710], par un chemin très court, très facile et très battu, se flatter de vivre un jour sous des lambris dorés, et, de millions en millions, s'élever par degrés jusqu'à mourir gendre ou beau-père de tout ce qu'il y avoit de mieux. Tout cela ne me gagna point: deux choses me rebutèrent de cette sorte d'élévation; l'aller et le revenir, la façon d'y parvenir et les désagrémens d'y être parvenu." Préface de *La Métromanie* (1756–57), *Œuvres Choisies* d'Alexis Piron (Paris: Haut-Cœur et Gayet, jeune 1823), I, 14.

Piron was a perennially gay Burgundian, fond of better wine and better food than his constant penury made possible. Although not a fervently religious man, he was scornful toward those whose only standard of judgment was the possession of money. One day, when he was elaborating a magnificent scheme which he had imagined, it is reported that a friend interrupted him with the question: "But you are not rich, are you?"

Piron replied, "No. I am not. But I don't care a damn and that makes it just the same as if I were."

It is not hard to imagine why such a lighthearted individual, with no great literary talent, did not prosper in the frequently venal society of Paris. But it seems incontrovertible that he came nearer to knowing happiness on earth, in spite of his continual poverty, than many of his contemporaries.

IV

A modern reader may be amazed at the frequent incidents of violent conduct in stories of contemporary life, as he reads through French novels of the 1720–40 period. Thus, Des Grieux, the hero of Prévost's best novel, *Manon Lescaut,* made several attempts to rescue his beloved from detention in Paris and later from the armed men guarding her on the way to exile, in his description of heartrending sentimental adventures. These scenes of lawless and violent action are realistically recounted and seem to be adventures remembered, compared to the vague and incredible last parts of the novel, which take place "among the hills of Louisiana, near New Orleans."

Examples which have already been given show that violence was indeed an everyday feature of life in the 1720's, not only in Paris, but along the highways as well. In real life, as well as in the novels of that period, noble gentlemen and ladies were sometimes captured at sea and held for ransom, or simply sold as slaves by pirates from North African ports. In Prévost's youth, it was common, as everyone knew, for young ladies to be "rescued" from convents by violent young gentlemen. But proper young ladies were not found in jails. What is unusual in the adventures of Des Grieux and Manon is that the young Chevalier, who had begun his studies for the priesthood, broke out of the prison where he had been confined and tried to remove his distinctly lower-class mistress from another Parisian jail! Of course, the author's long association with his Dutch mistress, also of low status, may help to explain the book's psychology, which is unusually realistic for a novel of that period. A few more contemporary laments about violence will suffice to make the point when added to those already given earlier, from viewpoints other than literary. The moral tone of Du Hautchamp's *History of the Financial System,* published in 1739, is as vivid as any other testimony concerning the year 1720 in Paris—the year that Law's *System* fell apart.

> A body was found in the river, chopped to pieces and enclosed in a sack. . . . A merchant, returning home from the rue de Quincampoix between seven and eight in the evening, was stabbed while on the Quai des Augustins. One day it was a provincial murdered just after collecting a cash payment; the next day a master whose throat was slit by his former servant. Lack of control had reached such a point that coachmen were attacked right in the streets. Such frightful disorder could only foreshadow an entire loss of confidence, which is so necessary to society and to public peace. All this, furthermore, foretold a state of poverty which was bound to follow the abundance of which some had made wrongful use.[35]

To explain the violence in society after 1700 with the simple statement that grinding poverty caused desperate Frenchmen to take the law into their own hands is not sufficient. Though doubtless one of the chief causes of violence was the extreme conditions of the poor, the fact remains that others who were not poor were also lawless and sometimes violent. One partial explanation was thought by some to lie in the preaching of the clergy. As early as 1715, Nicolas de Gueudeville's book, *The Censor,* stated bluntly that the preaching of that day was often an exhibition of talent.

> One cannot pay attention for, frequently, an hour and a half to a florid discourse, spoken with art and intended rather to please than to instruct. This being so, what people do is admire. And what is it they admire? The

[35] "On avoit trouvé dans la rivière un cadavre, enfermé dans un sac et haché par morceaux. . . . Un Négociant, revenant de la ruë Quinquempoix entre sept et huit heures du soir, fut poignardé sur le quay des Augustins. Aujourd'hui c'étoit un homme de Province assassiné immédiatement après avoir reçu ses Remboursemens; demain un Maître égorgé dans son lit par son ancien domestique. La licence en étoit venue à un point, qu'on attaquoit les cochers en pleine ruë. Un désordre aussi affreux ne pouvoit qu'annoncer la perte totale d'une confiance si nécessaire à la société et au repos public; ce qui faisoit prévoir une misère qui alloit infailliblement succéder à l'abondance dont plusieurs abusoient." Du Hautchamp, *Histoire du . . . finances,* Livre III, pp. 44–45.

inflexions of the preacher's voice, the regularity of his gestures, his choice of words! . . . If we know the man who declaims thus and spend time with him, then (Oh, corruption of our times!) it often happens that we see him in practice violate the rules of virtue. . . . Often, he even falls into the very vice against which he has preached.[36]

Gueudeville was a latter-day Theophrastus, by his own statement. But Marivaux's *Marianne,* some twenty years later, repeats this charge against florid preaching:

> The service began. There was a very fine sermon. I do not say a good sermon, for it was with the vanity of preaching elegantly that he inveighed against the vanity of earthly things. That is the fault of many preachers: their preaching is less for our instruction than for their own pride, and thus sinfulness preaches virtue from our pulpits.[37]

Some years after Marivaux began publishing his *Vie de Marianne,* the far less gifted author La Barre de Beaumarchais put out a volume entitled *Literary Entertainment for the Year 1738,* a mixture of comment and narratives. This author's criticism of the attitude of fashionable congregations in Paris in certain churches also gives an idea of the mentality of some socially prominent people.

> It is stylish to be enthusiastic about their sermons. Even unbelievers rush to hear them, either because it is the thing to do, or because it suits their taste. The eloquence of a man like Massillon, simple and clear, but majestic, serious and overwhelming, would terrify them, but the kind of preaching which is popular now occupies them pleasantly. One person remembers one passage of the sermon, another person another. This makes material for conversation in social gatherings afterwards, and the passages are judged with cool deliberation, as an academic discourse would be. . . . These sermons are less designed to convert than to please, and in that respect they

---

[36] "On ne peut fournir une attention souvent d'une heure et demie à un discours fleuri, prononcé avec art, et plûtôt dans la vüe de plaire que d'instruire. Ainsi on se contente d'admirer; quoi? Les infléxions de la voix, la régularité du geste, le choix des mots. . . . On connoît le Déclamateur, on le fréquente, et souvent (ô corruption de notre Siècle!) on le voit démentir dans la pratique, les règles de vertu . . . souvent même il tombe dans le Vice qu'il aura combattu." Nicolas de Gueudeville, *Le Censeur, ou mœurs de La Haye* (The Hague: H. Scheuleer, 1715), p. 4.

[37] "Le service commença; il y eut un sermon qui fut fort beau; je ne dis pas bon; ce fut avec la vanité de prêcher élegamment qu'on nous prêcha la vanité des choses du monde; et c'est là le vice d'un grand nombre de prédicateurs; c'est bien moins pour notre instruction qu'en faveur de leur orgueil qu'ils prêchent; de sorte que c'est presque toujours le péché qui prêche la vertu dans nos chaires." Marivaux, *La Vie de Marianne* (1731–41), IVᵉ partie, p. 171.

constitute one of the amusements in Paris. Sometimes one pays as much for a chair in church as at the Opera.[38]

In *Letter III* of this book, there are stories of two young ladies. The first ran away from home with a poor young nobleman and married him but was brought back to Paris by her outraged parents and put into a convent. Her serving-woman, who had gone away with her, was sent to prison, as was the priest who had performed the ceremony. A second young girl of noble family fell madly in love with "a charming man-servant" and: "She took her jewels and 1500 gold-pieces and with a pistol in her hand, forced her timid lover to accompany her to England."[39]

Perhaps even Cartouche, the most notorious highwayman in French history, might have been less bold in 1719, both before and after he was incarcerated at the Châtelet prison in Paris, if lawlessness had been less prevalent among "the better people." Certainly, those among them who went to church "to be entertained, as they went to the Opera" had little of the intimate conviction of religious values which seems to have, in all periods, restrained men of weak will from dishonesty and from acts of violence.

The cynical action of the Regent in making a Cardinal and Prime Minister of the Abbé Dubois, at a time when he was scorned by many as a shameless scoundrel, was of no help to those of the minor clergy who earnestly continued to preach humility and obedience. Whether one has democratic and equalitarian political beliefs or not, it must be admitted that the actions of conspicuous people are of great importance. The many are always inclined to follow the example set by those whom they consider "of better family," or whom they know to be "successful."

---

[38] "Il est du bel air de s'empresser à leurs sermons. Les Indévots mêmes y courent par mode ou par goût. L'éloquence simple et claire, mais grave, majestueuse, foudroyante, enfin Chrétienne d'un Massillon les effrayeroit, et celle-là les occupe agréablement. L'un retient un passage du Sermon, l'autre un autre, on s'en entretient dans les Compagnies, on en juge froidement comme d'un Discours Académique . . . ces Sermons semblent moins faits pour convertir que pour plaire, et c'est en ce sens-là qu'on les regarde comme partie des amusemens de Paris, et quelquefois on paye les chaises dans les Eglises aussi cher qu'à l'Opéra." La Barre de Beaumarchais, *Amusemens littéraires: ou Correspondance politique, historique, philosophique, critique, et galante* (The Hague: Jean Van Duren, 1741), Lettre I, p. 4.

[39] "Elle prend ses bijoux et quinze cens louis, et le pistolet à la main force son timide Amant de la suivre en Angleterre." *Ibid.,* Lettre III.

V

French Protestants in exile penned many documents accusing Louis XIV of injustice and deceit. These exiles resented the persecution of their fellows for years before the official Revocation of the Edict of Nantes. They made similar protests against the edicts of 1688 and 1689, which portended to hand over the property of refugee Protestants to their relatives who had remained and had abjured their beliefs, but then reversed the decision so that the recipients under the first decree could be stripped of their newly acquired wealth by the second. Their accusation against the king of downright trickery, as well as other attacks against dishonesty and double-dealing, continued for years after his death in 1715. The authors quoted in this chapter were frequently men who had nothing to gain by criticism of those in high places.

In December, 1689, Vauban, nobleman and high officer in the French army, wrote his *Memoir on the Recalling of the Huguenots,* which was addressed to the Minister Louvois. This document was not printed until long afterward, but its spirit is noteworthy. After lamenting the loss of citizens, manufacturing, and commerce, Vauban recalls a relevant historical fact:

> Sending delinquent Protestants to the galleys, or having them tortured in no matter what manner will only serve to increase their feelings of martyrdom. . . . The blood of martyrs of all religions has always been very fruitful. . . . In this connection we should remember the Saint Bartholomew Massacre of 1572, a short time after which there were 110,000 more Huguenots than there had been before.[40]

Vauban's reasons for having the Protestants return was not in any sense an emotional plea. It was his patriotism which led him to assert that the best of them had left the country, and he had no sympathy for those who had become "converted" and remained in France: "With regard to those who have remained in the Realm, one would not be able

[40] "Envoyer aux galères ou faire supplicier les délinquants, de quelque façon que ce puisse être, ne servira qu'à grossir leur martyrologie . . . le sang des martyrs de toutes religions a toujours été très fécond. . . . On doit se souvenir sur cela du massacre de la Saint Barthélemy, en 1572, où, fort peu de temps après l'exécution, il se trouva 110,000 huguenots de plus qu'il n'y en avait eu auparavant." Vauban, "Mémoire pour le rappel des Huguenots, adressé à feu M. de Louvois, en décembre 1689," in *Vauban: Sa Famille et ses Ecrits* (Paris: Berger-Levrault, 1910), p. 468.

to say that a single one of them was really converted."[41] The first requirement for a citizen was loyalty to the king—a requirement by which Vauban lived himself, to his own eventual sorrow, for the king in 1707 refused to consider Vauban's proposal for a single tax or to allow it to be published. With respect to Louis XIV's breaking of treaties, Vauban had written in a letter to his friend, Puyzieulx, dated October, 1701: "We have so spoiled our reputation that no one can believe what we say."[42]

Three months later, the refugee French Protestant editors of the *Historical and Political Mercury*, published at The Hague, were much more emotional and emphatic:

> It has been common knowledge that for forty years the King of France has been trying to establish Universal domination, which he has constantly sought by all methods of violence, rapine, and injustice. It is also common knowledge that he has not respected Oaths, Treaties, or Religion except as solemn pitfalls to surprise and trap everyone.[43]

Chasles, who is often quoted in these pages, in all probability was not a devout Catholic. He was beyond a doubt more interested in his own fortune and less of a patriot than Vauban. But Chasles believed in fair dealing and abominated trickery, particularly that which sought to hide under the cloak of religion. The anonymous person responsible for the preface of Chasles' *Journal of a Voyage to the East Indies* (published in 1721, but written much earlier), declared that Chasles was not a Protestant. Part of that preface reads:

> He was unprejudiced enough to do justice most of the time to people of all Nations and even all Religions, except the English and the Protestants, against whom he sometimes shows ill humor. Although a Roman Catholic, he could not tolerate persecution. He wished everyone to have the liberty to follow the light of his own conscience. And this single point will doubtless make all decent people regard him with esteem.[44]

41 "A l'égard des restés dans le royaume, on ne saurait dire s'il y en a un seul de véritablement converti." *Ibid.*

42 "Nous avons tellement gâté la nôtre [réputation] que personne ne peut se fier en nous." Lettre à Puyzieulx, 27 octobre 1701, in Vauban, *Lettres intimes (inédites) adressées au marquis de Puyzieulx (1699–1705)*, (Paris: Bossard, 1924).

43 "C'est une chose notoire que depuis 40 ans, le Roi de France a affecté la Monarchie Universelle, qu'il a constamment recherché par toutes les voyes de violence, de rapine et d'injustice; et qu'il n'a regardé les Sermens, les Traitez et la Religion, que comme de Pièges solennelles, pour surprendre et enlacer tout le Monde." *Mercure historique et politique* (La Haye: 1692–1720), janvier 1702, p. 100.

44 ". . . assez désintéressé pour rendre le plus souvent justice à toutes les Nations, et même à toutes les Communions, si l'on en excepte les Anglois et les Réformez, contre lesquels il est quelquefois d'un peu trop mauvaise Humeur. Tout Catholique-Romain

If we believe that estimate, Chasles was a freethinker, nominally a Catholic. It is reasonable to suppose that, having been on various continents among men of many different beliefs, any strictly defined religious ideas which he had possessed in youth had become blurred. He had not, however, lost the moral conviction of the sin of deceit, nor of injustice. In his *Memoirs,* all of which were written by 1716, there are almost fifty pages angrily denouncing taxgatherers and moneylenders.[45] Seven chapters (21 to 27) are devoted to a scornful hatred of those who profited by others' misery to become enormously rich themselves, thanks to devious and dishonest practices. Chasles does not hesitate to call these men by name: Thévenin, Bourvalais, Miotte, Le Normant, Deschiens, Hénault, Legendre.

Not only was Chasles critical of contemporary lowborn Frenchmen who had attained great wealth by trickery; he was equally free in criticizing the injustice of persons in high places, particularly if they used religion as a shield. A Maharajah in India is described thus in his *Journal of a Voyage:* "Remrajah . . . imagined, as did any number of other nobles, that religion should give way to material considerations. How many Christians, how many Popes even, have been of this opinion!"[46]

Although Chasles finished writing his *Memoirs* in 1716, they were not published until 1931, thanks to Augustin-Thierry. It is curious to read what he wrote within a year of Louis XIV's death about that monarch's shortcomings, and to note how much less loyal he was than Vauban had been a few years earlier. The first chapter of the *Memoirs* contains the following:

> I repeat again: this prince was born a decent person but he became completely corrupted by those damnable court pests [the flatterers]. . . . It is really they who ruined France, Louis having reigned but through them, or

---

qu'il étoit, il ne pouvoit souffrir la Persécution: il vouloit qu'on laissât à chacun la Liberté de suivre les Lumières de sa Conscience; et ce seul Point le fera sans doute regarder avec estime par les Honnêtes-Gens." Chasles, *Journal d'un voyage,* Avertissement.

[45] Chasles, *Mémoires.*

[46] "Remraja . . . s'imagina, aussi bien que quantité d'autres Grands, que la Religion doit céder à l'intérêt. Que de Princes Chrétiens, que de Papes même, ont été de ce sentiment!" Chasles, *Journal d'un voyage,* III, 21–22.

rather they having reigned in his name. . . . Certainly, his greatest short-coming was his love of flattery, adulation and praise.[47]

Chapter 2 begins with the words: "However all this may be, it would have been of advantage for the reputation of Louis XIV, if he had died thirty years sooner. . . . He would then have died as the adored father of his people. . . ."[48] A year after the Sun King's death, this angry author wrote: "Everything which Louis XIV and his ancestors did for the grandeur of France seems to have turned against him, by God's permission, after that Revocation of the Edict of Nantes."[49]

Since a Catholic gentleman and distinguished soldier like Vauban could write as he had, attempting to make known his ideas on the harm done to the country by exiling the Protestants, there is no reason, on the basis of the above quotations alone, to take Chasles as a disgruntled Protestant. All those in France at the time who believed in fair dealing and detested the misuse of power must have shared to some degree the opinions of Vauban and Chasles.

Marivaux, in his *Le Spectateur françois* of 1722–23, pictured the capricious and unjust ways of the court in a passage which was certainly dictated by his feelings on the subject rather than by any abstract logic:

> [This gentleman] received an order to withdraw from the Court, because he had not been skilful enough to continue in [the king's] favor, because his ability at intrigue was not superior to that of his enemies, because he had not himself ruined those who ruined him. For ordinarily these are the crimes of the men who have fallen into disfavor.[50]

Marivaux had far less a political than a moralizing bent as a journalist. His real gift to posterity was beyond any possible doubt his sympathetic

---

47 "Je le répète encore: ce prince était né honnête homme. Mais il a été absolument corrompu par ces maudites pestes de Cour [les flatteurs]. . . . En effet, ce sont eux qui ont perdu la France, Louis n'ayant régné que par eux, ou plutôt eux sous son nom. . . . Certainement, c'était son plus grand vice que d'aimer la flatterie, l'adulation et l'encens." Chasles, *Mémoires*, pp. 7–8.

48 "Quoi qu'il en soit, il aurait été avantageux à la mémoire de Louis XIV qu'il fût mort trente ans plus tôt. . . . Il serait mort, dans ce temps-là, le père et l'adoration de son peuple. . . ." *Ibid.*, p. 17.

49 "Il semble que Dieu ait permis, depuis cette révocation de l'édit de Nantes, que tout ce que Louis XIV et ses ancêtres ont fait pour la grandeur de la France, se soit tourné contre lui." *Ibid.*, p. 22.

50 "[Ce seigneur] a eu ordre de se retirer de la cour pour n'avoir pas eu l'adresse de se maintenir dans sa faveur [*du roi*], pour n'avoir pas eu une intrigue supérieure à celle de ses ennemis, pour n'avoir pas perdu lui-même ceux qui l'ont perdu, car ordinairement voilà les crimes de ces fameux disgraciés." Marivaux, *Le Spectateur françois*, (1722–23), 22e feuille, pp. 269–70.

understanding of the psychology of people he depicted, both in his stories and in his brilliant plays. It is therefore germane to the question of injustice that he understood and felt sympathy for a cobbler, who talked without looking up from his work while a crowd was cheering the arrival of the Infanta of Spain:

> That's too fine for little people like me; it don't belong to the likes of us to see those beauties: that's all well and good for people like you, who know where their bread is coming from. . . . You see, sir, when a fellow has work he has to deliver, or else go hungry without intending to, well, even if the bronze horse of that statue was to walk on his four hoofs, I'd rather believe it than go see it. . . . When I see so many fine carriages and all the fine people in them, my bench and shoes make me angry and then I get sad and don't have any heart for my work. By Gosh, since God made me to mend old shoes, I have to go along doing it, leave other people alone, and live as a good servant of the king and his family.[51]

A dozen years later, in Marivaux's novel about Jacob (the peasant who had made a fortune in Paris and had then retired to the country), there was more bitterness about the injustice of society than there had been in the story of the patient cobbler.

> What a wretched country, Madame, where they put those who are honorable into prison cells, and those who are not into well-furnished quarters! Marry a chambermaid to help some man out of trouble, and you'll have plenty of money. Take a decent girl for a wife, and there you are, between bare walls![52]

In Prévost's periodical, *Le Pour et Contre,* for 1735, an English tale of the revolt of Negro slaves in Jamaica is recounted at length for the benefit of French readers. As Lahontan had used an imaginary North American Indian to flay French civilization, so in this English story a much more credible Negro freedman criticizes the white man's ferocious

[51] "Cela est trop beau pour de petites gens comme nous; cela ne nous appartient pas, de voir ces beautés-là: cela est bon pour vous autres gens qui avez votre pain cuit . . . voyez-vous, monsieur, quand on a de l'ouvrage qu'il faut rendre, ou jeûner sans en avoir envie, le Cheval de bronze marcherait de ses quatre pattes, que j'aimerais mieux le croire que de l'aller voir . . . sitôt que je vois tant de beaux équipages, et tout ce monde qu'il y a dedans, mes escabeaux et mes savates me fâchent; et je deviens triste; je n'ai plus de cœur à l'ouvrage. Pardi! puisque Dieu m'a fait pour raccommoder de vivre bon serviteur du roi et des siens." *Ibid.,* 5e feuille, pp. 67–68.

[52] "Quel misérable pays, madame, où l'on met au cachot les personnes qui ont de l'honneur, et en chambre garnie celles qui n'en ont point! Epousez des femmes de chambre pour un homme, et vous aurez des rouleaux d'argent; prenez une honnête fille, vous voilà niché entre quatre murailles." Marivaux, *Le Paysan parvenu* (1735–40), 1ère partie, p. 32.

injustice. Moses Bom-Saam, the Negro orator, for many years a freed slave having some education, has become the leader of the black revolt. He harangues the white masters with feeling:

> It is not difference in ability, but upbringing and simple chance that give white people the superiority which they use to scorn black men and tread them underfoot. By that mysterious God which our persecutors claim to worship, what is that superiority of which they boast in their pride? What advantage do they find in their washed-out and disgusting whiteness, above the noble and majestic color that we have received from Nature? . . . As soon as I began to read, I learned in the most holy of all books, in the source of the religion of white men, that all men are the work of a single Creator, descended from a single father, and that they are all born with the same freedom and the same rights. . . . What right have the whites to object to our revolt? Will they say that our ancestors were slaves? Those who were delivered from slavery by Moses also had been slaves.[53]

A large number of Frenchmen probably read these words, thanks to Prévost's popularization of English writings in *Le Pour et Contre*. The contrast between the basic doctrine of the New Testament on the one hand and the injustice of social institutions on the other was gradually delineated—as much because of such emotional statements, probably, as because of the cooler, more logical statements of the *philosophes*.

The next chapter will present the vehement denunciations of injustice and double-dealing written by Protestant authors in exile.

VI

In contrast to the reprobation of cruelty, injustice, or pride in rank, little outcry evolved against sexual laxity, whether in life or in literature. Only in comparatively recent times has reprobation of adultery and dalliance been severe, and then only in certain places. Traditionally, blasphemy, deceit, perjury, and even anger were worse sins; thus Dante

---

[53] "Ce n'est point la différence du génie, mais l'éducation et le seul hazard, qui donnent aux Blancs cette supériorité dont ils abusent pour mépriser les Noirs et pour les fouler aux pieds. Eh! par ce Dieu mystérieux, que nos Persécuteurs prétendent adorer, quelle est donc cette supériorité dont leur orgueil se vante? Quel avantage croyent-ils tirer de leur fade et dégoutante blancheur, sur la couleur noble et majestueuse que nous avons reçûe de la nature? . . . Aussitôt que j'ai commencé à lire, j'ai appris dans le plus saint de tous les Livres; dans la source de la Religion des Blancs, que tous les hommes sont l'ouvrage d'un même Créateur, les descendans d'un même père, et qu'ils naissent tous avec la même liberté et les mêmes droits. . . . Qu'ont-ils à objecter contre la justice de notre révolte? Diront-ils que nos Ancêtres étoient esclaves? Ceux du Peuple qui fut délivré par leur Moyse l'étoient aussi." Prévost, *Le Pour et Contre*, No. 90, p. 223.

placed souls guilty of sins of the mind much deeper in Hell than those that had erred through the normal passion of love. Unfaithfulness of men to their wives had for a very long time been a subject treated lightly by the best authors. In North America slaveowners in the South were not visibly ashamed of having illegitimate offspring. Neither was Benjamin Franklin, by the way. Even today, in countries having a dowry system and little facility for divorce, marital unfaithfulness of men may be quite calmly accepted as a fact of masculine behavior.

It is therefore not surprising that sprightly and amusing tales of "immoral" tone were written by Montesquieu and Voltaire, among others, for a sophisticated public in eighteenth-century France. Such stories were apparently enjoyed by adults who had no morbid or sickly notions about sex. The husband whose wife was unfaithful was still a comic figure; her sins were a joke on her husband and the subject of gaiety among men.

An extreme statement like the following is surprising, however, coming from such a harsh critic of society as Pierre Bayle:

> Although our century is no more chaste than other times, it is at least more refined and decent externally. The laws of propriety are more strict and more widespread now than they have ever been. Authors intent on pleasing the best society have never before been required to write as decorously.[54]

Bayle went on, in his Article for June, 1684, in the *Nouvelles de la République des Lettres,* to castigate lewd authors such as Juvenal and Martial "who had no urbanity at all."[55] The fact is that light and amusing treatment of sexual sins was controlled by a strict observance of verbal propriety. Nothing coarse or vulgar was said, for example, by the very unethical characters in Dancourt's comedy, *Le Moulin de Javelle* (1696), even if they happened to be in the business of supplying a meeting place for illicit couples.

The reading public which knew La Barre de Beaumarchais' *Amusements Littéraires pour 1738,* quoted above, doubtless took pleasure in reading about the young ladies who escaped parental control in their

---

[54] "Encore que notre Siècle ne soit pas plus chaste que les autres, il est du moins plus poli, et plus honnête pour l'extérieur. Les loix de la bienséance sont à présent plus sévères et plus étenduës, qu'elles n'ont jamais été. Jamais les Auteurs qui ont voulu plaire au beau monde n'ont été obligez d'écrire si honnêtement." Pierre Bayle, *Nouvelles dé la République des Lettres* (1684–1718), juin 1684, Art. IV: *Commentaires de M. Vossius sur Catulle (en latin),* (London, 1684).

[55] ". . . ces anciens temps pour lesquels on témoigne une si grande vénération, n'avoient aucune teinture de la véritable *urbanité." Ibid.*

adventures with lovers. Neither the violence of the first girl's parents nor the atrocious violence of the second young lady, who used a pistol to make a lover of her manservant, is accompanied by the use of any vulgar words. These would certainly have revolted the readers' sense of the proprieties.

The second edition of *Letters of Heloïse and Abelard, Put into French Verse,* by M. Pierre-François Godart de Beauchamps, appeared in Paris in 1721. In the preface to this curious work, the author made a statement quoted in the review that appeared a few months later in the *Journal des Sçavans:* "Modesty is now only an imbecility of which people are ashamed."[56]

The Swiss author Muralt wrote at greater length about French ladies in his *Letters on the English and the French:*

Women of quality especially disdain timidity and modesty, thinking these something small-minded and constrained—perfectly fitting in middle-class women. To avoid that extremity, they shun modesty itself. . . . In their love-affairs, to which they are naturally inclined, fine ladies abandon the proper role of women. They do not yield to tenderness, which might win some indulgence for their weak and tender sex, exposed as ladies are, by the manners of the country, to men who are bold and practiced in such matters. Instead, they are won by lavish spending and public notice. The risk of their affairs becoming public knowledge does not stop them at all. As men are intrepid in war, so these ladies are in love: they brave all dangers and pay no heed to the examples of indiscretion around them.[57]

But this serious-minded Swiss author had grown to manhood in the more restrained society of his own country and had come to France after a stay in England, where there apparently was more restraint in the manners of well-born ladies.

[56] "La pudeur n'est plus qu'une imbécilité dont on a honte." *Journal des Sçavans,* novembre 1721, review of *Lettres d'Heloyse et d'Abailard, mises en Vers françois,* seconde édition, revue et corrigée, par M. de Beauchamps (Paris, 1721).

[57] "Les Femmes de qualité, surtout, dédaignent cette Timidité, cette Pudeur scrupuleuse. Elle leur paroit quelque chose de petit et de contraint, qui sied bien à des Bourgeoises, et pour s'éloigner de cette extrémité, elles s'éloignent de la Modestie. . . . Dans les Intrigues, vers lesquelles elles se trouvent portées plus naturellement, elles sortent encore du Caractère de Femmes: ce n'est pas à la Tendresse qu'elles se rendent, ce qui pourroit enfin mériter quelque indulgence à ce Sexe foible et tendre, exposé par les Mœurs du Païs aux entreprises des Hommes hardis et aguerris dans ce métier; on les gagne avec de la Dépense et du bruit. En tout sens le Bruit ne les rebute point: comme les Hommes sont intrépides à la Guerre, les Femmes le sont en Amour; elles bravent les dangers, et tous les exemples d'indiscrétion qu'elles ont devant les yeux." Béat de Muralt, *Lettres sur les Anglais et sur les Français* (Cologne, 1725), pp. 191–92.

The Marquise de Lambert wrote a book of *New Reflections on Women*, published in 1727 from a pilfered copy of her manuscript. (She tried to buy up the whole edition to avoid its publication, but a "New Edition" appeared in London in 1730 based on a copy of the 1727 book which had escaped her efforts.) Three short quotations from this London edition will suffice to show that, in some cases at least, French ladies had puritanical feelings about the behavior of their sisters:

> Has society benefited by such a complete change-over in women's behavior? They have put wild excess in the place of learning; they have substituted lack of decency for the exaggerated overrefinement for which they were reproached. Thus they have become degraded and have fallen from their dignity.[58]

> At present, lack of decorum has reached the point of one's no longer trying to hide weaknesses.[59]

> When luxury and money have lustre, true honor loses its.[60]

There were certainly many readers in 1735 for Marivaux's *Paysan parvenu*, in which Jacob recalled the various forms of immoral conduct in Paris, both his own and other people's, and told of them as a man born a peasant might have remembered them. He did not omit sexual sins from the number of those he had observed, but the emphasis is rather upon pride, dishonesty, injustice, and pretense. In telling his life story, the peasant Jacob still seems astonished at the rapidity of his rise to wealth:

> Just imagine what a young country bumpkin like me was at that age . . . married to a rich girl and the lover of two upper-class ladies. . . . Ten or twelve days earlier, everyone had called me "Jacob," but the loving stimulus of those two ladies and especially the charming but impure art which Madame de Ferval had used to conquer me, that leg of hers so richly stockinged, so fashionable, which I had looked at so much . . . what a

---

[58] "La Société a-t-elle gagné dans cet échange du goût des Femmes? Elles ont mis la débauche à la place du savoir; le précieux qu'on leur a tant reproché, elles l'ont changé en indécence. Par-là elles se sont dégradées, elles sont déchûës de leur dignité." Mme de Lambert, *Réflexions nouvelles sur les femmes*, nouvelle édition corrigée (London: J. P. Coderc, 1730), p. 6.

[59] "Mais à présent l'indécence est au point de ne vouloir plus de voile à ses foiblesses." *Ibid.*, p. 11.

[60] "Quand le luxe et l'argent sont en crédit, le véritable honneur perd le sien." *Ibid.*, p. 15.

schooling in soft living, pleasure, corruption, and consequently sentiment! For a man's soul becomes refined in proportion as it is corrupted.[61]

The paucity of printed criticism of sexual behavior may not, in itself, indicate the attitude of a majority of the French people in the first half of the eighteenth century, but it probably is an indication of the taste of the French literary public. The five statements quoted above, the result of an extensive reading of French works written between 1690 and 1740, highlight the rarity of such criticism in the period.

Today, particularly in Protestant countries, we would look with a sort of compound horror upon the idea of a duel being fought over a mistress by a pair of young *abbés* in 1720 or 1730. But it is not at all sure that the majority of Parisians at that time had similar feelings. The contemporaries of those young chaps, who had not as yet been assigned to regular priestly duties, apparently took it for granted that young men who had sufficient money should have mistresses. Nor was it a secret that young men at times quarreled over fickle and luxury-loving females. It was the fighting of duels that Parisians so bitterly condemned—a crime against law and order ever since the time of Richelieu.

These facts must be kept in mind if one would avoid the misunderstanding which results from judging one period by the standards of another.

[61] "Figurez-vous, ce que c'est qu'un jeune rustre comme moi . . . devenu le mari d'une fille riche, et l'amant de deux femmes de condition. . . . moi qu'on appelait Jacob dix ou douze jours auparavant; les amoureuses agaceries de ces deux dames, et surtout cet art charmant, quoique impur, que Mme de Ferval avait employé pour me séduire; cette jambe si bien chaussée, si galante, que j'avais tant regardée . . . quelle école de mollesse, de volupté, de corruption, et par conséquent de sentiment! car l'âme se raffine à mesure qu'elle se gâte." Marivaux, *Le Paysan parvenu,* IVe partie, pp. 209–10.

CHAPTER VII

Recriminations of Protestants

STATEMENTS OF outraged feelings of Protestants and of their sad lot in France long antedated the Revocation of the Edict of Nantes. After 1685, print shops in Holland, in Switzerland, in cities on the Rhine, and in England, were frequently in the hands of refugee Frenchmen and contributed a fair proportion of the bitter attacks leveled at the regime and the Catholic Church. Strong Catholics became convinced that the many statements in the seventeenth century about the disloyalty of Protestants had been true; that the vehement protestations by Calvinist ministers regarding the loyalty of their parishioners had been a tissue of lies. Those who are familiar with the works of the French rationalists and *philosophes* of the eighteenth century will find great similarity between their writings and the statements by Protestants of the time, for the hostility of these two quite divergent groups toward absolutism in government as well as toward the policies of the Church often coincided. Some of the statements quoted here, written by God-fearing Protestants, could easily be thought to come from the works of the "Fathers of the Revolution."

143

I

The association of political dissent with unorthodox religious views is old and well grounded. In the period which we are studying, there is no doubt that what brought Protestants and freethinkers together was their opposition to the use of political power against nonconformist ideas and to the exercise of social and material advantage to freeze the status quo. The Protestants, with support from the New Testament, early became champions of the poor as against the rich and powerful, often—as in the following passage—equating poverty with goodness, wickedness with wealth.

> Here you have the signs and marks of those who are good and those who are wicked. The wicked are noble, rich, educated, powerful, given to mockery and to persecution. They are cruel, proud, famous, ambitious. . . .
>
> Those who are good and kind are of low estate and without public esteem. They are poor, vulgar, ignorant, weak, disabled, mocked and scorned, pursued and afflicted. They are peaceable, gentle-natured, humble and abject, beaten down and cast out, low and despised. Such men are objects of horror to society. They are zealous to honor God and return good for evil. When they are cursed and reviled they bless; they follow Christ, the Lamb of God, through all trials and tribulations. . . .[1]

Sebastien Châteillon wrote those emphatic sentences in a book published in 1554, before the beginning of the Religious Wars in France.

Probably very few of the wealthy Protestants who left France after 1685 and took their wealth and manufactures elsewhere knew or heeded Châteillon's words. But the humble pastors in the mountainous Cévennes in central France had preached just this doctrine to the same parishioners who later faced and fought the royal troops, after the seizure and removal of their pastors. Rustic and poor Protestant subjects of Louis XIV were of the same "subversive" cast of mind as the Early Christians had been in the Roman Empire—for no one imagines that these last were

---

1 "Tu as ici les signes, et marques des bons, et des mauvais. Les mauvais sont nobles, riches, savants, puissants, moqueurs, persécuteurs, cruels, orgueilleux, renommés, et ambitieux. . . .
   Les bons sont gens de basse condition, et de nulle estime, pauvres, et malôtrus, ignorants, débiles, infirmes, moqués, et méprisés, harcelés, et affligés, pacifiques, débonnaires, humbles et abjects, abaissés et rejetés, viles et contemnés, et tels que le monde a en horreur, zélateurs de l'honneur de Dieu, qui rendent bien pour mal: lesquels étant maudits et injuriés bénissent, et suivent Christ l'agneau de Dieu par toutes croix, tribulations. . . ." Sebastien Châteillon, *Traité des hérétiques, à savoir, si on les doit persécuter.* . . . (Rouen [probably Lyon]: Pierre Freneau, 1554; Geneva: A. Jullien, 1913), pp. 192–93 (1913 edition).

persecuted simply for announcing one more god to the Romans, who already had hundreds. They, like the French Protestants, were politically "unreliable," in part at least because they believed that the wealthy and the mighty were evil men—a belief as intolerable to the authorities in Christian France as it had been in pagan Rome.

Esteem for the poor and downtrodden easily became associated with religious tolerance in Protestant thinking, as the following passage, also from Châteillon, illustrates:

> Would that good Kings and Princes considered diligently the story [of Daniel in the Old Testament] which has been handed down to them in writing, like all of Holy Writ, to teach and to instruct them, so that they might distrust those who urge them to kill and to burn alive any man in the cause of Faith and Religion, which must above all be free. For religion resides, not in the body, but in men's hearts, which the sword of Princes and Kings cannot reach. These rulers should rather forbid the wicked to harm the good, either in their goods or in their persons. . . .
>
> If someone disturbs the State by beating or striking anyone under the pretext of defending religion, a good Magistrate may punish him, as he does other malefactors who harm good men in their persons or their possession, but not for his religion.[2]
>
> It often happens that those who come to believe in the New Testament and in Christ feel and judge religious matters very well, as long as they are themselves poor and afflicted, for affliction and poverty are richly capable of approaching the truths of Christ, who was himself poor and afflicted. And yet later on, those very men, once they are raised to wealth and prosperity and are set up in authority over others, grow worse and change so greatly that they, who formerly defended Christ and his truth, now defend and approve murders and identify true piety with force and violence.[3]

[2] "Que les bons Rois et Princes considérassent diligemment cette histoire [Daniel, Vieux Testament], laquelle leur est laissée par écrit, comme toutes les autres écritures, pour les enseigner et instruire: afin qu'ils se gardent de croire à ceux qui les poussent à tuer et à brûler aucun pour la foi et la religion, laquelle sur toute chose doit être libre. Car elle gît non au corps, mais bien au cœur, auquel ne peut atteindre le glaive des Rois et Princes; mais bien se contenter de défendre que les mauvais ne nuisent aux bons, tant en leurs biens, qu'en leurs corps. . . .

Si quelqu'un trouble la République en battant, ou frappant aucun sous couleur de religion, le bon Magistrat le peut punir, comme celui qui fait mal au corps et biens, comme les autres malfaiteurs, mais non pour sa religion." *Ibid.,* p. 4.

[3] "Car il advient souventes fois que ceux-là qui viennent à l'Evangile et connaissance de Christ sentent et jugent très bien des affaires de religion, cependant qu'ils sont pauvres et affligés: pource que affliction et pauvreté est grandement capable de la vérité de Christ, lequel aussi a été pauvre et affligé: mais que ceux-ci même étant élevés par après en richesse, et prospérité, et constitués en autorité s'abâtardissent, et aliènent tellement, qu'eux, qui paravant défendaient Christ, et la vérité, défendent maintenant et approuvent les meurtres, et colloquent la vraie piété en force et violence." *Ibid.,* p. 22.

The belief that kings and sovereign princes should not favor one religious belief over another, the belief that the poor are virtuous and the rich wicked and prone to afflict the good, and the belief that men become corrupted by wealth and by being given power over others—these were Protestant tenets from the beginning of the movement in the sixteenth century.

Pastors knew these doctrines, whether or not they ever heard of Châteillon, for they were in the French New Testament, which pastors and literate Protestants studied most of the days of their lives—perhaps even in the translation by Châteillon.

The traditional Protestant belief that the poor were victims of the rich persisted in the early 1700's from Châteillon to ministers like Daniel de Superville (the elder). Superville published three volumes of *Sermons* at Rotterdam, from 1702 to 1705, and other works of Christian piety in 1708 and later. More important, as Jean Marteilhe's editor, he undoubtedly inserted some of his own educated beliefs into the first-person story of one of the few galley slaves in the time of Louis XIV who left a record of his life.

Jean Marteilhe was a self-confessed ignoramus, a humble young man from Bergerac in Gascony, who, because of the forcible removal of the pastors, had been unable to become confirmed a Protestant. Attempting to escape from France, he was apprehended near the northern border of the country and sent to row in the royal galley then being used in the English Channel. It seems likely that, when the tale of his sufferings was published (Rotterdam, 1757), it had been considerably enriched by its editor, the learned Superville. The following reflection on law may be one of the many such cases: "This law is a political one . . . it is unjust, for one man is punished by it for the crime of another. But as laws are made to defend the Rich, where can the Poor, where can a Galley Slave find Justice?"[4]

About the time Marteilhe was born at Bergerac, the French pastor Jurieu (or perhaps a Jansenist named Le Vassor) had published a series of memoirs entitled *Sighs of Enslaved France,* passages of which have already been quoted. It is Memoir V which concerns us here:

> The fourth means which has been used to hold peoples in slavery is to ruin them and humble them. Nothing destroys courage as effectively as low social status and poverty. Tyrants have all recognized that they could not

[4] Marteilhe, *Mémoires,* I, 265.

reign in a tyrannical manner over a rich people. . . . It is by this means that the Arabs, Turks and Tartars established their dominion from the Strait of Gibraltar to the frontiers of Siam and China.[5]

The true glory of a monarch is to reign over a people which blesses him, while they live quietly in their homes, each of them in peace and plenty.[6]

The author of this passage, unlike Châteillon, obviously thought property important. But the comparison of Louis XIV with the Arabs, Turks, and Tartars was plainly a subversive attack of which both stiff-necked Jansenists and stiff-necked Protestants were capable when they were oppressed by an absolute ruler.

II

The passionate conclusion of the *Memoirs* of Marteilhe should rank high among statements concerning political liberty and freedom of conscience in the eighteenth century:

I am equally sensible of my own Inabilities as a Historian, as of the want of importance in my subject to deserve that title. But if there is any Nation whom Heaven has blessed with Freedom, they may learn to value the blessing, by reflecting on the Persecutions to which I was exposed, by the arbitrary Will of a Tyrant. If there be any [Nation] whom Virtue loads with Calamity, they may learn by my Example to take comfort, for Heaven will surely at least reward its Votaries.

May true Religion and true Liberty be diffused throughout the world, till all Nations become virtuous and happy. Calamity will not then afflict the good Man; for as he cannot enjoy temporal Felicity in a Nation of Slaves, so he cannot be miserable, while the rest of his fellow Creatures are free from Distress.[7]

Pastor Jean Claude's *Laments of Protestants, Cruelly Oppressed in the Kingdom of France* was published, in both French and English, in

---

[5] "Le quatrième moyen dont on s'est servi pour retenir les peuples dans l'esclavage, c'est de les ruiner et de les abaisser. Rien n'ôte le courage comme la bassesse et la pauvreté. Les tyrans ont tous reconnu qu'ils ne pouvoient régner tyranniquement sur un peuple riche. . . . C'est par cette voie que les Arabes, les Turcs et les Tartares ont établi leur domination depuis le détroit de Gibraltar jusqu'aux frontières de Siam et de la Chine." Jurieu, *Les Vœux d'un Patriote, ou Les Soupirs de la France esclave* (1689–90), (Amsterdam, n.p., 1788), p. 81.

[6] "La véritable gloire d'un Prince, c'est de régner sur un peuple qui le charge de bénédictions, en vivant paisiblement chacun chez soi dans l'abondance et dans la paix." *Ibid.*, p. 83.

[7] Marteilhe, *Mémoirs*, p. 179.

1686. In a long preface (166 pages, for a book of 122 pages) written by the prominent minister, Jacques Basnage, distrust of high officials of the Church is combined with a belief in freedom. In a quotation from a 1713 edition, Basnage says:

> The Emissaries from Rome to Great Britain blatantly say that there is no persecution in France . . . that if there was harsh treatment there in the past, it is now ended, there being no Protestants left there.[8]

> Man, born free, has the right to choose his dwelling place.[9]

This was part of a general protest against Louis XIV's refusal to permit Protestants to leave the country, after the order of banishment had been given.

The belief in freedom was expressed also in the *Nouvelles de la République des Lettres* for April, 1709. Subscribers to that literary periodical could read that "Slavery did not originate in Nature, since by nature all men are born free."[10] It is well known that Pierre Bayle, founder of the *Nouvelles de la République des Lettres* and one of the major figures in the movement of French rationalism, had asserted that freedom of thought is a "natural right" a few years before Locke wrote his *Letters on Toleration*. Bayle's death in 1706 left the direction of his periodical to others, who built upon his philosophical foundation and sometimes went even further in revolutionary spirit than he had done.

The similarity between the Protestants remaining or detained in France and the ancient Hebrews enslaved in Egypt became an easy analogy for Calvinist preachers. One of these, who corresponded with many ministers in other countries, was François Turrettini of Geneva, a *Collection* of whose sermons was published there in 1687. In a foreword to that thick volume, the pity of the author for his fellow-Protestants in France appears in the following emotional simile, which recalls the opening lines of Book II of Lucretius' *De Rerum Natura:* "And like

---

8 "Cependant à entendre les Emissaires de Rome dans la Grande Bretagne, ils disent encore effrontément, qu'il n'y a point de Persécution en France . . . que s'il y a eu cy-devant des Rigueurs, elles ont fini, n'y ayant plus de Réformez de delà." Jean Claude, *Les Plaintes des Protestans, cruellement opprimés dans le Roiaume de France,* Nouvelle édition augmentée d'une Préface [par J. Basnage] . . ., (Cologne: Pierre Marteau, 1713), Preface, p. ii.

9 "L'homme, né libre, a le Droit de choisir une Habitation." *Ibid.,* p. vi.

10 "L'Esclavage ne tire point son origine de la Nature, puisque naturellement tous les hommes naissent libres." Gui Patin, *Nouvelles de la République des Lettres* (Amsterdam: 1684–1718, avril 1709), Art. VI.

those who are safe in port, who see others in a storm. . . . Thus, we see our poor brothers exposed to the furious tempest which is attacking them, from this restful place where the Providence of God has preserved us until now. . . ."[11] A blunt attack on the sins of the powerful occupies a number of pages at the beginning of this volume:

> He [Moses] knew perfectly well that it is in the courts of the great that the greatest sins reign, that impiety, licence, debauchery, impurity, fraud and deception, profanity and Atheism are, so to speak, enthroned.[12]

> . . . [Pharoah] the cruel tyrant who held them in bondage, not content to force them into the low and contemptible trade of making bricks . . . made their lives bitter and painful; worst of all, he caused an edict to be published, that all Hebrew males born should be killed and thrown into the River. . . .[13]

III

Thousands of years before French Protestants began lamenting their exile by Louis XIV, other men had emotionally related similar trials. Odysseus and Jason longed for home, when kept afar by tyrannical gods; the cry of Greek soldiers finally reaching the sea—which meant the possibility of reaching their homes again—has rung down the ages in the words of Xenophon. The poetry and the profoundly tragic sense of yearning for their Promised Land by the Hebrew people first enslaved in Egypt, then later struggling through a desert, stirred the emotions of French Protestants of the French seventeenth century even more deeply. Persecution at home and enforced exile abroad were lamented by other contemporary Frenchmen as well, not for religious reasons, but for the same fundamentally human yearning for home. Two of these writers

---

[11] "Et comme ceux qui sont dans le port, qui voyent les autres dans la tourmente. . . . Ainsi, voyant nos povres frères exposez à la furieuse tempête qui les agite, dans ce lieu de repos, où la Providence de Dieu nous conserve jusques à present. . . ." François Turrettini, *Recueil de Sermons* (Geneva: Samuel de Tournes, 1687), pp. 2–3.

[12] "Il [Moise] savoit bien que c'est dans les Cours des Grands, où regnent le plus souvent les plus grands vices, que c'est là où l'impieté et la licence, la débauche, l'impureté, la dissimulation et la tromperie, la profanité et l'Atheïsme sont comme sur le trône." *Ibid.*, p. 17.

[13] ". . . le cruel Tyran qui les tenoit en esclavage ne se contentant pas de les attacher au vil et contemptible métier de faire des briques, . . . rendoient déja par ce moyen leur vie amère et douloureuse; mais sur tout, par l'Edit sanglant et inhumain qu'il avoit fait publier, de tuer et de jetter dans la rivière tous les mâles des Hébreux qui viendroient au monde. . . ." *Ibid.*, p. 25.

have already been quoted in preceding chapters—Robert Chasles, who spent years keeping records at sea after losing his fortune, and Baron Louis-Armand de Lahontan, embittered by legal chicanery which had deprived him of his wealth and driven him to adventures in far-off Canada.

A much more celebrated French author than either man had expressed the feeling of exiles in the 1660's and early 1670's, during the period that the anonymous Portuguese Nun and Madame de Sevigné had also written of their self-pity. Charles de Marguetel de Saint-Denis, Seigneur d'Evremond, having written a pamphlet against Prime Minister Jules Mazarin, was thereafter unable to live in France, in spite of his brilliant career as a soldier. From 1661 until his death in 1703, Saint-Evremond remained most of the time in England. He is best known as a clever literary and moral critic, or as an aging member of a gay French coterie in London, from 1675 until his death. Yet in certain of his letters to friends, he confessed his emotions and formulated the theory that grief makes men tenderhearted.

> Exiles are fine ones to be hard of heart. It is not fitting in them, and if you had been the victim of some unfortunate affair, you would realize that no one is as tender as an unfortunate man. I have written somewhere that ill fortune not only brings us unhappiness; it makes our feelings more tender, so that we suffer the more. You Gentlemen, living like kings in Paris, lacking nothing for the satisfaction of the mind and for the pleasures of the senses, you who are young and vigorous, which I think more important than all the rest, you pleasure-seekers (to put it in a word) do not really bother about those who are suffering.[14]

The passage which Saint-Evremond wrote "somewhere" is found in a letter written five years earlier to Marshal de Grammont:

> Ill fortune does more than bring us unhappiness. It makes us more capable of being wounded by all sorts of things. Nature, which should resist ill

14 "C'est bien aux exilés d'avoir de la dureté, il ne leur appartient pas, et si vous aviez eu quelque méchante affaire, vous sauriez que rien n'est si tendre qu'un malheureux. J'ai écrit en quelque part que la mauvaise fortune ne se contente pas de nous apporter des malheurs, elle nous rend les sentiments plus tendres pour mieux souffrir. Vous autres, Messieurs, logés à Paris, comme des rois, à qui rien ne manque pour la satisfaction de l'esprit, et pour les plaisirs des sens, jeunes, vigoureux, dont je fais plus de cas que du reste, vous autres gens voluptueux, en un mot, ne vous mettez guère en peine de ceux qui souffrent." Lettre à M. D'Hervart, de La Haye, 10 avril 1670, in Charles de Saint-Evremond, *Œuvres,* éd. René Planhol (Paris: Cité des Livres, 1927), p. 60.

fortune, is its ally, making our feelings more tender so as to suffer from all the evils that ill fortune brings us.[15]

Only the final paragraph in this letter of 1665 reveals the critic and the mocker that Saint-Evremond was in public. As a concession to the seventeenth-century French canon of taste which condemned the expression of heartfelt emotion, he concluded: "I shall end this annoying conversation: usually those who have fallen from favor ridiculously color everything with their own misfortune; filled as they are with it, they try to infect others with it as well."[16]

Other instances of this more logical attitude at the end of a statement of self-pity have been quoted in the chapter on the Growth of Compassion. At the very least, after a confessional passage of deep feeling, a return to balanced self-control and to reason was required by French classical taste.

In a sense, Voltaire was still following the older tradition in retaining his reasonable and jocose spirit even after he had been twice in the Bastille and then in exile in London. Immediate and great literary success and no penury to make him miserable may, of course, have helped to keep him optimistic. But he quite obviously had a nature different from that of Defoe and, particularly different from that of Prévost, who was so often on the verge of tears and anxious to make others weep.

It is too well understood to require emphasis here that there was much deep sympathy for French Protestants and even considerable political action in their favor during the time of Queen Anne in England. It is well known too that the people of Geneva, Lausanne, Basel, the cities along the Rhine, and many Dutch cities welcomed French refugees, who were also protected farther to the east by the Elector of Brandenburg. An example from Switzerland of this sympathy in regions enjoying political and religious freedom appears in the writings of Johann Heinrich Tschudi, deacon of Schwanden and historian of the canton of Glarus. His books, written in far from elegant German, were intended

15 "La mauvaise fortune ne se contente pas de nous apporter des malheurs: elle nous rend plus délicats à être blessés de toutes choses; et la nature, qui devrait lui résister, est d'intelligence avec elle, nous prêtant un sentiment plus tendre pour souffrir tous les maux qu'elle fait." Lettre à M. le maréchal de Grammont (1665), *ibid.*, p. 218.

16 "Je finis un si fâcheux entretien: c'est un ridicule ordinaire aux disgraciés d'infecter toutes choses de leurs disgrâces; et possédés qu'ils en sont, d'en vouloir toujours infecter les autres." *Ibid.*, p. 220.

for his German-speaking fellow nationals and his pages are studded with the caressing diminutives often used by South German, Swiss, and Austrian peasants. A walk taken, *ein Spatziergang,* becomes *ein Spatziergänglein; Lamm* and *Kalb* become *Lämmlein* and *Kälblein* in the text of this unpretentious man.[17]

Tschudi knew and reflected the opinion of his more widely reputed scientific contemporary, Dr. Scheuchzer, concerning the nostalgia felt when living abroad.[18] Tschudi's second and more interesting work bore the title, *Beschreibung des Loblands Glarus,* and appeared in 1714. In it Tschudi tells, in just over eight hundred pages, about the "Estimable Canton of Glarus" with an unashamed patriotism often approaching a lyric quality. It is his view that whoever is not interested in the history of his Swiss country and does not tell it to his children is unworthy of the liberty which God has vouchsafed to the Swiss, who have bought it at such cost of sacrifice.[19] This emotional political belief explains the fact that Tschudi's history of Glarus for the year 1685 contains an account of the Revocation of the Edict of Nantes written with feeling about "the poor Protestants, chained on the galleys" of Louis XIV.[20]

The three Protestant writers to be quoted next were not in any sense "great authors." Yet the intensity of their feelings as unwanted citizens of their homeland warrants quoting them, as examples of a broad emotional movement becoming widespread at the same time that "The Enlightenment" was being urged by other French authors of more logical and reasonable mind.

The name of Maximilien Misson appears on a number of pages in *Le Sentiment de la Nature et le Retour à la Vie simple,* for he expressed a far greater appreciation of the out-of-doors and of nature, as well as of the "Simple Life" (1708), than did his illustrious contemporaries. Luckily for Misson, many readers of his time also welcomed his accurate descriptions of other European countries, particularly of Italy. His *Nouveau Voyage d'Italie* was by far the most used of the travel guides published during this period, both in England and in France. In his preface to this book, Misson expresses the feeling of homelessness com-

---

[17] Johann Heinrich Tschudi, *Das gesunde und lange Leben* (Zurich: J. H. Lindinner, 1710), pp. 45, 54.

[18] Tschudi uses both the technical word *Nostalgia* and the more emotional German word *Heimweh. Ibid.,* p. 67.

[19] Johann Heinrich Tschudi, *Beschreibung des Lobl. Orths und Lands Glarus . . .* (Zurich: J. H. Lindinner, 1714), Vorrede 9.

[20] "Diese arme Leuth auf die Galeeren Gefesselt," *ibid.,* pp. 664–65.

mon to the Protestant refugees: ". . . the haven of refuge where I now am has made me recognize that I have no particular homeland here on earth."[21] The preface of another book had been recognized as Misson's work long before the text of the book itself was found to be an amalgam of earlier accounts which he had put together in the form of a novel. The desert island story, whose preface is quoted next, antedated *Robinson Crusoe* by eleven years and was printed both in French and in English at London. The spirit of its pages has been recognized as a possible influence on *Robinson Crusoe*[22] by scholars primarily interested in Defoe since 1922. Few men before Defoe had written with such fervor as is found in Misson's preface to *Le Voyage de François Leguat:*

Weary of the bustle of the world and of the troubles I had suffered in society, I left its vanity and tumult with no regret. And already at an advanced age, I thought of living and dying in peace beyond its ordinary and frequent dangers. Having no longer anything to lose, I took no risk and could hope for a great deal. I could hope to have for the rest of my life the delightful repose which I have found only for a time, on the Island where I very quietly spent two years. . . . Without bread or servants, I was fed like a Prince. I was rich there, without diamonds or gold, and without ambition. . . . Deeply withdrawn into myself, my serious reflections showed me with perfect clarity the emptiness of an infinite number of things which are in high esteem among the inhabitants of this unfortunate earth, where Art almost always destroys Nature, under the pretext of beautifying it, where Artifice, worse than Art, where Hypocrisy, Deception, Superstition and Rapacity exert a tyrannical power; where, as it were, all is Error, Vanity, Disorder, Corruption, Malice, and Wretchedness.[23]

[21] ". . . le refuge où je suis m'ayant d'ailleurs assez fait connoistre que je n'ay point de patrie particulière icy bas." Maximilien Misson, *Nouveau voyage d'Italie* (Quatrième éd., La Haye: Henri van Bulderen, 1702 [éds. en fr., 1691, 1694, 1698, 1702, 1717 (2 éds.), 1731, 1743, etc.; en angl. 1695, 1699, 1714, 1744, 1749, 1774]), Preface.

[22] G. Atkinson, "A French Desert Island Novel of 1708," *PMLA*, XXXVI (December, 1921), 509–28; also more fully in Atkinson, *The Extraordinary Voyage in French Literature from 1700 to 1720* (Paris: E. Champion, 1922), pp. 35–65, 113–33.

[23] "Las du tracas du Monde, et fatigué des peines que j'y avais souffertes, j'en quittai la vanité et le tumulte sans aucun regret; et dans un âge déjà avancé, je songeai à tâcher de vivre et de mourir en paix, hors de ses ordinaires et fréquents dangers. N'ayant plus rien à perdre, je ne risquais rien, et je pouvais espérer beaucoup. Je pouvais espérer pour toujours le délicieux repos que je n'ai trouvé que pour un temps dans l'Ile où j'ai très doucement passé deux années . . . J'y ai été nourri en Prince, sans pain et sans valets. J'y ai été riche, sans diamants et sans or, comme sans Ambition. . . . Recueilli très profondément en moi-même, mes sérieuses réflexions m'ont fait voir là, comme au doigt et à l'oeil, le néant d'une infinité de choses qui sont en grand'-vogue parmi les habitants de cette malheureuse Terre; de cette Terre, où l'Art détruit presque toujours la Nature, sous prétexte de l'embellir: où l'Artifice, pire que l'Art, l'Hyprocrisie, la Fraude, la Superstition, la Rapine exercent un tyrannique Empire: Où

A second Protestant author, Jean Olry, not nearly as successful as Maximilien Misson, had been a lawyer and notary in the city of Metz, in Lorraine. His *Persecution of the Church at Metz* describes the sufferings of his fellows there on the way to exile and later on the Island of Martinique in the West Indies. In 1687, Olry and others were seized and taken to prison at Verdun, then taken across France in chains to the port of La Rochelle and shipped to the Antilles. Before 1690, he and several companions had escaped to one of the Dutch islands, returned to Europe, and from Holland had reached a German city where Olry found other members of his family. His book, printed at Hanau in Hesse-Nassau before the end of 1690, contains an excellent sample of emotional description:

> After the departure of our dear pastors, the pain of such a great loss was extended to our own persons and our families; tears and sighs were common among us; we busied ourselves at that time by reading and meditating on the scriptures and by seeking in good books, which we had until then neglected, solace to raise our downcast spirits, hoping to learn from them the means whereby we might appease the wrath of God, which appeared so inflamed against His people, upon whom he had unleashed his terrible judgments. Our fellow-citizens, who had formerly shown liking for us, then abused us insolently when they came upon us by chance, whether in the streets or in public places, calling us *damned heretics, Calvinists and schismatics, rebels who refused to obey their King.*
>
> What could a person reply to wildly passionate men, incapable of reason, who had banished all trace of charity from their hearts?[24]

---

tout, pour ainsi dire, n'est qu'Erreur, Vanité, Désordre, Corruption, Malice, et Misère." Maximilien Misson, *Voyage et aventures de François Leguet et de ses compagnons, en deux isles désertes des Indes orientales* . . . (2 vols.; London: David Mortier, 1708), Préface, p. xxiii.

24 "Après le départ de nos chers Pasteurs, la douleur d'une si grande perte s'estendit sur nos personnes et sur nos familles, les larmes at les soûpirs n'y furent pas épargnez; on s'occupa pour lors à lire et méditer les Saintes Ecritures, et chercher dans de bons livres, que nous avions jusqu'alors négligez, des consolations qui réjouïssent nos esprits abbatus, et nous apprissent les moyens, dont nous devions nous servir, pour appaiser la colère de Dieu, qui paroissoit si embrasée contre son peuple, sur lequel il avoit déployé ses terribles jugemens. Non concitoyens, qui auparavant témoignoient nous aimer, nous insultoient insolemment, lors qu'ils nous voyoient dans la recontre [*sic*], soit dans les rües, soit dans les places publiques, nous traitant de *maudits hérétiques, Calvinistes et Schismatiques, de Rebelles qui refusoient d'obéir à leur Roy.*

Que pourroit-on repondre à des furieux, et à des hommes incapables de raison, lesquels avoient bannis de leur esprit toute sorte de charité?" Jean Olry, *La Persecution de l'Eglise de Metz, descrite par le Sr. Jean Olry, cydevant Avocat au Parlement et Notaire Royal en la dite Ville et dédiée à sa Famille* . . . *son exil dans l'Amérique* (Hanau: Samuel Ammon, 1690), pp. 14–15.

[In the prison at Ile de Ré, before embarking] we recognized, by seeing various passages of Scripture scratched on the stone, that brethren of ours had been incarcerated there before us.[25]

Of their stay in Martinique, this former lawyer and notary wrote, expressing the despair of many men who had become separated from their families: "My whole occupation was to seek out lonely places, so as to think about the harsh captivity of my poor wife and children, and about the small likelihood, at my advanced age, of ever seeing them again, or of returning to Europe."[26]

Pity was as marked in Marteilhe, whom we have met before, but in him there was a revolutionary spirit:

In every Expedition, the Poor and those of humbler Stations, who suffer most, are least taken notice of; the Miseries of the Great are held up to engage our Compassion and Attention, while the Slave who feels the most complicated Distress, seldom finds even Pity to soften his Sorrows.[27]

The author's pity for his fellow galley slaves is shown on many pages. A good example is the tale of a young fellow who had been apprehended for saying: "The King [Louis XIV] and his family may go to the Devil!"

This distressed Gentleman [his father], throwing himself before his Majesty . . . offered, old as he was, to lead his three sons to the Field of Battle, and there shed his blood in the Service of his Country; but besought his Majesty not to spill it ignominiously under the Lash of a Task-master [on a galley]. The King was still inflexible; a plain Instance that the Great seldom forgive injuries committed against themselves.[28]

[25] "Nous reconnûmes par divers passages de l'Ecriture, qui se voyoient gravés sur la pierre de taille, qu'il y avoit eu de nos Freres enfermés en ce lieu auparavant nous." *Ibid.,* p. 90.

[26] "Toute mon occupation étoit de chercher des lieux écartés, pour rêver à la dure captivité de ma pauvre femme, et de mes enfans, et au peu d'apparence qu'il y avoit qu'à l'aage avancé auquel j'étois parvenu, je les dusse jamais revoir, ny retourner dans l'Europe." *Ibid.,* p. 108.

[27] The original of this passage could not be located in the edition of 1865. Professor Atkinson indicated I, 195, as its location in the Goldsmith translation (ed.).

[28] "Monsieur son père, vénérable vieillard, fut se jeter aux pieds du Roi avec ses deux autres fils, implorant la clémence de Sa Majesté pour celui qui était en galère. Il exprima avec tant de force la tendresse d'un père pour ses enfants, en promettant à ce monarque, d'aller, tout vieux qu'il était, à la tête de ses trois fils, répandre gaiement son sang pour son service; il parla d'une façon si touchante et si pathétique, que tous ceux qui étaient présents en furent attendris jusqu'aux larmes. Il ne put cependant fléchir le Roi, . . . ce qui fait bien voir que les injures que l'on fait aux grands, sont des taches pénétrantes qui ne s'effacent pas aisément." Marteilhe, *Mémoires,* I, 242; Goldsmith trans., p. 227.

It is interesting to note, early in the second volume of Marteilhe's story as printed in Goldsmith's translation, that Protestant slaves on the king's galleys possessed and read sermons by Elie Saurin and by Jurieu. Books and money, supplied from Holland, came to the unfortunates apparently through Protestants who had remained in France as Catholic converts. The gratitude of Marteilhe toward the "Turks" on board (who, being easily recognizable, were allowed to leave the galley and go into the town) is mentioned more than once. The merciful infidels brought books and money to their Protestant fellow-sufferers and refused any reward.

Marteilhe's remarkable account of a battle at sea, in which several rowers on his bench were killed and in which he himself lost the use of one arm, is too long to reproduce here. But two briefer examples of this young peasant's adeptness with realistic touches and with the expression of the feeling of personal experience will be quoted. The tale of his imprisonment was, we may assume, told viva voce to his friendly scribe, Superville, who probably added some of the Protestant reflections but could not have been responsible for the authentic ring of the pain and agony.

When the galleys on the English Channel were given up by the French Navy, the rowers were marched across France to the Mediterranean coast in winter:

> We entered Charenton at six in the evening by moonlight. It froze excessive hard, but the weight of our chains, being according to the Captain's calculation a hundred and fifty pounds upon every man, with the swiftness of our pace, had kept us pretty warm. And we were all actually in a sweat, when we entered Charenton.[29]

When the Protestant galley slaves were freed, they reached Nice and were well treated there for some time, before starting north toward Switzerland: "We accordingly left Nice in the beginning of July, everyone separately mounted. Our old men, however, gave us some trouble, as they were unable to sit on horseback."[30] Many of the young man's

[29] "Nous arrivâmes à Charenton sur les six heures du soir au clair de la lune. Il gelait, comme on dit, à pierre fendre. La peine que nous avions à marcher, et l'excessive pesanteur de nos chaînes (qui était de cent cinquante livres pesant pour chacun, suivant le dire du capitaine même) nous avait réchauffés du grand froid que nous avions enduré . . . arrivant à Charenton, nous étions en sueur, comme si on nous avait plongés dans l'eau." *Ibid.,* Goldsmith trans., II, 82.

[30] "Nous partîmes donc de Nice, au commencement de juillet . . . chacun sur sa monture. Nous avions quelques vieillards décrépits, qui nous donnèrent bien de la peine, ne pouvant se tenir à cheval." *Ibid.;* Goldsmith trans., p. 148.

contemporaries might have continued ignorant of the desperate lives of those who grew old as galley slaves, if it had not been for this unadorned statement of fact.

In addition to Protestant authors who naïvely confessed their emotions, there were those who apparently read into the writings of others feelings which were not there. An example of this kind is the unnamed author who wrote the preface for a French translation of Wollaston's *Natural Religion,* published at The Hague in 1726. Part of that preface reads: "There never was a more perfect, decent man than Mr. Wollaston: his outspoken and frequent praise of Truth, Order, Fair-dealing, and Love for one's neighbor and God can only be the natural outpourings of a heart filled with all these Virtues."[31] However, a reading of Wollaston's text is cause for surprise, for Wollaston proceeds from one logical step to the next in his treatment of virtues and vices among men, without much evidence of passion or emotion, in the same calm way that he demonstrates, to his own satisfaction, certain "errors" among the ideas of Spinoza. One can only conclude that his translator was reading emotions into its pages, or else that he may have been counting upon the emotional nature of prospective readers. As for the "natural outpourings of a heart . . . ," those qualities are precisely what is most absent in this theoretical work.

IV

The spirit of revolt against contemporary morality was expressed in many ways by the French refugees. The editors of the *Mercure historique et politique* (published at The Hague), for example, sometimes complained of the duplicity of the French government. In 1692 the *Mercure* published letters from eyewitnesses in France who told the correct details of a battle lost by Louis XIV's troops, which had been reported as a victory and for which a Te Deum was sung in Paris by order of the king![32] Jean Marteilhe attacked his countrymen by lavishing praise on

---

[31] "Il n'y eut jamais de plus parfait honnête homme que Monsieur Wollston: ces éloges si vifs et si fréquens de la vérité, de l'ordre, de la bonne foi, de l'amour de Dieu et du Prochain, ne peuvent être que les naturels épanchemens d'un cœur charmé de toutes ces vertus." Wollaston, *Ebauche de la Religion naturelle,* traduite de l'Anglois, avec un supplément . . . (The Hague: Jean Swart, 1726), p. vi.

[32] *Mercure historique et politique* (The Hague, 1692–1720), septembre 1692, pp. 1055 ff.

the English for their "Charity, public and private,"[33] a technique not new in French literature.

Pierre Bayle sometimes displayed a sense of humor in his bitter denunciations of the French government and of the Catholic clergy. After his death in 1706, however, one rarely finds a refugee Protestant author who was given to mockery or sarcasm. One small example of light fun on a religious subject occurs in 1716 in a review of Woodes Rogers' *Voyage Around the World,* which contained the story of Selkirk on the Island of Juan Fernandez. Details of goats, loneliness, and religious fervor on a desert island (which were to appear three years later in *Robinson Crusoe*) are given in a review in the *Nouvelles de la République des Lettres* for September, 1716: "The first eight months he found it very difficult to conquer his melancholy and overcome his horror of such frightful solitude. . . . Never had he been so good a Christian, which is not hard to believe."[34]

Mention has already been made of a volume dedicated to "The Lord Public," rather than to some nobleman: *Letters of a Savage Far from Home, Containing a Criticism of the Morals of this Century, and Reflections on Religious and Political Matters.* The heavy-handed satirical manner of Joubert de la Rue, to whom this mediocre book is generally ascribed, is a second example of the "levity" among Protestant authors:

> Gold and Silver . . . would always have remained imperfect, if your Reason, infinitely more clever than Nature—that Mother of all things— had not discovered the secret . . . furnaces and crucibles. . . .
>   Your Reason, constantly increasing discoveries, found the means of purifying the souls of heretics; burning pyres, wheels, and gibbets had the same effect in this respect that furnaces and crucibles had had in the case of precious metals.[35]

33 ". . . je ne puis qu'admirer leur piété, leur zèle pour la gloire de Dieu et leur amour pour le prochain, qui les porte à se conformer constamment au saint précepte de faire du bien à tous, mais principalement aux domestiques de la foi." Marteilhe, *Mémoires,* p. 429; Goldsmith trans., II, 178.

34 "Durant les huit premiers mois il eut beaucoup de peine à vaincre sa mélancolie et à surmonter l'horreur d'une si affreuse solitude. . . . Jamais il ne fut si bon Chrétien, ce qui n'est pas difficile à croire." *Nouvelles de la République des Lettres* (1684–1718), septembre 1716, article sur Woodes-Rogers, *Providence Displayed, or a very Surprizing* [*sic*] *Account of one Mr. Alexander Selkirk. . . . Written by his own Hand* (London: J. Read, 1712; 2 vols.; French tr. Amsterdam, 1716).

35 "L'or et l'argent . . . auroient toujours resté imparfaits, si votre Raison, infiniment plus habile que la Nature, cette Mère commune de toutes choses, n'eût trouvé le secret . . . des Fourneaux et des Creusets . . .
Votre Raison allant toujours croîssant en Découvertes, trouva le moyen de purifier

Few Protestant authors who attempted irony or sarcasm on the subjects of oppression and intolerance, after the time of Pierre Bayle, were felicitous in their use. The cleverness of the *philosophes* was not possible for the Protestants. Their solemn training and their emotional involvement, by being excluded from their country, made it unlikely that they could often achieve the gay manner and the light touch of the Voltaires and Montesquieus.

The Protestant writers in exile—as might be expected—gave considerable attention to the merits of religious tolerance. Bayle early set the tone for himself and his fellow-Protestants—and indeed, generally for the proponents of religious toleration. In Article VI of the *Nouvelles de la République des Lettres* for 1684 he praised an anonymous book entitled *De la Tolérance des Religions:*

> The Author even thinks that those who are brought up in the falsest religions sincerely believe them to be true: he infers that one must not use violence on anyone. . . . He says it is not in a man's power to believe this or that, and he lists various advantages which result from toleration.[36]

Marteilhe (with the help of his editor, Superville) expressed these ideas well in reporting the conduct of Mahometans:

> Those good men [so let me call them, those Followers of Mahomet], came one after the other, offering to serve me, and testifying the greatest Pity and Goodness of Heart. They generally called us Protestants their *Brothers in God;* and testified the utmost regard to our Opinions. . . . Yet those are they whom Christians call Barbarous! Would to God that Christians would but imitate their Integrity and Virtue; the Wicked can never with Justice be called polite, nor the virtuous reproached with barbarity.[37]

---

les Ames des Hérétiques; et les Bûchers, les Roués, et les Gibets, firent à cet égard le même effet, que les Fourneaux et les Creusets avoient fait à l'égard de ces Métaux précieux." J. de la Rue Joubert, *Lettres d'un Sauvage dépaysé, contenant une critique des mœurs du siècle, et des réflexions sur des matières de religion et de politique* (Amsterdam: Jean François Jolly, 1738), pp. 4–5.

[36] "L'auteur croit même que ceux qui sont nourris dans les Religions les plus fausses, les croyent bonnes fort sincèrement: il infère de là qu'on ne doit violenter personne. . . . Il dit qu'il n'est pas au pouvoir de l'homme de croire ceci ou cela, et il rapporte diverses utilitez qui naissent de la tolérance." Pierre Bayle, *Nouvelles de la République des Lettres* (1684–1718), Art. VI.

[37] "Ces bonnes gens donc . . . vinrent tous, les uns après les autres, me prier de me servir d'eux, me marquant des sentiments si pieux et me témoignant tant d'affection pour ceux de notre religion, qu'ils appelaient leurs frères en Dieu, que j'en fus touché aux larmes. . . . Ce sont ces gens que les chrétiens nomment *barbares*, et qui, dans leur morale, le sont si peu, qu'ils font honte à ceux qui leur donnent ce nom." Marteilhe, *Mémoires*, pp. 255–56; Goldsmith trans., II, 9.

The limits of religious toleration were stated in 1715 as follows by the editors of the *Journal littéraire:*

> . . . Each man believes himself Orthodox in his opinions and everything which is outside the sphere of his opinions seems to him quite remote from Sacred Doctrine. Thus, no matter what position we might take, we should find it impossible to avoid the odious name of "Heretics," which is used so generously in our time. We do not, however, promise to have the same consideration for those who declare themselves to be against Religion in general.[38]

A curious case of intolerance on the part of Protestants and Catholics alike at the beginning of the eighteenth century was their common rejection of Pietism. Those inclined to mysticism, including Archbishop Fénelon, were punished by Rome for advocating the pietistic doctrine of "pure love." The condemnation of this religious movement in the *Nouvelles de la République des Lettres* for June, 1710, is complete and forceful:

> One could not better punish Pietists than by leaving them to their Pietism and keeping them from profiting by the advantages which the Arts and Knowledge procure for men. . . . Pietism is a ridiculous mysticism, an exaggerated Fanaticism, which would make all men into Visionaries, lacking all Knowledge and completely taken up with themselves.[39]

One general remark is fitting here. When Saint-Evremond in 1687 had written intolerantly about Confucius (which was not the case thirty or forty years later with French *philosophes*), he was quite as joyously satirical as he was about anything else:

> [Confucius' book contains] the most boring moralizing that I have ever read. His sententious statements are lower than the quatrains of Pibrac

---

[38] "Chacun se croit Orthodoxe dans ses sentiments, et tout ce qui est hors de la Sphere de ses opinions, lui paroît éloigné de la Sainte Doctrine. Ainsi quelque parti que nous prissions, nous ne saurions jamais éviter le titre odieux, d'Hérétique, dont on est si prodigue dans notre Siècle. Nous ne nous engageons pas à avoir les mêmes égards pour ceux qui se déclarent contre toute Religion en général." *Journal littéraire* (seconde édition, The Hague, 1715), Préface, pp. xv–xvi.

[39] "On ne sauroit mieux punir les Piétistes qu'en les abandonnant à leur Piétisme, et empêchant qu'ils ne profitassent des avantages que les Arts et les Sciences procurent aux hommes. . . . Une Mystique ridicule, un Fanatisme outré, qui fera de tous les hommes autant de Visionnaires, vuides de toute science et parfaitement pleins d'eux-mêmes." *Nouvelles de la République des Lettres,* juin 1710, Art. VI.

[died 1584] when he is comprehensible, and loftier than the Apocalypse when he is obscure.[40]

The earnestness of the condemnation of Pietism by both Catholics and Protestants a few years later is far from this triple comparison. In the society of Saint-Evremond, it was not common to regard moral preaching with great seriousness. There was, as we have observed earlier, a light-hearted and carefree attitude on the part of many in high society toward moral preaching—unless it was decorated with striking rhetorical figures and punctuated with solemn, but interesting, gestures.

V

The earnestness and anger directed against the clergy by Protestant authors was in striking contrast to the criticisms written by the *philosophes*. A quotation from one of these free-thinking *philosophes* will illustrate the difference between them and their more serious-minded Protestant contemporaries.

Jean-Baptiste de Boyer d'Argens, or the "Marquis d'Argens," perhaps best known for his correspondence with Frederick II of Prussia, published a quite shameless story of "Amorous Nuns, or Love in the Béguinage" in 1740. No French Protestant author of the period used that type of "immoral" fiction to make sport of Catholics. Like Voltaire, D'Argens had found it convenient to leave France, where his free-and-easy writing about serious subjects made him unwelcome to the authorities. After publishing his scandalous *Jewish Letters*,[41] this prolific author began putting out a periodical, *Les Lettres chinoises*, advertised to "appear twice a week, namely Monday and Thursday," and to be sold by specified booksellers in 1739 at Amsterdam, Rotterdam, Leyden, Utrecht, and Breda. By that date, D'Argens had become reasonably successful in supplying copy to printers, but at first his life in Holland had been difficult, as he confesses emotionally in the preface to these "letters" by a fictitious Chinese:

---

[40] "J'ai passé de ces relations [de la Chine] au livre de Confucius, le plus ennuyeux moral que j'ai jamais lu. Ses sentences sont au-dessous des quatrains de Pibrac, où il est intelligible; au-dessus de l'Apocalypse, où il est obscur." Saint-Evremond, Lettre à M. Le Fèvre, 1687, in *Œuvres*, p. 239.

[41] See chap. vi, note 27, above.

It is true that for the first three months I spent in Holland, I was in a very sad situation. But as soon as I made up my mind to inform my brother of the place to which I had withdrawn, I was enabled to stop writing for publication, whenever I pleased. I am happy to give public testimony of my brother's Kindness and generosity, an example which has not often been equalled.[42]

The tone of the First Letter, in contrast, is of the mocking variety which had been made famous by Montesquieu in his *Persian Letters* in 1721:

My hostess asked me: "Do you believe in the Pope in your country, my dear Sir?" "No," I told her, "we have a different religion from his. But we get along very well with those who are of his persuasion. . . ." "Mon Dieu!" the woman replied, "you surprise me. How is it possible for Huguenots and Jansenists in your country to be such kindly people? . . . Our Priest says he had rather the wheat should freeze and all the apples should rot, than that he should put his hand to his hat on meeting the Jesuit Rector."[43]

Elsewhere, D'Argens' Chinese wrote of the scoundrelly actions of priests in all countries in much the same spirit best known today in the work of Voltaire.

The Protestants' attacks on the cruelty and intolerance of the Catholic priesthood were usually filled with passion and gave these utterances a quite different tone. Thus, Jean and Samuel Masson, in their periodical called *Histoire critique de la République des Lettres,* explained as follows how the refugees felt about King and Church:

We must perpetuate the memory of all this down to the most distant posterity, so that future centuries may understand, to the shame of humanity, what a King who called himself *Very Christian,* and what a Church which calls itself *Apostolic* have been capable of doing to poor, innocent

---

42 "Il est vrai que les trois premiers mois que j'ai passés en Hollande, je me trouvai dans une situation assez triste; mais dès que j'ai voulu faire savoir à mon frere l'endroit où j'étois retiré, j'ai pû cesser d'écrire toutes et quantes fois il m'a plû. Je suis bien aise de rendre ici un témoignage public à la tendresse et à la générosité de ce frere, dont l'exemple est bien rarement imité." J.-B. Boyer d'Argens, *Lettres chinoises, ou correspondance philosophique, historique et critique. . . .* par l'auteur des *Lettres juives* et des *Lettres cabalistiques* (2 vols.; The Hague: Pierre Paupie, 1740).

43 "L'hôtesse me demanda: Croïez-vous au Pape dans votre païs, mon cher Monsieur? Non, lui dis-je, nous avons une Religion différente de la sienne. Cependant nous vivons fort bien avec ceux qui sont de sa croïance. . . ." "Mon dieu! repliqua cette femme, vous me surprenez. Comment est-il permis que dans votre païs les Huguenots et les Jansénistes soient de si bonnes gens? . . . Notre Curé dit qu'il aimeroit mieux que les bleds gelassent et que les pommes fussent toutes pourries, que de donner un coup de chapeau au Père Recteur des Jésuites." *Ibid.,* I, 4.

people, who have never been criticized for anything, except that they wished to serve God according to the dictates of their own conscience.[44]

This statement was inspired by the death at Bremen, in 1715, of Pastor Icard, whose sad life story appeared in the same issue of the periodical as the above quotation. Charles Icard, born in the Cévennes in 1636, was condemned to be "broken alive on the wheel" for resisting authority. He escaped to Turin, then went to Geneva, spent two years at Neuchâtel as a pastor, and then, until his death, was pastor at Bremen.

Equally virulent criticism may be found in other periodicals. In the *Nouvelles de la République des Lettres* for September, 1709, there appeared the following scathing remark about the Pope:

> The Pope could have got out of all these difficulties [about Catholic Decrees regarding China] by canonizing Confucius and thereby rendering him worthy of the religious honors accorded him. This Chinese philosopher was a very decent person and a virtuous one as well. Why should the Pope, who has made saints of individuals who never existed, have any scruples against canonizing Confucius?[45]

One of the most readable of the periodicals published by French Protestants in Holland in the early eighteenth century is the *Journal littéraire,* published at The Hague by a superior group of editors, whose collaboration in writing single articles gave their journal such standing that it was republished in book form several times before 1740. In Volume II, Article VIII, 1713, there is a long review of the second edition of Bayle's two-volume *Philosophic Commentary . . . Treatise on Universal Toleration,* a work which is still read today by students of religious toleration. Bayle's text is quoted in the review as follows:

> Judges, Courtiers, Churchmen, Bourgeois, Peasants, all were responsible for, praised, approved, or hoped for the persecution [of Protestants in

---

44 "Il est nécessaire qu'on en perpetuë la mémoire jusqu'à la Postérité la plus reculée, afin que les siècles futurs voient, à la honte de l'humanité, ce qu'un Roi qui se disoit *très Chrétien,* et ce qu'une Eglise qui se nomme *Apostolique,* ont été capables de faire contre de pauvres innocens, à qui on n'a jamais eu rien à reprocher, si ce n'est qu'ils vouloient servir Dieu suivant les mouvemens de leur conscience." Jean et Samuel Masson, *Histoire critique de la République des Lettres, tant ancienne que moderne* (15 vols.; Amsterdam: J. Desbordes, 1717–18), Vol. XIV, Art. XI, 284.

45 "Le Pape eût pu se tirer de tous ces embarras en canonisant Confucius et le rendant digne par ce moyen des honneurs Religieux qu'on lui adresse. Ce philosophe de la Chine a été un tres-honnête homme, qui avoit de la vertu; pourquoi le Pape, qui a canonisé des saints qui ne furent jamais, se feroit-il un scrupule de canoniser Confucius?" *Nouvelles de la République des Lettres,* septembre 1709, Art. VII ("Réflexions sur le nouveau Décret . . . de la Chine").

France]. . . . Violence and broken promises are the two plain characteristics of the Catholic Church. . . . Though vicissitudes continually appear
in this world, the Church always keeps its character, it always stands on its
two feet—*broken promises and violence.*[46]

The editors of the *Journal littéraire* had promised in the preface of their
first volume that they themselves would not express their opinions in
religious matters, but this did not, apparently, prevent them from
quoting others, like Pierre Bayle. Another passage in the same review,
although it is not a direct quotation, is as harsh as the preceding: "The
author concludes by saying that, if it should happen that Monks gained
power in the country where he had sought and found refuge, he would
depart for Greenland the next day."[47]

In the *Journal littéraire* for July–August, 1714, there is an article on
Bayle's *Letters* (Art. V) and another on a proposed new edition of his
Dictionary (Art. VI), in which last the editors mention "Pope Joan."
In Article VII, the celebrated line of Lucretius on religion is quoted, with
reference to the Catholic Church: *Tantum religio potuit suadere
malorum.* (So many evils religion has brought about.)[48]

The last volume of the *Nouvelles de la République des Lettres,* published in 1718, contains a review of the *New Letters* of Guy Patin, a
French iconoclast who had died in 1672. According to the review, those
letters had been in the possession of Charles Spon, a doctor of medicine
in Lyons, and had been brought out of France by Jacques Spon, his son
and heir, in 1685. The violent hatred for the Catholic Church appears
in quotations like the following:

> . . . the fact is that the Devil never shows himself, or dares to make
> his voice heard, except in countries where there are too many monks.
> Nothing like this is observed in England, in Holland, or in Germany.
> Formerly, the Devil made trouble in Rome, but the Pope of today, who is
> a clever and wily politician, has set up so many precautions and rules that,
> if the Devil from Hell is afraid of exorcisms and of Holy Water, that

---

[46] "Juges, Gens de Cour, Gens d'Eglise, Bourgeois, Païsans, tous ont causé, loué,
approuvé ou souhaité la persécution [des Protestants en France]. . . . La violence et la
mauvaise foi sont les deux marques caractéristiques de l'Eglise Catholique. . . . Quoique
l'univers soit un Théatre de vicissitudes continuelles, cette Eglise garde toûjours son
caractère, elle se trouve toûjours sur ses deux pieds, *la mauvaise foi et la violence.*"
Journal littéraire, II (septembre et octobre 1713); reference here is to 4th ed. (The
Hague: Jean Van Duren, 1739), pp. 156–57.
[47] "L'Auteur finit en disant, que s'il arrivait aux Moines de s'impatroniser dans le
Païs de son Refuge, il en partiroit dès le lendemain pour la Groenlande." *Ibid.*
[48] *De Rerum Natura,* I, 95.

supposed Devil is no less afraid of the bailiffs and of the executioner at Rome.[49]

Luther and Calvin did away with Purgatory. If they could only take Hell away from us too, we should be as well-off as rats in the meal-barrel [straw-rick]. The Devil would be really dead then, and we should have nothing left but to enjoy ourselves, no longer having any fear of that ugly, metaphysical beast, which has horns and is very ugly, as Monks assure us to be the fact—and Monks, according to what they say themselves, are upright and honorable men![50]

It is doubtful that the emotions of upright and honorable Protestants always sanctioned such violence of language as the following, also quoted from Guy Patin's *New Letters:*

What a fine clearing-out it would be, if all those Monks, together with a like number of "Lady Monks," were put into boats and sent to cultivate Purgatory in the Islands of America, or at Mozambique, where the inhabitants of those regions have not yet seen birds of that feather! That would be the real means of unburdening France of so many useless mouths and so many idle men.[51]

The convergence of views between enraged Protestants and the more lighthearted, scoffing *philosophes* is clear in the willingness of the refugee French editors of the *Nouvelles de la République des Lettres* to print the preceding passages.

The *Journal des Sçavans,* yet another periodical published in Holland by French Protestants, devoted a review in May, 1731, to Voltaire's epic poem, the *Henriade,* with four whole pages of direct quotations, includ-

---

[49] ". . . c'est que le Diable ne se montre, ou ne se fait entendre qu'aux païs, où il est trop de Moines. Il ne se voit rien de pareil en Angleterre, en Hollande, ni en Allemagne. Il a fait autrefois du bruit à Rome, mais le Pape d'aujourd'hui, qui est un fin et rusé politique, y a tant apporté de précautions et tant de règles, que si ce Diable d'enfer a peur de ses Exorcismes et de son Eau Bénite, ce Diable supposé n'a pas moins peur du Barrigel et du Bourreau de Rome." *Nouvelles Lettres de Feu Mr. Gui Patin* (2 vols.; Amsterdam, 1718), Lettre XII, in *Nouvelles de la République des Lettres,* mars-avril, 1718, Art. VII.

[50] "Luther et Calvin ont ôté le Purgatoire. S'ils pouvoient aussi bien nous ôter l'Enfer, nous serions comme Rats en paille. Le Diable seroit mort cette fois-là, et nous n'aurions plus qu'à nous gaudir, sans plus avoir aucune crainte de cette vilaine bête métaphysique, cornue et fort affreuse; à ce que nous assurent les Moines, gens de bien et gens d'honneur, à ce qu'ils disent!" Patin, Lettre XIV, *ibid.*

[51] "Que ce seroit un beau déblai, si l'on mettoit tous ces Moineaux dans des batteaux, avec autant de Moinesses, et qu'on les envoyât cultiver le Purgatoire des îles de l'Amérique, ou à la Mozambique, où les habitans de ces lieux n'ont point encore vû d'Oiseaux de tel plumage! Ce seroit là le vrai moyen de décharger la France de tant de bouches inutiles, et de tant d'hommes oiseaux." *Ibid.*

ing, of course, the stanzas on the Saint-Bartholomew Massacre. The two lines of the poem which perhaps rankled most among Catholics in France when that poem first became known there as *La Ligue* about 1723 appeared again in the review in Holland: "Those furious monsters, thirsting for blood,/ Spurred on by the voices of sanguinary Priests."[52]

Marteilhe and Superville wrote in the following interesting and cynical terms of two Catholic religious orders:

> Among Ecclesiastics, Ambition is an epidemical Disease, which only preys inwardly. Thus the Lazarists fed this growing passion in their hearts, while their external deportment bespoke the most profound humility. . . . They saw how well the humble deportment and the mortified air had profited the Jesuits . . . and were accordingly resolved to have the appearance of merit, but not of happiness.[53]

The *Letters Addressed to J.-A. Turrettini*, the Protestant pastor in Geneva, collected and published in 1887, constitute a useful compendium for the study of his fellow pastors outside of Switzerland. It is only fair to the Protestant refugees to show by quotations from two learned correspondents of Turrettini that some of them were broad-minded enough to be distressed by the agonizing rigidity of certain theologians of the Reformed Church. Beaulacre, for instance, wrote from Leyden on November 24, 1713:

> I heard a young man at Amsterdam last Sunday preach to us on the imputation of the Fall of Adam as if he knew all about it, *ex professo*. He was not troubled by the most unpleasant consequences of that dogma; and to prepare our minds for the subject, he had us sing Psalm CIX, which is filled with the most horrible imprecations. They had had me preach in the morning. For a long time I had refused to preach among such barbarous theologians.[54]

---

[52] "Ces monstres furieux de carnage altérez,/ Excités par la voix de Prêtres sanguinaires." *Journal des Sçavans*, mai 1731, compte-rendu de Voltaire, *Henriade* (London: Hierôme Bold Truth, Sous presse à Amsterdam chez E. J. Ledet et Jacques Desbordes, 1730).

[53] "Parmi les ecclésiastiques l'ambition est une maladie épidémique qui n'affecte que l'intérieur: aussi ce fut sous le manteau de l'humilité que nos Lazaristes couvrirent leurs vues ambitieuses . . . Ils savaient combien avaient servi aux Jésuites, l'extérieur humble, l'air mortifié et composé; pour aller plus sûrement à leurs fins, ils les imitèrent dans leur maintien et leur habillement, et renchérirent même sur leurs originaux . . ." Marteilhe, *Mémoires*, pp. 269–70; Goldsmith trans., II, 21–22.

[54] "J'entendis dimanche dernier à Amsterdam un jeune homme qui nous prêcha *ex professo* l'imputation du péché d'Adam. Toutes les conséquences les plus fâcheuses de ce dogme ne lui faisoient pas la moindre peine, et pour nous préparer à la matière il nous fit chanter le Psaume CIX qui est rempli des plus horribles imprécations. On

Here is a letter from Jean (?) Le Clerc which accuses theologians of hardness of heart:

> I praise the Lord that a spirit of moderation and peace is coming to be acceptable, and I pray with my whole heart that the Lord may continue to spread it in greater abundance. Good books can greatly contribute, and you have very properly turned your efforts thereto in your writings. Continue in the same direction with your usual prudence. I have no doubt that the works about which you wrote to me were well received, whether in French or in Latin, but one cannot be assured of not shocking the fanatics who are everywhere. When I consider the Protestant Powers and the present state of affairs, I see no likelihood of bringing people's minds to peace. Here, the theologians are just as violent and just as sordid as they have ever been.[55]

Even if it could be demonstrated that the books and sermons of Protestant pastors abroad did not shake the convictions of any practicing French Catholic, it would still be possible to believe that the persistent attacks by the refugee editors of periodicals printed in Holland, particularly after Pierre Bayle's death in 1706, may have had an influence in France in seconding the writings of the *philosophes*. Embedded in the more literary journals from Holland, many of the opinions which emotional Protestant editors shared with the *philosophes* were read by Frenchmen at home, month after month. After 1715, relaxation of government controls in a time of violence and cupidity doubtless made it possible for much which would have been censored, if published in France, to come over the northern borders on men's backs and to supply a market which from all appearances must have been considerable.

---

m'avoit fait prêcher le matin. Il y a longtems que je refusois de prêcher parmi des Théologiens si barbares." *Lettres inédites adressées de 1686 à 1737 à J.-A. Turrettini* (3 vols.; Paris, Geneva, 1887), I, 197.

[55] "Je loue Dieu de ce que l'esprit de modération et de paix commence à venir à la mode, et je le prie de tout mon cœur qu'il le répande encore et en plus grande abondance. Les bons livres y peuvent beaucoup contribuer et vous avez pris un tour très propre pour cela dans vos écrits. Continuez toujours sur le même pied avec votre prudence accoutumée. Je ne doute pas que les ouvrages dont vous me parlez ne fussent très bien reçus, soit en François, soit en Latin, mais on ne peut pas se promettre de ne pas choquer les Fanatiques qui sont répandus partout. Quand je considère les Puissances Protestantes et l'état où sont les choses, je ne vois aucune apparence de ramener les esprits à la paix. Ici, les théologiens sont aussi violens et aussi crasseux qu'ils l'aient jamais été." *Ibid.*, II, 136–37.

CHAPTER VIII

Conclusion

THANKS TO THE investigations of Daniel Mornet, there is no doubt that copies of the various editions of Pierre Bayle's *Dictionary* were to be found in a great many private libraries in France during the eighteenth century. That monumental compilation of heresies and religious aberrations constituted a vast storehouse of the kind of information wanted by French *philosophes* and, in English translation, served the purposes of freethinkers across the Channel. It would be hard to prove that very many people in France were emotionally affected by the indignant writing of other exiled Huguenots to the extent that skeptics were intellectually stimulated by Bayle's works.

Vehement denunciations by exiled Protestants, particularly in literary and learned periodicals, did come into France from other countries regularly on the backs of smugglers, and recriminations against the Catholic Church in such writings by exiles often coincided with mocking statements by the *philosophes* before 1740. Nevertheless, good reasons exist for separating most heartfelt statements of Protestants in exile from other examples of emotional writing in the foregoing pages. Many Frenchmen of the period from 1690 to 1740, both those of religious conviction and those of only nominal Catholic membership, still shared their ancestors' prejudice that Protestants were traitors. Not only Frenchmen but others as well have a curious trait: the very persons who feel free to criticize their own country and to denounce individuals in high positions react unfavorably and at once to similar statements made by foreigners or by those of a different political faith. The venomous political seriousness in the works by exiled Huguenots very probably did not delight a sophisticated public in Paris to such an extent therefore as did the clever and mocking statements with regard to church and state by those of nominally Catholic faith.

Fortunately, adequate contemporary evidence exists to demonstrate the emotional dissatisfaction of impoverished nobles and of self-consciously virtuous commoners in France during the half century following 1690. Protestant writers abroad at that time seemed to have been far less influential in France than the emotional and compassionate authors who had not gone into exile and whose feelings were not affected by partisan and political convictions.

I

More than one of the authors quoted in the foregoing chapters confessed that they had grown more compassionate after having suffered themselves. If this were true of most people who were somewhat sensitive, it is easy to understand the considerable number of expressions of pity written by Frenchmen from 1690 to 1740. The frequency of those expressions indicates more than a mere change in literary taste from that of the preceding period.

Even if there had not been several famines and a severe plague during those fifty years, it was inevitable that many French people who had been relatively well off financially in the 1680's should have become poverty-stricken well before 1730. Continuing warfare at great national expense, a ruinous system of taxation, and desperate efforts to retain value in a currency which continued to decline until paper took the place of coins—all these changed the fortunes of many and completely destroyed the fortunes of others. There had been much poverty in France before 1690, but, as a French saying has it, "One becomes

used to being poor, but no one ever gets used to not being wealthy."
And it was precisely those of substance or of social standing as landed
gentry who suffered great losses, particularly after 1715.

On the other hand, during the first third of the eighteenth century,
taxgatherers, moneylenders, and some few fortunate speculators became
very rich in a short time, and powerful as a result. They were not
usually honest men, and were scorned both by nobles who had suffered
losses and by middle-class people in trade or commerce. Furthermore,
the display of wealth by notorious individuals angered all, including
working people. On several occasions, in the troubled days of the
Regency, they attacked expensively decorated private coaches in the
streets of Paris.

One effect produced by the great increase in the number of literate
middle-class people during this fifty-year period was that it became
possible to earn a living by writing. Novels and periodicals by professional authors flourished. A number of upper-class ladies and gentlemen
also besieged publishers with their manuscripts. Protests of editors about
too much material in the early eighteenth century indicate both the
increased size of the reading public and the increased literary activity.

Professional authors of the middle class or of the recently impoverished petty nobility who wanted to make a living by their work had
two choices: either to entertain by composing comedies and sentimental
tales of love and adventure, or to instruct as well as entertain by writing
more serious prose. Material lay at hand for dealing realistically with
contemporary characters which could be appreciated by a "vulgar"
public. The Regency and the period following provided more than
enough cause for moralistic laments in prose. Not only taxgatherers and
moneylenders but also prominent people, including the Regent himself,
were observed to be venal and rapacious with regard to other people's
money.

It was not altogether fortuitous that, toward 1720, the most celebrated of French highwaymen, Cartouche, and gangs of criminals led
by others of less fearsome reputation, operated not far from the center
of Paris, where the Protestant Scotsman, Law, who was favored by the
Regent, was reducing thousands to destitution by his Mississippi Company shares and by his banknotes. The scramble for money caused
violence, robbery, and murder in the city to an extent that appalled

decent citizens, including serious-minded authors, whose works were published, and keepers of diaries and journals, which were not.

Some of these writers were equally appalled in 1722, when the Regent made the Abbé Dubois a Cardinal and Prime Minister, in spite of the fact that he had not been of high standing in the Church and that he was widely reputed to be avaricious, violent in his ambition, and generally a very doubtful sort of Christian. By the time Dubois was elevated to the highest positions of Church and state, it was plain to everyone who thought about it that noble birth, a reputation for honesty, and even common decency were no longer required for eminence and influence in France. Men of strong principles, who had either noble or middle-class concepts of good government, were revolted by this particular action of the Regent. But doubtless many of weaker will and convictions were influenced in their conduct by the example of those in higher positions in society, as many are influenced in all periods of history.

Emotional indignation at the Regent's injustice and love of money is not difficult to find in contemporary writing. His well-known lascivious conduct, contrary to the judgment of later moralists, was not considered to be as reprehensible as his debasement of the idea of royalty, resulting from his lack of a sense of dignity, his neglect of his obvious duties as head of a state, and his cynical favoring of men like Law and Dubois, who were clearly harmful to the kingdom.

Long before the catastrophic 1720's, at least one Protestant in exile had expressed astonishment that the impoverished and oppressed French people did not rise up in a general revolt against Louis XIV's government. Because of scandalous goings-on at the Court in the early 1720's, a sensitive and high-minded French lady who has been quoted in these pages wrote, in a letter to a friend, that she looked forward without hope to the destruction of the monarchy. Prophets of doom were mistaken, however, by underestimating the number of patient and patriotic people in the country, particularly in the provinces. Even in the worst days of famine, pestilence, and poverty during the 1720's, large numbers in France continued to believe in the traditional form of government. In spite of quarrels and even pitched battles, there was no politically conscious, forcefully led faction of any important size until long after 1740. Parisians did see and describe a mob pillaging food shops well before 1730; some discontented peasants had at times revolted and been disciplined in the provinces by the army; others had left their fields untilled in times of famine and gone to rob on the highways; embattled Protestants in the mountainous Cévennes had fought against royal troops. But no general uprising took place, as exiled Calvinists expected or as patriotic Catholics feared.

The political, social, financial, and literary activity in Paris no doubt led many to think that matters were proceeding at the same pace throughout the country, but there is no evidence to show that a majority of the sturdy peasantry had significantly changed from the state which La Bruyère had described in 1688—"bent over their work in the fields during daylight and withdrawing to their wretched lairs at night." One foreign observer among several who described the stark poverty of peasants in France was surprised that those wretched people had retained strong patriotic feelings and rejoiced at the success of French military forces.

It seems only fair, even in a brief conclusion of this study devoted to social change, to mention a distinctly middle-class and humble French priest, the Abbé Noël-Antoine Pluche. The tone of his writing has a broader significance than the fact that it pleased young Jean-Jacques Rousseau in the 1730's, for Pluche's attitude and his stable, even peaceful, views of society apparently prevailed among his fellow priests in the peasant parishes of France. An articulate "patriot," bent on conflict and revolution, would have had considerable difficulty in reaching the humble, patient subjects of whose existence Pluche's writings remind us.

II

Although there was nothing like a political revolution in France during the years from 1690 until 1740, there did take place during that half century a profound social upheaval, a social revolution. Like other changes before and since, this one was most conspicuous in what was observed and written in Paris. Diaries and journals, which have luckily been preserved, were kept in Paris by nobles and by some inconspicuous members of the middle class, presenting very divergent points of view. These bear striking witness to a profound change since the great days of the reign of Louis XIV only a short time before. Periodicals like Marivaux's *French Spectator,* as well as his novels, commented in moralizing manner on this change in the 1720's and 1730's. Print shops established abroad by refugee Protestants steadily continued to publish literary and learned periodicals after 1685, reporting with more or less moral indignation the decline of the fortunes of the nobility and the rise of a class of new rich.

At the time of the 1695 crop failure and famine, conditions compelled an excellent landed family of old, noble name to marry its son to the daughter of a low-born banker. In the years that followed, the mingling for economic reasons of noble blood with middle-class blood, and even with that of men born in the lowest classes, became more frequent. By the 1720's, middle-class moralists were writing scathingly about some members of the nobility fawning on recently enriched taxgatherers, men generally judged to be unmitigated scoundrels. Apparently the nobles who acted in this manner continued to do so for reasons which they thought prudent in troubled times. In fact, the vending of "good names" to questionable characters in order to obtain large dowries is significant in the development of materialism and love of luxury, as well as in the decadence of noble values.

The breaking down of social barriers was definitely paralleled in the history of some literary forms, if not in uninspired lyric poetry of this period, or in the style of painting. It is surely symptomatic that the most noble of literary forms, the French *tragédie,* was bastardized to become a series of pathetic surprises and that the sublime gave way in the newly popular form of the novel before more mundane considerations. Of course, the writing of fairy tales did not cease at once, and lady novelists continued to produce tales of illustrious heroes. But professional writers created for a larger public. Amusing picaresque novels and satirical tales composed by such men were appreciated by both nobles and commoners. These changes and innovations are closely associated with the existence of a larger Parisian public of literate commoners. Moreover, middle-class writers and readers no longer felt, as many of their status had felt in the seventeenth century, any necessity to be apologetic about their position in society. Quotations given in the preceding chapters have demonstrated this new pride. There are even a few cases in which members of this class criticized others who attempted to conceal their origins by adopting names of more noble sound.

It was only a short step from conscious pride in their own status to open criticism of noblemen who did not share their virtues: industriousness, living within one's income, setting a good example of conduct to one's children, paying bills when due, and preserving a reputation for business integrity (this last virtue being understood as the only enduring basis of prosperity). Commoners often scorned the prejudices of nobles quite as earnestly as nobles had scorned them and their values a generation earlier.

The growing self-respect and consequent moralizing judgments of French commoners constituted one significant indication of the great social change which was under way, not dissimilar from transitions which had occurred elsewhere in Europe. Thus a regard for their own worth among commoners in Switzerland had existed centuries earlier, when they had killed many of the local nobility and successfully resisted the domination of foreign princes. At least two centuries before the 1720's the burghers of Ghent, Antwerp, and cities farther north had already endowed the terms "middle class" and "citizen" with respectability in the minds of men in the Low Countries. Civil war and alternating rule by kings and commoners in seventeenth-century England had resulted in a self-respecting middle class there, when Louis XIV's glory was at its height in France. The freeing of citizens from domination by hereditary nobility had been accomplished in Swiss cantons long before Luther and Calvin.

What was written by French *philosophes* before 1740 is, of course, much better known today than the work of their contemporaries, whose plodding seriousness and moralizing tone are admittedly less entertaining. In fact, the names of many of these serious-minded authors have long since been removed from the annals of good literature, with justification. But because of their appeal to their contemporaries, particularly of the middle class, these minor authors deserve to be taken as testimony of the profound social change which was occurring in France.

To assume that the emotions of the middle class were alone responsible for the French Revolution would be foolish. It would probably be futile to attempt to measure the relative importance of that influence against the influence of the more judicious and logical statements by the *philosophes* and *encyclopédistes*; yet the intelligence of the few could not have brought about the events of 1789 without the sentimental and far from intellectual feelings of the many.

Bibliography

Adams, John. *Défense des Constitutions américaines.* 2 vols. Paris: Buisson, 1792.

Addison, Joseph, and Richard Steele. *The Spectator.* London: 1711–14.

Aïssé, Mlle de. *Lettres à Mme C——, depuis l'année 1726 jusqu'en 1733.* Paris: La Grange, 1787.

Alcoforada, Marianna. *Lettres portugaises traduites en françois.* Paris: Cl. Barbin, 1669.

Anonymous. *Les Charmes de la Société du Chrétien.* Paris: J. Etienne, 1730.

——. *Le Code Noir, ou Edit du Roy servant de Règlement pour le Gouvernement et l'Administration de la Justice . . . le commerce des Esclaves Nègres dans la Louisiane.* Versailles: 1724.

——. *Les Femmes Militaires; Relation Historique d'une Isle nouvellement découverte.* Paris: Claude Simon, Pierre de Batz, 1735.

——. *The Matchless Rogue: or an Account of the Contrivances, Cheats, Stratagems and Amours of Tom Merryman, commonly called Newgate Tom, who stiled himself, Baron of Bridewell . . . Marquis of Newgate.* London: A. Moore, 1725.

——. *Mémoires du Chevalier de T——.* The Hague: Pierre Gosse, 1738.

——. *Recueil de toutes les Feuilles de la Spectatrice.* Paris: Vve Pissot, 1730.

——. *De la Tolérance des Religions.* Rotterdam: 1684.

Argens, Marquis d'. *See* Boyer d'Argens, J.-B.

Argenson, René-Louis d'. *Journal et Mémoires du Marquis d'Argenson.* Paris: Société de l'histoire de France, 1859.

Atkinson, Geoffroy. *The Extraordinary Voyage in French Literature from 1700 to 1720.* 2 vols. Paris: E. Champion, 1922.

——. "A French Desert Island Novel of 1708," *PMLA,* XXXVI (December, 1921), 509–28.

——. *Les Idées de Balzac, d'après la Comédie humaine.* 5 vols. Geneva: E. Droz, 1949–50.

——. *Les Nouveaux horizons de la Renaissance française.* Paris: E. Droz, 1935.

————. *Les Relations de Voyages du XVIIe siècle et l'évolution des idées.* Paris: Champion, 1924.

————. *Le Sentiment de la nature et le retour à la vie simple.* Geneva: E. Droz; Paris: Librairie Minard, 1960.

Augustin-Thierry, A. *See* Chasles, Robert.

Auvigny, Du Castre d'. *Aventures d'Aristée et de Télasie.* 1731.

————. *Mémoires du Comte de Comminville.* 1735.

Barbier, E.-J.-F. *Journal historique et anecdotique du règne de Louis XV.* Paris: Jules Renard, 1847.

Bayle, Pierre. *Nouvelles de la République des Lettres* (1684–1718). London: n.p., 1684.

Blondel, Marshal. *Nouvelle Manière de fortifier les places.* The Hague: n.p., 1684.

Boisguilbert, Pierre le pesant de. *Le Détail de la France: La Cause de la Diminution de ses Biens, et de la facilité du Remède. En fournissant en un mois, tout l'argent dont le Roy a besoin, et en enrichissant tout le monde.* 1695.

Bossuet. *Œuvres complètes.* Paris: Lachat, 1863.

Boursault, E. *Lettres de respect, d'obligation, et d'amour.* Paris: Guignard, 1698.

Boyer, Paul. *Véritable Relation de l'Amérique occidentale.* Paris: Rocolet, 1654.

Boyer d'Argens, J.-B. *Lettres chinoises, ou correspondance philosophique, historique et critique . . . par l'auteur des Lettres juives et des Lettres cabalistiques.* 2 vols. The Hague: Pierre Paupie, 1740.

————. *Lettres morales et critiques sur les différens états et les diverses occupations des hommes.* Amsterdam: Michel Charles Le Cene, 1737.

Burnet, Gilbert. *Histoire de ce qui s'est passé . . . en Angleterre pendant la vie de Gilbert Burnet, Evêque de Salisbury.* The Hague: Jean Neaulme, 1735.

————. *Travels through France, Italy, Germany, and Switzerland.* London: T. Payne, 1750.

Bussy Rabutin, Comte de. *Lettres du comte de Bussy Rabutin.* Paris: F. et P. Delaulne, 1697.

Buvat, Jean. *Journal de la Régence* (1715–23). 2 vols. Paris: Plon, 1865.

"Catalde." *Mémoires de Monsieur le Comte de Claise.* Amsterdam: n.p., 1738.

————. *Le Paysan Gentilhomme, ou Aventures de M. Ransau.* The Hague: De Hondt, 1738.

Chansierges, M. *L'idée d'un roy parfait.* Paris: G. Saugrain, 1723.

Chasles, Robert. *Un Colonial au temps de Colbert: Mémoires de Robert*

Chasles, Ecrivain du Roi (1717), edited by A. Augustin Thierry. Paris: Plon, 1931.

———. *Histoires françoises galantes et comiques*. Amsterdam: 1710.

———. *Les illustres Françoises, histoires véritables*. Utrecht: E. Neaulme, 1737.

———. *Journal d'un voyage fait aux Indes orientales par une escadre . . . commandée par Mr. Du Quesne*. Rouen: J.-B. Machuel le Jeune, 1721.

Châteillon, Sébastien. *Traité des hérétiques, à savoir, si on les doit persécuter. . . .* Geneva: A. Jullien, 1913.

Claude, Jean. *Les Plaintes des Protestans, cruellement opprimés dans le Roiaume de France*. Cologne: Pierre Marteau, 1713.

Claude, Jean-Jacques. *Sermons sur divers textes de l'Ecriture Sainte*. Geneva: Du Villard et Jacquier, 1724.

Corneille, Pierre. *Examen de "Mélite."* 1630.

Crébillon fils. "Portrait de M. de Pranzi" in *Les Egarements du cœur et de l'esprit*. Paris, 1736–38.

Crousaz, J.-P. de. *Traité du beau*. Amsterdam: François L'Honoré, 1715.

Dancourt. *Chefs-d'œuvres de Dancourt* in *Choix de pièces du théâtre françois*, Vols. I and II. Paris: Les Libraires associés, 1783.

Dangeau, Marquis de. *Journal*. Paris: Didot, 1859.

Defoe, Daniel. *The History of Colonel Jack*. London: W. Meadows, 1721.

———. *A Plan of the English Commerce*. London: W. Meadows, 1728.

———. *Robinson Crusoe*. London: W. Meadows, 1719.

———. *The Shortest Way with Dissenters*. London: W. Meadows, 1703.

[Defoe, Daniel]. *The Protestant Monastery*. London: W. Meadows, 1727.

———. *Reasons Why this Nation Ought to Put a Speedy End to this Expensive War*. London: J. Baker, 1711.

Du Castre d'Auvigny. *See* Auvigny, Du Castre d'.

Duclos, Charles Pinot. *Considérations sur les mœurs*. London: Cambridge Univ. Press, 1939.

Dufresny, Charles. *Amusemens sérieux et comiques* (1699). Paris: Bossard, 1921.

———. *Le Double Veuvage* in *Chefs-d'œuvres des auteurs comiques*. Paris: F. Didot, Frères, 1845.

Du Hautchamp. *Histoire du système des finances, sous la minorité de Louis XV, pendant les années 1719 et 1720*. 2 vols. The Hague: Pierre de Hondt, 1739.

Farquhar, George. *Love and a Bottle*. N.p., 1698.

Fénelon, François de Salignac de La Mothe. *Directions pour la conscience des rois . . .*, The Hague: J. Néaulme, 1747.

———. *Lettres*. Paris: 1702–13.

Foullon, Jean-Erard, S. J. *Les Causes des guerres et de toutes les afflictions publiques.* Liége: B. Broncart, 1648.

Froger, François. *Relation d'un voyage en 1695, 1696, 1697, aux côtes de l'Afrique.* Paris: M. Brunet, 1698.

Gacon, François. *Discours satiriques en vers.* Cologne: n.p., 1696.

Germain, Joseph, S. J. "Letter of 1711" in *Jesuit Relations, Canada,* Vol. LXVI. Cleveland, Ohio: The Burroughs Bros. Co., 1897.

Goldsmith, Oliver. *See* Marteilhe, Jean.

Gueudeville, Nicolas de. *Le Censeur, ou mœurs de La Haye.* The Hague: H. Scheuleer, 1715.

Guillot de Marcilly. *Relation historique et théologique d'un voyage en Hollande.* Paris: Jacques Estienne, 1719.

Jesuit Relations and Allied Documents. Travels and Explorations of the Jesuit Missionaries in New France, 1610–1791. 76 vols. Cleveland, Ohio: The Burroughs Bros. Co., 1900.

Joubert, J. de la Rue. *Lettres d'un Sauvage dépaysé, contenant une critique des mœurs du siècle, et des réflexions sur des matières de religion et de politique.* Amsterdam: Jean François Jolly, 1738.

Journal des Sçavans. Amsterdam: June, 1724.

Journal littéraire. The Hague: T. Johnson, 1715.

Jurieu. *Les Vœux d'un patriote* (also known as *Les Soupirs de la France esclave*). Amsterdam, 1788.

Keith, George. *An Exhortation and Caution to Friends concerning Buying or Keeping of Negroes.* New York: n.p., 1693.

La Barre de Beaumarchais. *Amusemens littéraires: ou Correspondance politique, historique, philosophique, critique, et galante.* The Hague: Jean Van Duren, 1741.

———. *Le Hollandais, ou Lettres sur la Hollande, ancienne et moderne.* 2nd ed. Frankfort: Fr. Varrentropp, 1738.

Lahontan, Louis-Armand, Baron de. *Dialogues curieux entre l'auteur et un sauvage de bon sens qui a voyagé . . .* (1703). Baltimore, Md.: Johns Hopkins Press and Oxford Univ. Press, 1931.

La Loubère, de. *Du Royaume de Siam.* 2 vols. Amsterdam: A. Wolfgang, 1691.

Lambert, Abbé Claude-François. *La Nouvelle Marianne.* The Hague: n.p., 1740.

Lambert, Marquise de. *Réflexions nouvelles sur les Femmes.* London: J. P. Coderc, 1730.

Langford, Jonas. *A Brief Account of the Sufferings of the Servants of the Lord Called Quakers: From Their First Arrival in the Island of Antegoa . . . from 1660 to 1695.* London: T. Sowle, 1706.

La Rue, J. Joubert de. *See* Joubert, J. de la Rue.

LaTouche, Jacques-Ignace de. *Le Militaire en solitude, ou le philosophe chrétien.* The Hague: P. de Hondt, 1736.

Lenfant, J. *Sermons sur Divers Textes de l'Ecriture Sainte.* Amsterdam: Pierre Humbert, 1728.

Le Noble. *L'Ecole du Monde, ou Instruction d'un Père à son Fils, touchant la manière dont il faut vivre dans le monde.* 4 vols. Paris: M. Jouvenel, 1700.

Le Pelletier, Jean. *Mémoires pour le rétablissement du commerce en France.* Rouen (?): n.p., 1701.

Lesage, Alain-René. *Œuvres.* Paris: A. A. Rebouard, 1821.

Lescarbot, Marc. *La Conversion des Sauvages qui ont esté baptisez en la Nouvelle France, cette année 1610. Avec un bref récit du voyage du sieur de Poutrincourt.* Paris: J. Millot, 1610.

Lillo, George. *The London Merchant, or the History of George Barnwell.* London: John Gray, 1734.

[Maillard]. *Le Triomphe de la Pauvreté et des Humiliations, ou la Vie de Mademoiselle de Bellere du Tronchay, appellée communément, Sœur Louïse, avec ses Lettres.* Paris: G. Martin, 1732.

Marcilly, Guillot de. *See* Guillot de Marcilly.

Marivaux, Pierre de Chamblain de. *Le Cabinet du Philosophe.* 1734.

———. *Les Fausses Confidences.* 1737.

———. *Le Paysan parvenu.* 1735–40.

———. *Le Spectateur françois.* 1722–23.

———. *La Vie de Marianne.* Paris: Charpentier, 1842.

Marteilhe, Jean. *Mémoires d'un Protestant, condamné aux galères de France pour cause de Religion . . . depuis 1700 jusqu'en 1713,* edited by Daniel de Superville. Rotterdam: J. et D. Beman, 1757. Translated by Oliver Goldsmith, *The Memoirs of a Protestant Condemned to the Galleys of France.* London: J. M. Dent, 1895.

Martin de Nantes. *Relation Succincte et sincère de la mission du Père Martin de Nantes, Prédicateur Capucin . . . dans le Brézil.* Quimper: Jean Périer, 1707.

Masson, Jean et Samuel. *Histoire Critique de la République des Lettres, tant ancienne que moderne.* 15 vols. Amsterdam: J. Desbordes, 1717–18.

Méheust, Mme. *Les Mémoires du Chevalier de ——.* Paris: Dupuis, 1734.

Melon, J. F. *Essai Politique sur le Commerce.* 1734.

Mercure historique et politique. The Hague, 1692–1720.

Misson, Maximilien. *Nouveau Voyage d'Italie.* The Hague: Henri van Bulderen, 1702.

———. *Voyage et aventures de François Leguet et de ses compagnons, en deux isles désertes des Indes orientales.* . . . 2 vols. London: David Mortier, 1708.

Moncrif, de. *Essais sur la Nécessité et sur les moyens de plaire.* Geneva: Pellissari, 1738.

Montesquieu. *Lettres.*

Moreau, P., S. J. *Relation du Brésil.* 1651.

Moreton, Andrew. *See* Defoe, Daniel.

Mouhy, Charles de Fieux, Chevalier de. *Paris, ou le mentor à-la-mode.* Paris: Au dépens de la Compagnie, 1735.

Muralt, Béat de. *Lettres sur les Anglais et sur les Français.* Cologne: n.p., 1725.

Nau, S. J. Letter from Quebec, October, 1735; in *Jesuit Relations*, Vol. LXVIII.

Naudé, Philippe. *Histoire abrégée de la naissance et du progrès du Kouakerisme, avec celle de ses dogmes.* Cologne: P. Marteau, 1692.

Olry, Jean. *La Persécution de l'Eglise de Metz, descrite par le Sr. Jean Olry, cy-devant Avocat au Parlement et Notaire Royal en la dite Ville et dédiée à sa Famille . . . son exil dans l'Amérique.* Hanau: Samuel Ammon, 1690.

Patin, Gui. *Nouvelles de la République des Lettres.* Amsterdam: n.p., 1718.

Penn, William. *An Essay towards the Present and Future Peace of Europe, by the Establishment of an European Dyet, Parliament, or Estates.* London: n.p., 1695.

Peregrine (pseud.). *The Compleat Mendicant: or, Unhappy Beggar, Being the Life of an Unfortunate Gentleman.* London: E. Harris, 1699.

Pinot Duclos, Charles. *See* Duclos, Charles Pinot.

Piron, Alexis. *Œuvres choisies.* Paris: Haut-Cœur et Gayet, 1823.

Pitt, Moses. *The Cry of the Oppressed, Being a True and Tragical Account of the Unparallelled Sufferings of Multitudes of Poor Imprisoned Debtors, in Most Gaols in England, under the Tyranny of Gaolers.* London for Moses Pitt, 1691.

Pluche, Abbé. *Le Spectacle de la nature.* Paris: Frères Etienne, 1764.

Prévost, Abbé. *Le Doyen de Killerine.* 1735.

————. *Le Philosophe anglois, ou Histoire de Monsieur Cleveland, fils naturel de Cromwell, écrite par lui-mesme, et traduite de l'anglois.* Paris, 1823.

————. *Le Pour et Contre, Ouvrage d'un Goût nouveau, par l'Auteur des Mémoires d'un Homme de Qualité.* Paris: Didot, 1733–35.

————. *Mémoires d'un homme de qualité.* 1731.

————. *Œuvres choisies.* Paris, 1823.

Rémond des Cours, Nicolas. *La Véritable Politique des personnes de qualité.* Paris: Jean Boudot, 1693.

Rogers, Woodes. *Providence Displayed, or a very Surprizing Account of one*

Mr. Alexander Selkirk . . . Written by his own Hand. London: J. Read, 1712; French translation, Amsterdam: 1716.

Rollin. *De la Manière d'enseigner et d'étudier les belles-lettres, par rapport à l'esprit et au cœur.* Paris: Vve Estienne, 1740.

Rousseau, Jean-Jacques. *Œuvres complètes.* Paris: Hachette, 1912.

Saint-Evremond, Charles de. *Œuvres.* Paris: Cité des Livres, 1927.

Saint-Pierre, Abbé Castel de. *Ouvrages de Politique par M. l'Abbé de Saint-Pierre, de l'Académie françoise.* 3 vols. Rotterdam: J. D. Beman, 1733.

Saint-Simon, Duc de. *Mémoires.* Paris: La Pléiade, 1947.

Sévigné, Mme de. *Lettres.* The Hague: P. Gosse, J. Néaulme et Cie, 1726.

"Sœur Louise." *See* Maillard.

Superville, Daniel de. *See* Marteilhe, Jean.

Tschudi, Johann Heinrich. *Beschreibung des Lobl., Orths and Lands Glarus.* . . . Zurich: J. H. Lindinner, 1714.

————. *Das Gesunde and lange Leben.* Zurich: J. H. Lindinner, 1710.

Turrettini. *Lettres inédites adressées de 1686 à 1737 à J.-A. Turrettini.* 3 vols. Paris and Geneva: n.p., 1887.

Turrettini, François. *Recueil de Sermons.* Geneva: Samuel de Tournes, 1687.

Tyssot de Patot, Simon. "Discours de M. Simon Tyssot, Sr. Patot, où dans la vuë de concilier les différentes Nations au sujet de la Chronologie . . ." in *Journal littéraire* (The Hague), XII (1723).

————. *Le Voyage de Jacques Massé.* Bordeaux: n.p., 1710.

Vallange. *Nouveaux Systèmes ou nouveaux plans de méthodes . . . pour parvenir en peu de temps et facilement à la connoissance des Langues et des Sciences.* . . . Paris: Jombert, 1719.

Vauban, Sébastien Le Prestre, Marquis de. *Lettres intimes adressées au marquis de Puyzieulx* (1699–1705). Paris: Ed. Bossard, 1924.

————. Mémoire pour le rappel des Huguenots, adressé à feu M. de Louvois, en décembre 1689," in *Vauban: Sa Famille et ses Ecrits.* Paris: Berger-Levrault, 1910.

————. *Mémoire pour servir à l'instruction dans la conduite des sièges.* Leiden: 1740.

————. *Projet d'une dixme royale.* Paris, 1707, 1851.

Wollaston. *Ebauche de la Religion naturelle,* traduite de l'anglois, avec un supplément. . . . The Hague: Jean Swart, 1726.

Index

Aïssé, Charlotte-Elisabeth: predicts ruin of France, 13; her treatment of sin, 115

Algonquin: condemned and killed, 14

Amyot, Jacques: his translation of Plutarch admired, 65

Animals: pity for, 77

Argens, J.-B. Boyer d': on social injustice, 125–26; example of light approach, 161–62

Argenson, René-Louis d': attitude toward the poor, 88; optimism, 89; on doing good, 108, 110, 111; influenced by Saint-Pierre, 111

Arnadin, d': royal censor, 12

Auvigny, Du Castre d': against war, 37; on pity, 94–95

Bacon, Francis: his view of man, 99

Balzac, Guez de: as example of restraint, 67

Balzac, Honoré de: role of, in his novels, 92; mentioned, 35

Bank: closure in 1720, 26

Barbier, E.-J.-F.: on closing of Bank, 26; on war, 33; on suffering of the poor, 80

Basnage, Jacques: on duels, 53; his social views, 148

Bayle, Pierre: loss of status, 71; against war, 71, 72; social and political views, 139, 148, 158, 159, 163; quoted in *Journal littéraire*, 164; importance of, 168; mentioned, 6

Beachy: defeat of French Navy at, 6

Beauchamps, P.-F. Godart de: on sexual laxity, 140

Beaulacre: his broad-mindedness, 166

Beaumarchais, Labarre de: on doing good, 111; on contemporary preaching, 131; on sexual laxity, 139–40

Bienfaisance: origin and meaning of the term, 89, 98, 99, 102; 99–112, *passim*

Black Code: intent of, 103

Boileau-Dépréaux, Nicolas: on expression of personal emotion, 66

Boisguilbert, Pierre le Pesant de: on state of commerce, 15–16; praised Vauban, 49

Bossuet, Jacques-Bénigne: harshness toward Protestants, 64; attitude to Fénelon, 73

Boursault, Edme: his lack of compassion, 76

Bourvalais: attacked for profiteering, 135

Boyer d'Argens, J.-B.: on social injustice, 125; as example of light approach, 161–62

Burnet, Bishop Gilbert: travels in France, 8–9; on middle class, 41; on vice in cities, 120

Bussy Rabutin, Roger de: recipient of letter on persecution of Protestants, 7; on Protestantism, 8

Buvat, Jean: on death of Louis XIV, 21; on funeral of Marquise de Louvois, 21–22; on visit of Persian ambassadors, 22; on lawlessness, 23; on poverty in south, 25; his prose style, 25, 79; his compassion, 79

Cambrai: Fénelon exiled to, 73

Canada. See New World

Cartouche: identified, 132; operated at Paris, 170

Catalde: on nobility, 60; on pity, 95–96

Catholics: accused of obeying the Pope, 69

Cerati, Gaspard: recipient of letter by Montesquieu, 117

Cévennes: fighting in region of, 30

Challes, Robert. See Chasles, Robert

Chapelain, Jean: as example of restraint, 67

Charron, Pierre: his view of man, 100

Chasles, Robert: on Louis XIV, 19; on toleration in England, 19; on corruption and injustice, 19–20, 52, 119, 135–36; on Protestants' rights, 19, 134, 136; on equality, 50; pity in writings